Ernest Hemingway Speaking...

"All stories, if continued far, end in death, and he is no true story-teller who would keep that from you."

"So far, about morals, I know only that what is moral is what you feel good after and what is immoral is what you feel bad after."

"Since he was a young boy he has cared greatly for fishing and shooting. If he had not spent so much time at them . . . he might have written much more. On the other hand he might have shot himself."

Ernest Hemingway, the giant of American
Letters; his legacy of genius remains with us . . .
forever.

ERNEST HEMINGWAY

THE LIFE AND DEATH OF A MAN

BY
ALFRED G. ARONOWITZ
AND
PETER HAMILL

A LANCER PAPERBACK EDITION PUBLISHED BY
LANCER BOOKS, INC. • 26 WEST 47 STREET • NEW YORK 36, N. Y.

A LANCER ORIGINAL · NEVER BEFORE PUBLISHED

For My Old Man
He likes to sing, he likes to drink, he likes to fight; he
does all of them well, and not necessarily in that order.

P. H.

For my own Brett

A. G. A.

Authors' Preface

FOR ONE of us the news came while he was sitting in the living room of a friend's home in a Philadelphia suburb watching the Dodgers play the Phillies on television. Junior Gilliam was at bat. Then the sound cut out, and while Gilliam took his swings an unseen announcer broadcast the news. The bulletin was terse, saying that Ernest Hemingway had accidentally shot himself to death in his home in Ketchum, Idaho. Then the game resumed.

For the other the announcement came over the radio and was equally as stark: Columnist Leonard Lyons, the announcer said, reports that Ernest Hemingway, the writer, accidentally killed himself with a shotgun blast at his Idaho home. There were no further details. Instead, there was a feeling of infinite personal sorrow, followed by the vague hope that, as on other occasions, there might have been a slight exaggeration.

On that sad early summer afternoon, neither of us knew that just about all there was left of the rugged outdoor face that had graced the public prints of the world was the jaw. Hemingway's lifelong odyssey through the world of violence had ended, inevitably, within its frontiers.

Any of us who had been nurtured on Hemingway had known, of course, that he would never die in bed. And yet, initially, at least, the manner of his death seemed a betrayal. Even when he had gone, like Jack Dempsey or Joe Louis, strangely out of style, he was still a champion to us. Hemingway, in the new dawn of enlightenment that seems to come every morning, had been wrong. That's what everyone had said. They had said Hemingway was wrong. You had to believe it, and yet you couldn't. Then Hemingway pulled the triggers of a shotgun and proved himself he was wrong. That's the way it seemed at first.

But as that day dragged on, and you stayed pinned to radios and made phone calls in an attempt to get more details, you began to feel a different emotion. It was if, while traveling in a strange and foreign place, you had heard of the dying fall of the old champion. You had rooted for him when you were young, and secretly when you grew older, but in the end he had been knocked out. And in that foreign place, where there had once been the sound of revelry by night, the chairs were stacked and the night-jazz of the arena was stifled by a mute silence. You had rooted for him because you wanted to believe there *could* be greatness in your time.

Then you began making the excuses. Perhaps his legs were gone, the reflexes shot, the brain punch-addled. He had been getting by, your champion, on guile and cunning after the old skills had tarnished and the end was inevitable. And yet he was the champion. There can be only one champion, and whether we liked it or not Hemingway was ours. But we demand more of our champions than we do of clubfighters.

No doubt there will be hundreds of thousands of words expended on Hemingway in the years to come. It is to be hoped that most of them will not be denigrating. If they are, it will be unfortunate, but typical. It has always been easier for those suffering from the dry rot of the academies to make a living nipping at the heels of the great.

For now, we hope this book will serve as a preliminary report on the life and good and bad times of a man who changed the way many of us wrote, and the way many of us talked. It was good to know, as Hemingway once said about Joyce, that you were alive in the presence of a great artist. If one young man in one of the hundred thousand Oak Parks of this country reads it and decides to challenge for the title, this book will have been worth writing.

PETE HAMILL and ALFRED G. ARONOWITZ

Acknowledgments

THIS BOOK could not have been written without the generous help and kind cooperation of Dr. Carlos Baker, Woodrow Wilson Professor of Literature at Princeton University; Mr. Harold Loeb; Mr. Earl Wilson of the *New York Post;* Mr. Leonard Lyons of the *New York Post;* Mr. Norman Mailer; Mr. Seymour Krim; Mr. Sam Boal; Mr. Prudencio de Pereda; Professor Arthur A. Fiedler of Montana State University; Professor Seymour Betsky of Montana State University; and all the other persons who consented to be interviewed and who are quoted in these pages.

The authors in particular also wish to thank Mr. John Hemingway and his mother, Mrs. Paul Scott Mowrer, for their aid in compiling and appraising the information in this book.

In addition, the authors wish to acknowledge the permission to quote material from the following books.

Ernest Hemingway, by Philip Young. New York: Rinehart & Company, Inc., 1952.

Hemingway, The Writer as Artist, by Carlos Baker. Princeton: Princeton University Press, 1956.

The Autobiography of Alice B. Toklas, by Gertrude Stein. New York: Random House, 1933.

Shakespeare and Company, by Sylvia Beach. New York: Harcourt, Brace and Company, 1956.

Love and Death in the American Novel, by Leslie A. Fiedler. New York: Criterion Books, 1960.

Advertisements for Myself, by Norman Mailer. New York: G. P. Putnam's Sons, 1959.

Hemingway, A Pictorial Biography, by Leo Lania. New York: The Viking Press, 1961.

The Far Side of Paradise, by Arthur Mizener. New York: Houghton Mifflin Company, 1949.

The Way It Was, by Harold Loeb. New York: Criterion Books, 1959.

Ezra Pound, by Charles Norman. New York: The MacMillan Company, 1960.

After the Lost Generation, by John W. Aldridge. New York: The Noonday Press, 1958.

The Third Rose, Gertrude Stein and Her World, by John Malcolm Brinnin. New York: Grove Press, Inc., 1959.

Exile's Return, by Malcolm Cowley. New York: The Viking Press, 1951.

Ernest Hemingway, by S. F. Sanderson. New York: Grove Press, Inc., 1961.

The Apprenticeship of Ernest Hemingway, The Early Years, by Charles A. Fenton. New York: The Viking Press, 1954.

The Spanish Civil War, by Hugh Thomas. New York: Harper and Brothers, 1961.

Permission is also acknowledged from Charles Scribner's Sons to quote material from the following books by Ernest Hemingway:

The Sun Also Rises, A Farewell to Arms, In Our Time, Death in the Afternoon, Green Hills of Africa, To Have and Have Not, The Fifth Column and the First Forty-nine Stories, For Whom the Bell Tolls, Across the River and Into the Trees, The Old Man and the Sea.

Permission is also acknowledged to quote material from the following periodicals:

The Noble Savage: The Starched Blue Sky of Spain, by Josephine Herbst, Spring, 1960.

Esquire: Old Newsman Writes, by Ernest Hemingway, December 1934; On the Blue Water, by Ernest Hemingway, April, 1936.

Life: Mister Papa, by Malcolm Cowley, January 10, 1949; The Dangerous Summer, by Ernest Hemingway, September 5, 12, 19, 1960; His Mirror was Danger, by Archibald MacLeish, July 14, 1961.

The New Yorker: How Do You Like It Now, Gentlemen?, by Lillian Ross, May 13, 1950; El Unico Matador, by Lillian Ross, March 12, 19, 26, 1949.

The Minnesota Review: Random Thoughts on the Twenties, by Allen Tate, Fall, 1960.

University of Minnesota Pamphlets on American Writers: Ernest Hemingway, by Philip Young, 1959.

The Paris Review: The Art of Fiction XXI, by George Plimpton, Spring, 1958.

Saturday Review: The Great and Small in Ernest Hemingway, by Max Eastman, April 4, 1959.

Look Magazine: Christmas Gift, by Ernest Hemingway, April 20, 1954 and May 4, 1954; A Visit With Hemingway, by Ernest Hemingway, September 4, 1956.

CHAPTER ONE

A Round with Papa

Since he was a young boy he has cared greatly for fishing and shooting. If he had not spent so much time at them . . . he might have written much more. On the other hand he might have shot himself.

—ERNEST HEMINGWAY, writing about himself in *Portraits and Self Portraits* by George Schreiber, 1936.

I

HE WAS a tall, large and muscular man who liked to take advantage of that fact. He had a great, hairy torso and a stone wall abdomen on shanks that were both spindly and overwrapped with sinew and his strength sometimes seemed to burst through his arms the same way his arms sometimes burst through his shirts. He had cheeks that were too full for his face and a smile that almost extended beyond them. His frown, of course, was another matter, when it mattered at all, dark beneath the shadow of his early mustache, fierce in the jungle of his later beard. With his demeanor and his shape he was, to some, an approximation of the bull, an analogy that might have given him as much pleasure as he used to get from watching the death of that animal. By his own description, he also was pretty close to a bear, so close, in fact, that in Montana, once, he lived with a bear, slept with it and got drunk with it, or so he said. "I love to go to the zoo," he once told a friend. "But not on Sunday. I don't like to see the people making fun of the animals, when it should

13

be the other way around." Often, in the world-wide haunts where shades of him must remain even today, Paris, New York, Havana, Venice, Madrid, Nairobi, and the great mass of trees, rivers, mountains and details in between, he would stop in his tracks as if he were hunting and suddenly sniff the air. He knew the scent, he always said, of possum, deer, elk, coon and other animals, an attribute of living his life with a shotgun and of a refined nose, so refined that he never smoked. "Cigarettes," he said "smell so awful to you when you have a nose that can truly smell." His eyes, too, were sensitive. He arose each day at daybreak, or rather, with the sun he also rose, a light and punnish hint perhaps that his greatest title didn't come entirely from *Ecclesiastes*. "I have seen all the sunrises there have been in my life," he told Lillian Ross in 1950, "and that's half a hundred years." His eyelids, he said, were too thin to hide the morning light, and it seems strange now that the sun continues to rise without him.

He was the Paul Bunyan of the typewriter, although he actually wrote by pencil, whittling them down forests at a time. He was the shadow boxer of American Letters, throwing punches even as he talked and often as he wrote. He loved a brawl, knock-down, drag-out, usually the other fellow, but he saved what he called his big ones for the adversaries who weren't there. ". . . I started out very quiet and I beat Mr. Turgenev," he once said. "I trained hard and I beat Mr. de Maupassant. I've fought two draws with Mr. Stendhal, and I think I had an edge in the last one. But nobody's going to get me in any ring with Mr. Tolstoy unless I'm crazy or I keep getting better." It was the sun, too, that gave him his beard, although he always had, after his first boyhood exhilaration from it, disliked shaving. In his youthfulness, he wore a black mustache the length of his smile, a badge, so to speak, of himself. Afterwards, with his age, came his beard, first black, then iron gray and finally white. "When you have a slight case of skin cancer from the rays of the sun off the sea," he told a group of school children, "you grow a beard and quit shaving." With the beard, of course, he became Papa.

II

The circumstance of how he first came to be called Papa by everyone beyond the rightful heirs to that privilege

14

remains only one of the thousand-dollar-a-word treasures locked in Ernest Hemingway's inescapable memory. If he could have lived several more lifetimes than the several he did live, he might have found time to write about that strange and prophetic baptism, just as he might have found time to write about everything else which he never forgot. But then, if he could have lived several more lifetimes, he would have had several more lifetimes to write about. The fact is that whatever Hemingway could remember, he tripled by what he could invent. "Hemingway," said Carlos Baker, the Princeton University scholar who is among the best of Hemingway's literary biographers, "had a great memory, but he had an even greater imagination. Well, if he hadn't, he wouldn't have been the writer that he was." Or, as Hemingway himself said in 1959: "Fiction is inventing out of what knowledge you have. If you invent successfully, it is more true than if you try to remember it. A big lie is more plausible than truth. People who write fiction, if they had not taken it up, might have become very successful liars." The key to his inescapable memory, then, was his imagination. The artistry which Ernest Hemingway leaves behind him actually is merely the residue of his total artistry, now twice buried, once in his mind and once in the ground.

III

New York Post columnist Leonard Lyons, noting that Hemingway always called her "daughter," thinks it was Marlene Dietrich who first applied the nickname of Papa to him, "and it grew along with his beard."

"Oh, I don't think so," counters Hemingway's first son, John, not quite Miss Dietrich's sibling. "I'm sure I called him Papa before she ever did, fine lady that she is."

Some chroniclers think it was Papa himself who christened himself Papa, referring to himself as P. O. P., or Poor Old Papa, in *Green Hills of Africa*, written in 1934. Other chroniclers guess it might have been Hemingway' fourth wife, Miss Mary, who allowed the outside world in on his family label, although there also is some question as to who allowed the outside world to call *her* Miss Mary. In any event, he started out as Ernest and his first nickname was Hem, which is what most acquaintances called him before the advent of either his middle age or his beard. He also had some regional appellations. In Spain, for example, he was Ernesto, although,

15

most recently, matador Antonio Ordoñez, for one, called him *Papa* Ernesto.

Some called him Ernie, a name he tolerated only from close friends, but then there were so many who qualified as such. Others never called him anything but Ernest. During World War II, when, as a correspondent for *Collier's*, he traveled in a commandeered jeep sixty miles ahead of the advancing Fourth Division, armed with gin in one canteen, dry vermouth in another, and a few odds and ends that noncombatant war correspondents weren't supposed to be armed with, he was known by a wide variety of sobriquets. Some, in a group of French guerillas, called him *Mon Capitaine*. Others, among the American troops, called him the Kraut Hunter. Still others called him Old Dr. Hemingstein, a name, reportedly, which Hemingway applied to himself in the presence of anti-semites. Some called him what he called himself, Ernie Hemorrhoid, the poor man's Pyle. Some even called him Mr. Hemingway. But mostly they called him Pop or Papa, which were then, and until the day he died, the names he seemed to like best.

"Do you know," said Leonard Lyons, "that he even signed his letters, Papa, talked about himself in the third person as Papa?" Literary historian Malcolm Cowley, another friend, recalls that Hemingway sometimes signed his letters, "Mr. Papa," although that might have been merely in his more formal, business correspondence. He was *Papa*, anyway, when he returned after the war to Cuba, where the waiters in his favorite Havana cafes, the fishermen at Cojimar and his nine household servants at *Finca Vigia*, his fifteen-acre estate in the village of San Francisco de Paula, all addressed him by no other name.

"You order a Daiquiri, trying to explain how you want it made," Cowley once wrote in *Life* magazine, "and the waiter at the Cafe Florida says brightly, '*Como Papa?*' If you answer, 'Yes, like Papa,' a double Daiquiri without sugar appears in a shaker brimful of shaved ice. 'Papa, you write that we may drink,' said a Cuban lawyer in the Ambos Mundos while Hemingway reached for the check as always and beamed as if from the head of a family table. Sometimes his friends describe him as having a papa complex, which, they explain, is exactly the opposite of a father complex. Instead of seeking for a substitute father to support and protect him, he keeps trying to protect and lay plans for others. Younger men and women come to him for advice about their literary problems and their love affairs while he talks to them as if he were ninety years wise instead of only forty-nine. 'I was lucky enough,' he says, 'to associate with older people when I was young and with young people now that I'm older.'"

Papa to Hemingway was more than a name. It was a rank. "He encouraged it," says Carlos Baker. "He wanted the status. He wanted to have the status of a father, or a sort of father, among all his friends, the man to whom they always turned for advice." But Papa became an even greater rank. Papa to his friends became Papa to his enemies. Papa became, in fact, Papa to the world. He was the Papa of masculinity, the Papa of courage, the Papa of hunting, the Papa of fishing, the Papa, in many ways, of the bullring and, most specifically and probably most important, the Papa of American letters.

"No novelist in the world has produced such an effect on other people's writing," said author C. P. Snow. "I can't think of any other in history who directly influenced so many writers," echoed novelist John O'Hara. "He is not dead—generations not yet born of young men and women who want to write will refute that word as applied to him," added William Faulkner, who, of course, was another Nobel Prize winner.

And it's true. Hemingway's style, so easy to parody but so impossible to emulate, is today out of style. After two or more generations of trying to do one or the other, most writers today no longer try to write like Hemingway. And yet his impact remains visible, not only in their words but in their actions. The esthetic philosophy of a Norman Mailer or a Jack Kerouac is as different from Hemingway's as their sentences, and yet his Papa image still shines through their disaffection, as it does, incidentally, through the writing of most authors who have once read, for example, *The Killers*.

"For members of my generation, the young men born between 1918, roughly, and 1924, there was a special charm about Hemingway," said critic John Aldridge, speaking not entirely for himself. "By the time most of us were old enough to read him he had become a legendary figure, a kind of twentieth-century Lord Byron; and like Byron, he had learned to play himself, his own best hero, with superb conviction. He was Hemingway of the rugged outdoor grin and the hairy chest posing beside a marlin he had just landed or a lion he had just shot; he was Tarzan Hemingway, crouching in the African bush with elephant gun at ready, Bwana Hemingway commanding his native bearers in terse Swahili; he was War Correspondent Hemingway writing a play in the Hotel Florida in Madrid while thirty fascist shells crashed through the roof; later on he was Task Force Hemingway swathed in ammunition belts and defending his post single-handed against fierce German attacks.

"But even without the legend he created around himself, the chest-beating, wisecracking pose that was later to seem so incredibly absurd, his impact upon us was tremendous. The feeling he gave us was one of immense expansiveness and freedom and, at the same time, of absolute stability and control. We could put our whole faith in him and he would not fail us. We could follow him, ape his manner, his cold detachment, through all the doubts and fears of adolescence and come out pure and untouched. The words he put down seemed to us to have been carved from the living stone of life. They were absolutely, nakedly true because the man behind them had reduced himself to the bare tissue of his soul to write them and because he was a dedicated man . . ."

Even in the 1920s, when he first went to Paris, betting horses, managing prize fighters and boxing, earnestly, himself, the cult of Hemingway had begun to grow among other writers. He was to them, as a contemporary, Harold Loeb, remembered, the muscled proof that a he-man could be a writer and that a writer could be a he-man, and not necessarily have to be an Oscar Wilde, or vice versa. He had begun to make writing respectable among heterosexuals again, and its respectability has survived in writers who respect him for nothing else. "I wanted to be considered a big white lamb," says Kerouac, "but I'm a big Hemingway 'Jake' in the people's eyes." Norman Mailer, too, has become his own best hero.

". . . I was one of the few writers of my generation," Mailer wrote in *Advertisements for Myself*, "who was concerned with living in Hemingway's discipline, by which I do not mean I was interested in trying for some second-rate imitation of the style, but rather that I shared with Papa the notion, arrived at slowly in my case, that even if one dulled one's talent in the punishment of becoming a man, it was more important to be a man than a very good writer, that probably I could not become a very good writer unless I

18

learned first how to keep my nerve, and what is more difficult, learned how to find more of it . . ."

Perhaps Mailer was one of the *few* writers of his generation to do so, and perhaps one of the many. Like almost anyone else who tried to put words down in a creative spirit while under the shadow of a sun that also rose, Mailer wasn't just interested in Hemingway, he was *consumed* with Hemingway. *Advertisements for Myself,* insofar as it defines a lifestyle, is, to some extent, a new generation's *Death in the Afternoon* and, to another extent, an advertisement for Ernest Hemingway. "For years," Mailer wrote of Hemingway, "he has not written anything which would bother an eight-year-old or one's grandmother, and yet his reputation is firm—he knew in advance, with a fine sense of timing, that he would have to campaign for himself, that the best tactic to hide the lockjaw of his shrinking genius was to become the personality of our time. . ." And yet Mailer also was able to write: ". . . I have come finally to have a great sympathy for The Master's irrepressible tantrum that he is the champion of this and of all time, and that if anyone can pin Tolstoy, it is Ernest H. . ." Hemingway, in fact, is all through Mailer's book. At one point, Mailer nominates Ernest H. for president. At another point, Mailer, who by that time had written several novels, tells of having, finally, sent a copy of his third book, *The Deer Park,* to The Master inscribed as follows:

To Ernest Hemingway
—because finally after all these years I am deeply curious to know what you think of this.
—but if you do not answer, or if you answer with the kind of crap you use to answer unprofessional writers, sycophants, brown-nosers, etc., then F - - - you, and I will never attempt to communicate with you again.

—and since I suspect that you're even more vain than I am, I might as well warn you that there is a reference to you on page 000 which you may or may not like.

NORMAN MAILER

The package containing the book was returned to Mailer unopened. On it was stamped the Spanish equivalent of ADDRESS UNKNOWN—RETURN TO SENDER. Mailer, like so many other writers, was left to himself with his curiosity. He is still left to himself with it. "The one new thing I've written about Hemingway since *Advertisements* was a letter to Fidel Castro, an open letter," Mailer said shortly after Hemingway's death. "In it, I said we will curse Hemingway's memory if he dies in silence. He received that letter, I know. Some friends sent it to him but he never said anything about it . . . The big thing I feel about his death is that it was terribly, terribly depressing to me, peronally, like some relative I had cared about a great deal, an uncle or something, had died that way. I was depressing *that* way. But what was doubly depressing was that he died in silence. . . ."

Mailer paused. Then he continued: "I think Hemingway had a tremendous influence of a peculiar sort, which killed me because I think at the very end the influence he had was a lousy one. He became *Life* magazine's great American writer and whenever *Life* felt something was going wrong with American letters they'd rush Hemingway into the front like the U. S. Cavalry—you know, he'd come to the rescue when us Indians were about to burn one of *Life's* forts and he let himself be used that way, and to me it's damned depressing. And I think that one of the reaons he didn't have that much influence in the last ten years is because a lot of the young writers resented him. I resented him very much fifteen years ago. . ."

Again Mailer paused. He lit a cigarette. "You know," he resumed suddenly, "Hemingway wasn't wrong on the bullfight. That's what turned me towards him about five years ago. I hated *Death in the Afternoon* when I read it and then I was down in Mexico and I hated the bullfights for a long time, too. And then, after I had seen about five or six of them I slowly started liking them and in liking them I had to turn half my ideas inside out because, as a Socialist, what the hell was there to justify about a bull fight? I really had to start thinking. . .

"I almost met him one night. It killed me. I was all set to meet him and didn't. Am I sorry? Sure, I'm sorry, but why put it in? Where's your sense of Hemingway style? Just say I almost met him one night and didn't. Let the reader feel his sorrow."

There may be few writers other than Mailer and Kerouac who still try to live like Hemingway. Probably it's true that the new young leaders of American letters scorn, as Mailer says they do, Hemingway's image, or at least the Hemingway image of his later years. "But let's not say," Mailer adds, "that he didn't influence American letters. *Jesus!*"

Even Saul Bellow, who might be regarded as one of those new leaders scorning Hemingway, doesn't really scorn him. "He changed the way Americans talked and the way Americans wrote," Bellow said shortly before Hemingway's death. "He's our greatest writer." Deep in the soul of every American author is his first awakening to *The Sun Also Rises*. The probability is that Bellow, no less than Mailer, or Kerouac, or Nelson Algren, or James Jones, or Harvey Swados, or John O'Hara, or William Styron, or poor Tom Chamales, who survived years of guerilla fighting in Burma only to die of a cigarette fire in his drunken room, or dozens of other American writers, dead, alive, and about to be born, all of them are or were in some way obsessed with the idea of getting into the ring with Hemingway. Young writers no longer may try to write like Hemingway, but they forever will have to contend with the Hemingway legend. The tasks are equally difficult.

IV

"What I want to be when I am old is a wise old man who won't bore," Hemingway, who was then already Papa, told the *New Yorker's* Lillian Ross in 1950. "I'd like to see all the new fighters, horses, ballets, bike riders, dames, bullfighters, painters, airplanes, sons of bitches, café characters, big international whores, restaurants, years of wine, newsreels, and never have to write a line about any of it. I'd like to write lots of letters to my friends and get back letters. Would like to be able to make love good until I was eighty-five, the way Clemenceau could. And what I would like to be is not Bernie Baruch. I wouldn't sit on park benches, although I might go around the park once in a while to feed the pigeons, and also I wouldn't have any long beard, so there could be an old man didn't look like Shaw. . . Anyway, I would take up harness racing. You aren't up near the top at that until you're over seventy-five. Then I could get me a good young ball club, maybe, like Mr. Mack. Only I wouldn't signal with a program—so as to break the pattern. Haven't figured out yet what I would signal with. And when that's over, I'll make the prettiest corpse since Pretty Boy Floyd. Only suckers worry about saving their souls. Who the hell should care about saving his soul when it is a man's duty to lose it intelligently, the way you would sell a position you were defending, if you could not hold it, as expensively as possible, trying to make it the most expensive position that was ever sold. It isn't hard to die."

Papa, nevertheless, found it hard. He kept trying, it seemed, all his life. When he was ten, his father gave him his first shotgun. When he was fourteen, he began taking boxing lessons, sparring on his first day with a professional middleweight who broke his nose. Later, in another boxing match, he nearly lost an eye. When he was a senior at Oak Park High School, he made the football team only to be carried out, injured, from the two most important games.

"He was not a born sportsman who somehow learned to write, as if Luis Angel Firpo had been granted the gift of tongues," wrote Malcolm Cowley in *Life* magazine. "On the contrary, he was a born writer and student who taught himself painfully to be a sportsman."

He volunteered for various branches of the Army on twelve different occasions after World War I broke out but was rejected each time because of his injured eye. He joined, instead, the American Field Service, whose visionary requirements were somewhat less, and he was assigned as an ambulance driver with the Italian Army, near the tiny village of Fossalta di Piave. On July eighth, 1918, two weeks before his nineteenth birthday and seven days after his first admission to the trenches, he was handing out chocolate bars to Italian soldiers at a riverbank listening post when an Austrian trench mortar exploded nearby, filling his legs with two hundred thirty-seven fragments of sawed-off steel rods.

"I died then," Hemingway later told his friend, Guy Hickok. "I felt my soul or something coming right out of my body, like you'd pull a silk handkerchief out of a pocket by one corner. It flew around and then came back and went in again and I wasn't dead any more."

When he returned to Oak Park in the spring of 1919, he had the Italian *Croce de Guerra*, three citations, the *Medaglia d'Argento Al Valore Militare*, a pension from the Italian government of fifty dollars per year, a grafted bone in his foot, all the scrap metal which the surgeons had been unable to remove and an aluminum kneecap which will remain forever with his skeleton. But Hemingway wasn't through with life, or with courting an end to it.

22

He became, of course, an *aficionado*, playing with bulls from a range close enough to be gored by one. He resumed hunting, a sport which led him into other appropriate but, fortunately, unconsummate dangers. He returned to covering wars, first the Greco-Turkish War and then the Spanish Civil War, during which shells repeatedly scored direct hits on Madrid's Hotel Florida, where he happened to be. He also covered the Sino-Japanese War in China, but his emergencies there were nothing to speak of. At least he didn't speak much of them.

He was the victim of three serious auto wrecks, one in Cuba, where a rear-view mirror bracket was driven into his skull, one in Montana, where, on a hunting trip with John Dos Passos, he nearly lost an arm, and one in London, where, during the World War II blackout, his taxi rode into a stationary water tank, again injuring his head. The injury, which occasioned fifty-two stitches, did not prevent him, however, from joining the third wave ashore at Normandy on D-Day, twelve days later.

In 1949, while hunting near Venice, he was struck in the eye by shotgun wadding which caused an infection that later spread through his body, nearly killing him. In 1954, while hunting in Africa, he and his wife walked away from an airplane crash while newspapers throughout the world reported that he had been killed. When he boarded a rescue plane, that crashed, too. His skull was fractured, his bladder was pierced, his spine was injured and his kidney was crushed but even so. Hemingway, according to the legend of him, walked out of the jungle carrying a bunch of bananas in one hand and a flask of gin in the other. He laughed when he read his obituaries.

CHAPTER TWO

Fathers and Sons

SHORTLY AFTER ten a.m. on December sixth, 1928, Dr. Clarence Edmonds Hemingway, then sixty-seven years old but still the senior obstetrician at Oak Park Hospital, returned to the weathered squareness of his large, stucco, porchfront house after making an early morning call on a patient.

"I'm very tired," he told his wife, Grace Hall Hemingway, well known throughout the better neighborhoods of Oak Park as an artist. "I think I'll go upstairs and take a little nap."

Slowly, and with only slightly less effort than any man his age, the large, muscular, bearded Dr. Hemingway mounted the steps to his bedroom, closed the door and went to a cabinet where he kept an antiquated revolver which had been used by his father in the Civil War. He removed the gun, pointed it upward into his mouth and pulled the trigger.

The shot, of course, was not heard around the world, although, thirty-three years later, its echo would be. Aged out of a vigor which already had been inherited by his son, ridden by a diabetes that made life irretrievable, tortured by an angina pectoris that could kill him at any moment, Dr. Hemingway had killed himself. It was quite a sin to an Oak Park that had stood its ground amid growing erosion of propriety. But it was quite another sin to Dr. Hemingway's son Ernest.

"*Anyone has a right to do it,*" mused Robert Jordan,

waiting to die, lying on the hillside of *For Whom the Bell Tolls*, thinking of his father's suicide. *"But it isn't a good thing to do. I understand it, but I do not approve of it . . . But you do understand it? Sure, I understand it but. Yes, but. You have to be awfully occupied with yourself to do a thing like that . . . I'll never forget how sick it made me the first time I knew he was a* cobarde. *Go on, say it in English. Coward."*

There is today some question of whether Ernest Miller Hemingway, in the last expert moments of *his* morning with the trigger, might have reappraised those lines. Certainly there is much of what he wrote that will be reappraised by others. Perhaps no other writer in American literature left his life open to such hard scrutiny and then, with his death, seemed to render so much of it obsolete. Throughout his life and his fiction, his mystique of courage had always consumed Hemingway, although there forever will remain the question of its final consummation. Robert Jordan is not the only Hemingway character who called Hemingway's father a coward. His concept of his father haunted Hemingway, apparently until his dying day.

The good doctor, according to those who remember him, was a man who had a huge body and a head that was, by comparison, small. He had large, bushy eyebrows and black, tiny, piercing eyes and looked, despite these dissimilarities, much like his son. The doctor's own father had a house, stylishly cupolaed, in Oak Park, just across the city line from Chicago, and when Dr. Hemingway built his home nearby "there was," as Hemingway later wrote, "nothing but the North Prairie that ran all the way to the Des Plaines River." Hemingway was born there on July twenty-first, 1899, the second child and first son of the six children which circumstance and Dr. Hemingway accorded to Mrs. Hemingway, a woman who sang at the First Congregational Church and who named all her four daughters after saints. Hemingway's later remembrances of her weren't much more embracing than those of his father but then even in his derision it was his father that Hemingway embraced. Years later, after his *A Farewell to Arms* had been published, causing a furore in Boston and similar places of clean literary taste, she wrote him a letter telling him that the women's literary society in Oak Park had discussed his book that day. "I," she added loyally, "didn't go."

Although prosperous as a physician, Hemingway's father was much more inclined toward hunting and fishing and he gained his reputation not for his skill with the tools of saving lives but with the tools of taking them. He also was noted for his eyesight, which, it was said, enabled him to count potato bugs across a mile-wide lake on a bright summer day. He was, in addition, an expert wing shot, in and out of season. Once, according to Malcolm Cowley, a neighbor complained that he was breaking the law. "Never mind the law, madam," he shouted. "Shoot the birds!"

". . . *He wasn't any son of a bitch, though*," thought Robert Jordan, doomed on his Spanish hillside. "*He was just a coward and that was the worst luck any man could have. Because if he wasn't a coward he would have stood up to that woman and not let her bully him. I wonder what I would have been like if he had married a different woman. . .*"

According to the evidence of Hemingway's scattered and sardonic reminiscences, his mother set out to dominate him with the same authority she exercised over Dr. Hemingway. In their big brown house at six hundred North Kenilworth Avenue was a music room thirty feet square with a concert stage from which Mrs. Hemingway sang to invited audiences, and quite early in his life she gave young Ernest a 'cello.

My mother kept me out of school a whole year to study music and counterpoint," he told George Plimpton of the *Paris Review* in 1958. "She thought I had ability, but I was absolutely without talent. We played chamber music—someone came in to play the violin; my sister played the viola, and my mother the piano. That 'cello—I played it worse than anyone on earth. Of course, that year I was out doing other things too."

As Hemingway later implied, in a short story called *The Doctor and the Doctor's Wife*, the "masculine" interests won out over the "feminine" ones. By the time young Ernest was three, his father had given him a fishing rod. By the time he was eight, he was marching, according to ancient Oak Park recollections, in Decoration Day parades with his grandfather's Civil War pistol strapped to his side. By the time he was ten he had a shotgun. And when he was fourteen, his father gave him the gift he had asked for most of all, a course of boxing lessons advertised by a Chicago gymnasium.

According to Malcolm Cowley, the most important of the lessons came on the first day. Arriving at the gymnasium, young Ernest was invited to spar with one Young A'Hearn, a tough, tight-muscled professional middleweight who was training for his next bout.

"I'll take it easy," promised A'Hearn, but no sooner had they stepped into the ring when Hemingway wasn't stepping any more. He was lying on the canvas with blood running from his nose. With one punch, A'Hearn had broken it in three places.

"I knew he was going to give me the works the minute I saw his eyes," Hemingway told a friend.

"Were you scared?"

"Sure, he could hit like hell."

"Why did you go in there with him?"

"I wasn't that scared."

Not until he reappeared at the gymnasium the next day did Hemingway learn that A'Hearn had been Lesson No. 1 to other students as well. The other students, after paying their tuition in advance, had been satisfied with just that one lesson, but Hemingway, probably to both the admiration and dismay of his instructors, finished the course. By the time he was sixteen, he had suffered a number of further sparring injuries, one of them serious enough to impair the sight of his left eye and threaten the vision of his right. Big for his age, the boy, it seems, was also brittle. Yet he continued boxing and even other competitive endeavors, although more as a matter of course than of desire. As he later explained, it was not that he wanted to be an athlete.

"I had no ambition or choice," he said. "At Oak Park, if you could play football, you had to play it."

In 1959, he told an audience of high school students: "I played football in high school, and went right into basketball and then the track season and then baseball, and from all these sports I was always too tired to study. One year I had to have a private tutor for Latin and my father made me pay for him out of dough I had to earn. I had to have this tutor because in Latin class I had been sitting next to a very bright guy who moved away, and my average slumped. There are high schools like that where football practice uses up all the study time and leaves you so tired you can't study anyway. You should be guaranteed a good guy sitting next to you in Latin."

On the football team, famous for its day, if only for its neighborhood, he played right guard, a position which brought him more injuries, and certainly more injuries than glory. In his senior year at Oak Park High School, he had to be all but carried out of the two most important games, one for the scholastic championship, which Oak Park lost to Evanston, and one for an intersectional rivalry, which Oak Park lost to Evanston, and one for an intersectional rivalry, which Oak Park won from Toledo. Since, in addition, he not only happened to be the editor but also the sports writer for the school newspaper, *The Trapeze,* the young Hemingway was able to give himself adequate coverage. He concluded the account of one game with this late bulletin: "Hemingway is reported as convalescing, but the doctors fear his mind is irreparably lost." A later bulletin reported: "A large and enthusiastic crowd attended Hemingway's funeral. A pleasant time was had by all."

Whether carried or driven, young Hemingway went out for everything else in high school as well, or at least for enough to merit eight lines of extra curricular listings in the Class of '17 yearbook, the *Senior Tabula.* He was a member, for example, of the Hanna Club, which met to listen to prominent businessmen, of the Burke Club, which was dedicated to the practice of oratory and of the Boys' High School Club, which convened, according to the *Tabula,* to listen to addresses on "efficiency, Christianity and such things that are desirable to the life of a boy." What else was desirable to the life of a boy, Hemingway had to learn from other sources, but then, as the *Senior Tabula* said: "None are to be found more clever than Ernie." That was the legend printed in the yearbook along with the listings of his school activities, which, in addition, included the school orchestra, the school swimming team, the school athletic association, the class play and the writing of the class prophecy. In the prophecy, Hemingway predicted that classmate Morris Musselman would become a Hollywood writer, which Musselman did, that his sister Marcelline Hemingway would become a veterinarian, which she did not, and that he himself would become an aide to a general, which he was on at least several occasions.

Otherwise, Hemingway's major literary influences at the time were Margaret Dixon, an English teacher whose economic and social ideas were, a contemporary recalled, "somewhat at variance with the very conservative school and community;" Fannie Biggs, another English teacher whom Hemingway himself described as "very nice and especially nice to me;" his typewriter, which he kept in a third-floor room of that North Kenilworth Avenue house, insulated as much as possible from the rest of his family; and Ring Lardner, whose column, *In the Wake of the News*, appeared each day in the *Chicago Tribune*.

"Right half Smearcase of Bloomington kicked off to Cole, who returned the ball to his own one-yard line," Hemingway wrote in a *Trapeze* column entitled *A "Ring Lardner" on the Bloomington Game*. "Wilcoxen signaled for the hit and run play but Gordon was caught at second by a perfect throw from the catcher. Hemingway went over for the first touchdown by way of the Lake Street 'L.' Colville missed goal, the ball hitting the bar and causing havoc with the free lunch. Score, Oak Park 6, Bloomington, 0."

But Hemingway, even then, had his own inventiveness, and not just Ring Lardner's. It was as editor of the *Trapeze*, for example, that he created still another extra curricular listing for himself, the Boys' Rifle Club. Actually, according to Charles A. Fenton in his book, *The Apprenticeship of Ernest Hemingway*, there was not nor had there ever been a Boys' Rifle Club at Oak Park High. Faced one day, however, with the existence of a Girls' Rifle Club and with a blank space in the *Trapeze*, young Hemingway simply decided to make one up. From then until the end of the school year, he published stories about the club's matches and incredible skill. When, in the spring, the yearbook editors dutifully asked for a picture of the Boys' Rifle Club, Hemingway enlisted five friends, borrowed a shotgun for each of them and posed them before a camera. None, of course, had ever fired a gun in his life.

And yet, despite the clubs, the teams, the schoolboy camaraderie and this early display of what was to become his lifelong show of force, young Hemingway remained essentially a lonely boy, both at school and at home, where the loneliness was multiplied by each member of his family. "This is an awful thing to say," remembered Hemingway's first wife, Hadley, reminiscing later, a short time after his death, "but Ernest told me he didn't get along with any of the rest of his family as well as with one sister, Ursula. This sister, Ursula, understood him the best of anybody in the family. His parents, you know, disapproved of almost everything he did because almost everything he did was wild and adventurous."

He never went to school dances. His contemporaries remember that he showed a certain maladroitness with Oak Park girls, even though, as Hadley recalled him telling her, "he was a leader in the gang out there at Oak Park from a very young age, a gang of both boys *and* girls." Twice he ran away, leaving 'his cello behind and working as a day laborer, a farm hand, a dish washer, a sparring partner and riding the rails in a panorama of brooding that decorated many of his later stories. He never stayed away long enough to fall behind in school, but even so—and even then—he began to get the reputation among at least some of the sheltered sons and daughters of Oak Park that he was a tough guy. In a way, he was. When he was still fourteen, he later told his sons, he began boxing as a professional in Chicago under an assumed and now long-forgotten name. The victim of frequent overmatches, he came home to his father one night as a patient. His nose had been broken again. It was only in treating the injury that Dr. Hemingway learned how Ernest had gotten it, and, as a result of the ensuing argument, he ran away. According to what he told Earl Wilson, he went to Petoskey, Michigan, and promptly got another job as a professional boxer. He set himself up in a theater where the management offered five dollars to anyone who could stay a round with him. Overmatches in Petoskey, however, turned out to be something more lethal than overmatches in Chicago. When the lumberjacks of the area learned of the theater's offer, both it and young Hemingway were withdrawn.

Otherwise, Hemingway's escapes were *with* his father. Each summer, the two of them and others of the family would journey to their summer cabin at Horton's Bay in Northern Michigan, not far from Petoskey, where they would hunt and fish along the Big Two-Hearted River and occasionally minister to the medical needs of the Ojibway Indians, who were the chief inhabitants of that remote, primitive, old-time lumbering wilderness.

Although Hemingway never troubled himself or blessed his chroniclers with anything like an autobiography, many of his early short stories were dedicated to these summer adventures. In one, *Indian Camp*, he told of watching his father perform, with a jackknife, without anesthetic, and with fishing leaders for stitches, a Caesarean section on an Ojibway woman while her husband, unhinged by her screams, slit his throat in the double-decker bunk overhead. In another, *The Doctor and the Doctor's Wife,* he told how his father, during an argument with an Indian, threatened to knock the Indian's eyeteeth down his throat but then, at the last minute, went instead to his cabin and began cleaning his shotgun.

"His father came back to him in the fall of the year," Hemingway wrote in another, later short story, *Fathers And Sons,* published in 1933, *"or in the early spring when there had been jacksnipe on the prairie, or when he saw shocks of corn, or when he saw a lake, or if he ever saw a horse and buggy, or when he saw, or heard, wild geese, or in a duck blind; remembering the time an eagle dropped through the whirling snow to strike a canvas-covered decoy, rising, his wings beating, the talons caught in the canvas. His father was with him, suddenly, in deserted orchards and in new-plowed fields, in thickets, on small hills, or when going through dead grass, whenever splitting wood or hauling water, by grist mills, cider mills and dams and always with open fires. The towns he lived in were not towns his father knew. After he was fifteen he had shared nothing with him."*

The probability is that young Hemingway, applying the label of coward to his father long before his father's final act, dedicated himself to manliness at approximately the same time.

"He understood his father," Hemingway wrote of Robert Jordan in *For Whom the Bell Tolls, "and he forgave him everything and he pitied him but he was ashamed of him."*

Hemingway, then living in Key West, was on board a Pennsylvania Railroad train between New York and Trenton when he learned of his father's death. "I remember," said his oldest son, John, "Papa got off the train and left me in charge of a Pullman car porter all the way down to Key West. He didn't tell me at that time what it was all about. He just said, 'Something bad has happened. I have to go take care of it.'" In the moments that he had while he changed his route to Chicago, Hemingway penciled a short, unhappy note to his editor and friend, Maxwell Perkins. "He wrote, 'I feel terrible and sick',," said Carlos Baker. Hemingway's next recorded reaction to his father's death was in *Fathers And Sons:*

"The handsome job the undertaker had done on his father's face had not blurred in his mind and all the rest of it was quite clear, including the responsibilities. He had complimented the undertaker. The undertaker had been both proud and smugly pleased. But it was not the undertaker that had given him that last face."

It was years later that Hemingway told *New York Post* columnist Earl Wilson of having received a Christmas package from his mother while he was in Paris. Unaware of what the package might contain, he unwrapped it to find the revolver which his father had used to kill himself.

"I didn't know," Hemingway told Wilson, "whether it was an omen or a prophecy."

On the day that Ernest Hemingway killed himself, a man who had devoted his life to chronicling Hemingway's, sat in the silence of his completed work and wondered what went through Hemingway's mind in those final moments of his death.

"I had no doubt it was suicide," he said. "I could even imagine what he might have said to himself before he pulled the trigger. 'Well, here I come, Dad.' Or, 'I'm sorry I called you a coward.' In a way, he had it coming to him. . ."

CHAPTER THREE

The Discovery of Evil

ERNEST HEMINGWAY had shot himself once before. The circumstances, however, were somewhat less questionable. Marlin fishing from a cabin cruiser off the Florida Keys in the 1930s, he found the ship surrounded by sharks. With his companions, he began firing at them from the side of the cruiser, one of his favorite sea sports. Somehow his aim fell or the sea rose and, according to chronicler Carlos Baker, Hemingway shot himself in the leg with a submachinegun. He promptly vomited into a bailing bucket.

"The fact of the matter," said Baker shortly after Hemingway's death, "is that Hemingway had a whole history, all of his life, of being what they call accident-prone. Oh, there are a whole bunch of things. Once, when he was in Switzerland skiing, his little boy John inadvertently put his finger in his father's eye, scratched the eyeball and Hemingway was blind in that eye and sympathetically blind in the other eye for two days.

"Then again, he hit his head on a stanchion in London during the blackout, and once he hit his head badly on a skylight in one of the Paris garrets where he was living. The firearms accident—I believe it was his only one—happened in the 1930s, and then, of course, he had three bad automobile accidents and then the airplane accidents, two of them.

"All of those add up to a real accident-prone history, so that I don't know if you can rule out the possibility of accidental death. It's entirely possible that Hemingway's death was an accident, just as all those other times when he could have gotten killed were accidents. But if you're cleaning a shotgun, even if it's loaded, you're usually pointing it down, certainly not peering up the tube, seeing if it's clean. Because if you're cleaning a shotgun, you've got to break it to clean it."

Mathematically, it stands to reason that Hemingway should have suffered constantly from accidents. He was always flirting with the danger of them. In the formula of his success, he equated courage with what he persisted in calling the good and true, with an occasional detour in terminology toward the straight, and he stalked them continuously in what he thought was their natural habitat—violence. Sometimes, in fact, it seemed that what he actually was stalking was violence itself.

". . . This is the Hemingway 'code'—a 'grace under pressure'." wrote critic Philip Young in his study of Hemingway. "It is made of the controls of honor and courage which in a life of tension and pain make a man and distinguish him from the people who follow random impulses, let down their hair, and are generally messy, perhaps cowardly, and without inviolable rules for how to live holding tight."

Writers have always sought the underworld to satisfy themselves that nothing is above it. From his first conception of fatherly cowardice, Hemingway began to form his ideology that virility is man's proudest possession, that to be defeated is not necessarily to lose and that life is not a garden party. It was a matter of course, then, that he did not seek life in garden parties but in places where men risked defeat and proved their virility. Such places weren't always war, but they were almost always environmentally violent. "There is honor among pickpockets and honor among whores," Hemingway once said. "It is simply that the standards differ."

As his friends, for example, he sought out generals, prize fighters, spies, jockeys, matadors, escaped convicts, exiled revolutionaries, saloonkeepers, junkies, ski instructors, gangsters, hunters, drunks, and those pickpockets and whores and everyone else whom he described as living their lives "all the way up." And not only did he seek out their friendship; he also sought out their experiences.

"They are men and women," Malcolm Cowley once wrote

34

of Hemingway's friends, "who have taken risks, and that is one reason why the mortality among them has been high. Hemingway has taken risks and survived, but he carries scars—literally from the crown of his head to the sole of his right foot. One might say that the story of his life is engraved on his body."

Hemingway, of course, began this engravure at an early age. When he first used his fishing reel at three and his shotgun at ten, he literally was hunting through the bush of violence. As for his adolescent injuries, they were the first marks of his risks. But Hemingway also was marked by inner scars. When, in *Indian Camp*, the first of Hemingway's lightly disguised autobiographical short stories, the young Nick Adams watches his father perform a Caesarian section on an Ojibway woman while her husband slits his throat, the events are stark, gruesome and shocking, but Hemingway is not primarily interested in the events themselves.

"He is more interested." wrote Philip Young, "in their effect on the little boy who witnessed them. As a matter of fact the events do not seem, at the time, to have any remarkable effect on the boy. But later on this same Nick Adams is a badly scarred and nervous young man, and in this story Hemingway is relating to us one of the many reasons why."

In other words, Hemingway's search through violence led, inexorably and early, to what Robert Penn Warren and other critics have called the discovery of evil. "When the young man Hemingway came to the edge of the forest," wrote Wright Morris in *The Territory Ahead*, "when he saw what man had left in the place of nature, he found it something more than an unpleasant shock. He found it unacceptable. In that early judgment he has never wavered." Whether it was Hemingway's encounter with a punchdrunk, one-time prizefighter, or his first sexual intercourse with a teenaged Ojibway girl, or his father's cowardice, real or imagined, the discovery of evil, according to Young, made Hemingway "sick." Like Huckleberry Finn and most of America's youth, he was unprepared for his confrontation with it.

Not that his fellow townsmen were guilty of having permitted young Hemingway to make such a discovery in Oak Park. Often called the middle class capital of the world, Oak Park barred evil at the city line.

"The wonder to me," said one of his former teachers at Oak Park High after Hemingway had bequeathed his ado-

35

lescent years there, "and to a lot of other Oak Parkers, is how a boy brought up in the Christian and Puritan nurture should know and write so well of the devil and the underworld." Even by midcentury, Oak Park hadn't been able to reconcile itself with having been the birthplace of such a man of letters, or, rather, of a man of such letters. "It is a puzzle," another native told Hemingway biographer Charles A. Fenton in 1952, "and, too, an amazement to Oak Park that Ernest should have written the kind of books that he did."

Even so, Hemingway, by the advent of his Oak Park High School years, had begun to give some indication of his future literary bent, whether it was bent in Oak Park or elsewhere. "He wrote with an avid interest in realistic adventure," said one English instructor, remembering Hemingway's freshman themes. "I can recall that his writings in this class were different to the extent that it seemed to me they might not be acceptable as the assignment," recalled someone else who had been Hemingway's friend and neighbor. And history instructor John Gehlmann, who was faculty adviser to the school newspaper, *The Trapeze*, while Hemingway was one of its editors, remembered that Hemingway's early subject matter and style were the cause of much consternation to the school superintendent, M. R. McDaniel, and, consequently, the cause of much chagrin to Gehlmann. "I was always having to fight criticism by the superintendent," Gehlmann later said, "that Ernie was writing like Ring Lardner—and consequently a lost soul!"

Even after Hemingway's graduation into the literary ranks, Superintendent McDaniel blamed Gehlmann for Hemingway's fall from Oak Park grace. "He held me responsible," Gehlmann said, "for the malodorous writings from Ernie's pen." Oak Park, as a matter of fact, continued to hold its nose or point it upward for a long time after its unfavored son had become favored in other places. And among Oak Park's residents remained, of course, some of Hemingway's family. Earl Wilson, for example, tells the story of how, in 1925, a relative ordered ten copies of Hemingway's *in our time* to send out as Christmas presents to other members of the family. When she received the order and read the book, however, she sent all ten copies back with an angry note, explaining that if she had known Hemingway were going to write in such ungentlemanly language she wouldn't have ordered a single book.

Actually, whatever Hemingway was looking for he found in the wilderness beyond Oak Park, although he didn't fail to recognize Oak Park a a wilderness in itself. As far as Hemingway was concerned, Oak Park escaped him with as good fortune as he escaped it. "I had a wonderful novel to write about Oak Park," he said in 1952, "and would never do it because I did not want to hurt living people." That he considered Oak Park to have living people in it at all was an additional compliment. Probably the truth is that he never wrote about Oak Park because there was so much else which he found so much more vital. Even while he was still in high school, he was writing about other things and other places. One of his earliest manuscripts, *Judgment of Manitou*, printed in the February, 1916, issue of the school literary magazine, the *Tabula*, was a story about a trapper who murdered his associate in the Walloon Lake country near the Hemingway summer cabin. A second manuscript, *A Matter of Colour*, published in the next issue of the *Tabula*, was a story about a crooked prize fight based on material which had been impressed on him in the same Chicago gymnasium where he had been so impressed with Young A'Hearn's fist. And his third story, *Sepi Jingan*, was about an Ojibway killer who also happened to be a kind and decent man, tender with dogs and more deeply concerned about the merits of various pipe tobaccos than with the savage memories that made Hemingway's story. *Sepi Jingan* had dimensions Hemingway did not find in Oak Park:

The edge of the full moon showed above the hill to the east. To our right was a grassy bank. "Let's sit down," Bill said. "Did I ever tell you about Sepi Jingan?"

"Like to hear it," I replied.

"You remember Paul Black Bird?"

"The fellow who got drunk last fourth of July and went to sleep on the Pere Marquette tracks?"

"Yes. He was a bad Indian. Up on the upper penninsula he couldn't get drunk. He used to drink all day—everything. But he couldn't get drunk. Then he would go crazy; but he wasn't drunk. He was crazy because he couldn't get drunk."

There was no getting drunk, of course, in Oak Park, at whose boundaries the saloons stopped and the churches began. Hemingway never wrote an autobiography, but he did provide the approximation of one with his short stories, including even *Judgment of Manitou* and *Sepi Jingan*, despite their early displays of Hemingway's ebullient imagination. It was, however, in his short stories about his recurrent hero Nick Adams, ranging from *Indian Camp* to *Fathers And Sons*, that Hemingway revealed the insights and recollections closest to what actually happened. In these Nick Adams stories, which he wrote between 1921 and 1933, Hemingway traced the growth of his hero from the little boy watching his father perform a jackknife operation in *Indian Camp* to the grown Nick Adams telling his own son about his father in *Fathers And Sons*. It was Nick Adams who overheard the gunmen looking for Ole Andreson in the all-night diner of *The Killers*. It was Nick Adams who walked through the burned-out blackness of the forest fire in *Big Two-River*.

For Hemingway, tough guy that he might have become to his Oak Park friends, his discovery of evil was hardly among the little girls with bows in their hair and chin-high bodices who still peer with bashful smiles from the pages of the 1917 *Senior Tabula*. The distance between them and Trudy, the Ojibway girl of the Northern Michigan wilds, was something more than a day's train ride. Trudy, Hemingway wrote in *Fathers And Sons*, "did first what no one has ever done better . . . *Plump brown legs, flat belly, hard little breasts, well holding arms, quick searching tongue, the flat eyes, the good taste of mouth, then uncomfortably, tightly, sweetly, moistly, lovely, tightly, achingly, fully, finally, un-endingly, never-endingly, never-to-endingly, suddenly ended, the great bird flown like an owl in the twilight, only it daylight in the woods and hemlock needles stuck against your belly. . .*"

Hemingway left Oak Park in the fall of 1917, not for good perhaps, but eventually for better. His original intention had been to enroll at the University of Illinois, but the entrance of America into World War I left no other recourse for a youth with his emerging virile pretensions than to enroll instead in the Army. The Army, however, wouldn't have him. He was rejected because of his eye injury and he was rejected, in fact, twelve times. Somewhat blind but never daunted, he kept going from one branch of the military service to another trying to fool the opthalmologists. Unsuccessful, he decided instead to seek whatever turmoil he could find as a cub reporter on the *Kansas City Star*.

"I wanted to work on the *Star*," Hemingway said years later, "because I thought it was the best paper in the U. S." If it was not *the* best, it certainly was one of the best. On its staff at the time were Russel Crouse, who later became half of the playwriting team of Lindsay and Crouse; John Selby who turned into an editor and novelist, although of somewhat less impressive fame; Frances Davis, now better known as the Frances Lockridge of the Mr. and Mrs. North partnership; Wesley Stout, the eventual editor of the *Saturday Evening Post*; and a host of others who found further literary success of varying degrees. "Every newspaperman I knew," Crouse later remembered of the *Star* city room, "was secretly working on a novel."

Actually what brought Hemingway to Kansas City were the facts that his father's younger brother, Tyler Hemingway, was a successful businessman there and that a Horton Bay friend, Carl Edgar, worked in Kansas City for a fuel oil company. Young Hemingway often had rowed across to Edgar's Pine Lake cottage during their northern Michigan summers and had talked about joining him in the midwest metropolis. When Hemingway finally arrived in Kansas City, he added a year to his age and Uncle Tyler used a few well-placed connections to get him into the *Star* city room. It was there, at sixty dollars a month, that Hemingway met two famous journalistic institutions.

One was the *Star* style sheet, a long single, galley-sized page, which dictated the rules all *Star* writers had to follow and which today sounds like a guide to the surface characteristics of Hemingway's own writing mannerisms: "Use short sentences. Use short first paragraphs. Use vigorous English. Be positive not negative . . . Avoid the use of adjectives, especially such extravagant ones as *splendid, gorgeous, grand, magnificent,* etc. . . Never use old slang." In 1940 Hemingway told a young newspaperman: "Those were the best rules I ever learned for the business of writing. I've never forgotten them. No man with any talent, who feels and writes truly about the thing he is trying to say, can fail to write well if he abides by them."

The second famous journalistic institution was Lionel Calhoun Moise, a nomad newspaper journeyman of the old, or, rather, no school, who had become a legend in American city rooms by the time he was thirty, who loved to get drunk, brawl in barrooms, slug cops and, according to Russel Crouse, throw typewriters out of windows. No small part of Moise's legend also was the fact that he was one of the most fluent writers in the newspaper business, once contributing three hundred extremely unrepetitious words per day for thirty consecutive days all on the presence of Halley's comet. Moise was what might now be considered a character right out of Hemingway, and there is no doubt that he was one of the characters who went into Hemingway. The two became close friends during Hemenway's seven months at the *Star*, with Moise gaining the post of the most respected of Hemingway's many mentors there. "Pure objective writing is the only true form of storytelling," Moise would tell Hemingway. "No stream of consciousness nonsense; no playing dumb observer one paragraph and God Almighty the next. In short, no tricks."

At first Hemingway was assigned to share the Federal Building beat with Frances Davis, but, as she remembered, "He wanted to ride ambulances." After several weeks, Hemingway got what he wanted. "I covered the short-stop run," he recalled in 1952, "which included the Fifteenth Street police station, the Union Station and the General Hospital. At the Fifteenth Street station, you covered crime, usually small, but you never knew when you might hit something larger. Union Station was everybody going in and out of town . . . some shady characters I got to know, and interviews with celebrities going through."

"He liked action," recalled Hemingway's old boss, Pete Wellington, then assistant city editor of the *Star*. "When he was assigned to the General Hospital, he had an irritating habit of riding off with the first ambulance to go to some kind of cutting scrape without letting the city desk know that he was leaving the post uncovered. He always wanted to be on the scene himself. . ." Landon Laird, later a *Star* columnist, remembered that "Ernest was always bouncing up to the police station to ride squad cars with officer Bauswell and others. Officer Bauswell was a character, and much more productive of the excitement in which Ernest reveled than a city room could possibly be."

Hemingway continued to display this zest for action when, one day, he happened to be working at a city room typewriter on which every tenth letter or so would print above the line. As he pulled the finished sheet out of the typewriter and called for a copy boy, he turned around to find a young man, new in the office, who had been watching him. "That's rotten looking copy," Hemingway said, sheepishly. "When I get a little excited this damn type mill goes haywire on me." Then he got up and held out his hand. "My name's Hemingway," he said, "Ernest Hemingway. You're a new man, aren't you?"

The new man was Theodore Brumback, son of a Kansas City family with even better connections than Uncle Tyler's. Blind in one eye because of a golfing accident, Brumback had foresworn his senior year at Cornell to serve in France with the American Field Service as an ambulance driver attached to the *Chasseurs Alpins*. When his enlistment had expired, he had returned to Kansas City, had gotten a job on the *Star* and, on his first day, had noticed Hemingway attacking the typewriter.

The two young men became close friends, with Hemingway fascinated by the manner in which Brumback, despite his eye injury, had managed to get into the war anyway. Brumback confided that he wanted to go back, and Hemingway, of course, wanted to go with him. Finally, in April of 1918, the two of them happened to be in the vicinity of the cable desk when a story came over the wires reporting that the American Red Cross wanted volunteers to serve as ambulance drivers with the Italian Army on the Northern Italian front. The idea was that the presence of American uniforms, even if only on ambulance drivers, would be helpful to the morale of the Italian troops, and Hemingway immediately liked the idea.

According to the best recollections of those who were present, Hemingway and Brumback cabled their appplications to the Red Cross even before the wire story had gotten to a linotype machine. By May twelfth, they were in their uniforms as honorary lieutenants and by the following week they were in New York, marching downtown from Eighty-second Street to the Battery with President and Mrs. Wilson reviewing the parade. The one hundred and ten blocks were, for Hemingway, all part of the journey toward what he was seeking, although he knew he really would not know what he was seeking until he had found it.

On the troopship Chicago, sailing without lights or destroyer escort, Hemingway waited expectantly on the darkened deck amid rumors of U-boat sightings. At one point, when the ship suddenly changed course, Hemingway turned with elation toward Brumback with the thought that excitement was rising out of the sea. The excitement disappeared, however, when a reported German submarine turned out to be a barrel sitting upright on a floating raft.

"Hemingway felt he'd been cheated," Brumback later remembered.

Again, when the two of them arrived in Paris, they found they were just in time for the first shelling of the city by the new, long-range German Big Berthas. At the railroad station, the *Gare du Nord*, Hemingway promptly hailed a cab.

"Tell the taxi," he instructed Brumback, "to drive up where those shells are falling. We'll get a story for the *Star* that'll make their eyes pop out back in Kansas City."

Hemingway began stuffing money into the cab driver's hand and then ordered him to start off in what Brumback later described as "one of the strangest taxi drives I shall probably ever experience." For an hour, the cab raced through Paris trying to catch up with the falling shells. Although the race didn't end in a tie, it came close enough.

". . . The shell hit the facade of the Madeleine," Brumback later wrote, "chipping off a foot or so of stone. No one was hurt. We heard the projectile rush overhead. It sounded as if it were going to land right in the taxi with us. It was quite exciting."

Eventually, Hemingway and Brumback were sent to Milan, where Hemingway scribbled a post card back to a friend in Kansas City: "Having a wonderful time!!! Had my Baptism of fire my first day here when an entire munitions plant exploded." But for Hemingway, not yet nineteen, his first taste of blood had merely whetted his appetite. When, in the ambulance corps, he later found himself bedded down in a country club near enough to the front lines to be conscious of them but too far away to be in any danger, he asked for a transfer to one of the Red Cross canteens which had been established at the trenches. "I'm fed up," he said after a week of baseball and swimming at the country club. "There's nothing here but scenery and too damn much of that." With Brumback, he discussed quitting the ambulance corps altogether "to see if I can't find out where the war is."

At last he received the transfer. "I go to the front tomorrow," he wrote back to Kansas City. "Oh Boy!!! I'm glad I'm in it."

Seven days later, on July eighth, 1918, Hemingway, placed in charge of a canteen just west of the Piave River, bicycled through the darkness to a riverbank listening post about one hundred yards beyond the Italian lines. At the listening post were three Italian soldiers, and Hemingway was handing out chocolate bars to them from his supply bag when an Austrian trench-mortar, with both the size and the nickname of an ash can, exploded only a few feet away.

"*. . . Through the other noise I heard a cough, then came the chuh-chuh-chuh-chuh—then there was a flash, as when a blast furnace door is swung open, and a roar that started white and went red and on and on in a rushing wind,*" he later wrote in *A Farewell to Arms.* "*I tried to breathe but my breath would not come and I felt myself rush bodily out of myself and out and out and out and all the time bodily in the wind. I went out swiftly, all of myself, and I knew I was dead and that it had all been a mistake to think you just died. Then I floated, and instead of going on I felt myself slide back. I breathed and I was back. The ground was torn up and in front of my head there was a splintered beam of wood. In the jolt of my head I heard somebody crying. I thought somebody was screaming. I tried to move but I could not move. I heard the machine-guns and rifles firing across the river and all along the river. There was a great splashing and I saw the star shells go up and burst and float whitely and rockets going up and heard the bombs, all this in a moment, and then I heard close to me someone saying, 'Mama Mia! Oh, Mama Mia! . . .*"

The ash can had been filled with quarter-and half-inch pieces of sawed-off steel rods and when Hemingway recovered consciousness he found that the explosion had blown off the legs of all three Italian soldiers. Two of them were already dead and the third was screaming. Unaware that his own legs had been shattered by the shrapnel, Hemingway lifted the wounded Italian onto his back and carried him several hundred feet to a first aid dugout while two Austrian searchlights and a machine-gun battery followed him. As Hemingway made his way from the riverbank, staggering and crawling in a manner that he could not afterwards remember, one of the machine-gun bullets hit him again in the knee and another hit him again in the ankle. When he reached the safety of the trench, he collapsed. By that time the soldier he had carried on his back was dead.

"My feet," he wrote his family later, "felt like I had rubber boots full of water on (hot water) and my kneecap was acting queer. The machine-gun bullet just felt like a sharp smack on the leg with an icy snowball." Later, in *A Farewell to Arms,* he would write: "*I knew that I was hit and leaned over and put my hand on my knee. My knee wasn't there. My hand went in and my knee was down on my shin.*"

By the time Hemingway regained consciousness a second time he was being carried on a stretcher to another dressing station three kilometers away. The road, however, was being shelled and with each swoosh of an approaching projectile, his stretcher-bearers would abruptly drop him on the ground and dive for cover. "*They dropped me once more before we reached the post,*" Hemingway was to write. "*You sons of bitches,*" *I said.* When they arrived at the dressing station they found it had been evacuated. For two more hours, Hemingway lay in a stable under the continuing bombardment, waiting for an ambulance to take him to still another dressing station. When he arrived there the doctors found that he had been struck by two hundred and thirty-seven pieces of shrapnel.

At the dressing station, twenty-eight of the fragments were removed by the physicians. Later, as he told Guy Hickok, a total of one hundred and eighty were taken from his legs. How many pieces of the sawed-off steel rods stayed in him remains unclear, but thirty years afterwards he was still complaining about metal fragments working their way out through his skin. From his hospital bed at the time, he drew pictures indicating their size and mailed the drawings home to his family. Six weeks later he was to write to them: "I wouldn't really be comfortable now unless I had some pain."

According to biographer Charles A. Fenton, Hemingway spent five days in a field hospital before he was fit to be moved to the base hospital in Milan. There, he underwent a dozen operations. His right leg was still in a plaster cast when he was recommended for the *Croce de Guerra* with three citations and the *Medaglia d'Argento al Valore Militare,* which was the second highest Italian military decoration and which carried with it a pension of about fifty dollars a year. "As Ma Pettingil says," he wrote to his family, "'Leave us keep the home fires burning.'"

It took three months for Hemingway to receive his bone graft, his new aluminum knee cap and his release from the hospital. During his stay there, he had reassured Brumback that from then on he was going to stick to ambulance driving. By October of 1918, however, he had recovered enough of his health and his posture to inveigle the Italians into assigning him as a bona fide, fighting infantryman with one of their elite units, the *Arditi*. Actually, however, more than Hemingway's legs had been shattered.

"When you go to war as a boy you have a great illusion of immortality," he wrote later. "Other people get killed; not you . . . Then when you are badly wounded the first time you lose that illusion and you know it can happen to you."

When he returned to Oak Park in the spring of 1919, he found that he no longer could sleep except during the day. Having been blown up during the night, he imagined that if he ever closed his eyes in the darkness again, he might never be able to reopen them.

"I remember him distinctly," an Oak Park acquaintance later recalled, "walking up the street in his blue uniform and limping, with a cane."

Hemingway's uniform, according to Carlos Baker, consisted of a tunic which he "had traded someone out of," a pair of boots and a shirt purchased in Gibraltar and a black leather coat with sheepskin lining that had accrued to Hemingway through a friend's death. Years later, Hemingway told Earl Wilson that it wasn't his idea to wear the uniform in Oak Park. His family, he said, insisted on it. He kept wearing it, he added, until his family insisted he take it off.

Hemingway remained in Oak Park only briefly. Before he left, he was invited to speak at the high school. He stood up in the assembly hall, told the students it was his first speech, described what had happened to him and then held up the shrapnel-riddled trousers he had been wearing when he was wounded. Later, in a letter to Maxwell Perkins, he explained: "I have not been at all hardboiled since July eighth, 1918—on the night on which I discovered that that also was vanity." When he left Oak Park again, he never returned.

CHAPTER FOUR

The Fouled Generation

I

IN THE MIDI, the south of France, Gertrude Stein one day overheard a garagekeeper raging over the ineptitude of his apprentices with such problems as the monkey wrench and the screwdriver.

"*Vous êtes tous,*" he shouted at them, "*une génération perdue!*"

In the subsequence of events, Miss Stein did more than merely translate the garagekeeper's rage into English. What she did was translate it to mean an entire revolt of culture. To the cubist circle of war-tinted painters, socialite culture-seekers, garret-starved poets, great and little magazine editors, chamber pot novelists, real and unreal surrealists, and Bohemian scholars who gathered about her in her Paris salon, sometimes seeking intellectual crumbs and sometimes seeking alimentary ones, Miss Stein declared:

"You are all a lost generation!"

It was Ernest Hemingway, insisting that she was wrong, who eventually proved that she was right.

"After the last World War," she wrote on V-E Day in 1945, "there was the lost generation, they were successful but I called them sad young men because their life was finished by thirty, they dreaded their thirtieth birthday, that was the end of life for them, life began early, success was great and after thirty what was there to do, nothing. This was something that inevitably made for sadness, and it was because as a Frenchman explained, a man goes through his period of becoming civilized between seventeen and twenty-five, it is in these years that women mold him into shape, that he begins to measure himself in the real business of life against his contemporaries and competitors, he becomes civilized. The other war just destroyed that civilizing business, and they were a lost generation, their life became too easy as it did after the war was over, and life being too easy it looked as if it was over by thirty and so they were sad young men."

And among the sad young men was Ernest Hemingway. For all of his back-slapping, jaw-punching, tennis-courting, buck-hunting, Oak Park boisterousness, he was still the shattered, brooding soldier whose inner torment would become so explicit in his later stories, such as *Soldier's Home:*

". . . 'Don't you love your mother, dear boy?'

"'No,' Krebs said.

"His mother looked at him across the table. Her eyes were shiny. She started crying.

"'I don't love anybody,' Krebs said."

The sad young men who returned to the Oak Park of America were not the same romantic siblings who had gone into the Great War with slogans dancing bravely in their heads along with dreams of valor that would make the world safe for a democracy they would never know. They came back from trenches and barbed wire which still held pieces of their flesh, from poison gas and mortar bombs designed to maim whole regiments, from shells fired short from their own artillery batteries into their own midst, from wounded screams that filled the watery craters of no-man's land, from bayonets that spilled other men's entrails with their own hands, from officers who shot them in their frightened, defecating backs, from the forbidden, manly words of everyday language, from dead drunken nights in strange dead towns, from midnight doorway love affairs with girls whose names they never asked. They came back and found the Women's Christian Temperance Union.

"Nothing was changed in the town except that the young girls had grown up," Hemingway would write in *Soldier's Home.* *"But they lived in such a complicated world of already defined alliances and shifting feuds that Krebs did not feel the energy or the courage to break into it . . . Vaguely he wanted a girl but he did not want to have to work to get*

47

*her. He would have liked to have a girl but he did not want
to have to spend a long time getting her. He did not want to
get into the intrigue and the politics. He did not want to have
to do any courting. He did not want to tell any more lies. It
wasn't worth it . . . Here at home it was all too complicated
. . . That was the thing about French girls and German girls.
There was not all this talking . . . It was simple and you
were friends. . ."*

II

After several months of war-produced insomnia in Oak
Park and the Northern Michigan wilds of his already distant
boyhood, Hemingway, then twenty, decided to return to
newspaper writing, first in Toronto, where he wrote feature
articles for the *Daily Star* and the *Star Weekly*, and then in
Chicago, where he edited a house organ, the *Co-operative
Commonwealth.*

His job with the Toronto *Star*, like that in Kansas City,
was obtained for Hemingway by connections. One of his
father's friends in Horton Bay was Ralph Connable, then
head of the F. W. Woolworth chain in Canada, and, during
Hemingway's restless 1919 summer in Michigan, Connable
offered to help tie up his post-war loose ends by inviting him
to the Connable home in Toronto. There Hemingway acted
as a tutor to Connable's young son until Connable, Uncle
Ralph to Hemingway, was able to introduce him to the *Star*
through its advertising department. When Hemingway and
the *Star* finally met, they formed a relationship that was to
last four years, with only the brief interruption of Hemingway's activities in Chicago.

"A rap at the door followed by the entrance of my right-
hand man and special writer, Gregory Clark," Herbert Cran-
ston, then editor of the *Star Weekly*, later wrote of his
meeting with Hemingway. "He had in tow a tall, thin, loosely
jointed chap with flushed cheeks, black, glowing eyes, a thin
black mustache and careless black hair. He limped a little,
wore a peaked cap, a leather coat short in the arms, and
gray tight trousers, also short.

"'Boss, this fellow says he can write, and he wants to do
something for us,' said Clark. 'His name is Ernest Hemingway.'

". . . Greg Clarks recalls that Hemingway used to come
into the office and sit on the radiator while he talked and

interfered with the work the other fellows were trying to do. He was a good talker too, just like Greg, who would rather talk any day than take his typewriter in hand.

"Sometimes I listened in. I remember being fascinated by 'Hemmy's' tales of his adventures in eating. Seems he was ready to try anything once. If he heard of anything new that anybody was eating anywhere in the world he would swallow it himself to discover what it tasted like. He claimed to have masticated slugs, earthworms, snails, ants, and all sorts of other Epicurean delicacies. . ."

Hemingway returned to Chicago in the fall of 1920, dropped in at Oak Park just long enough to kiss everyone hello and goodbye and then found himself quarters on the saloon side of the city line. ". . . In Chicago," Charles A. Fenton wrote in his heavily documented book about Hemingway's early years, "he lived on the outskirts of the world of people like the retired gunman and the practicing bootleggers. . . He spent a great deal of time in the Chicago gyms, and in the Italian restaurants. For a while, very broke, he shared a furnished room with Bill Horne, his ambulance corps friend. Eventually he got a job through a want ad in the *Chicago Tribune.*" And eventually he met Sherwood Anderson.

The want-ad that Hemingway answered had been placed in the *Tribune* by the Co-operative Society of America, a venture formed by one Harrison Parker, who, as recently as 1948, was still getting into trouble with the federal government over the pocketing of other people's funds. Hemingway's task with the *Co-operative Commonwealth* was to publicize the society, from which he earned fifty dollars a week and from which Harrison Parker earned fifteen million. "I worked until I was convinced it was crooked," Hemingway said years later, "stayed on a little while thinking I could write and expose it, and then decided to just rack it up as experience and the hell with it."

More important experience for Hemingway, however, was gained in the Chicago apartment of still another Horton Bay friend, Y. K. Smith, where Hemingway eventually was given sleeping space with a conglomorate group of other aspiring writers and where he helped organize them into a sort of fraternity dedicated to literary and other horseplay. "He was by far the most colorful of us," Smith later recalled. "And very witty."

He also, perhaps, was the most serious about his writing. His typewriter remained the busiest in the apartment and he kept mailing out stories, essays, articles, poems and newspaper correspondence as fast as the Post Office could reward him with rejection slips.

"Will it sell?" he would ask his co-tenants at the apartment after reading one of his stories aloud. "Do you think it will sell?"

"There was a real irony in his concentration upon salability," wrote biographer Fenton. "While the others discussed art and the artistic verities, and urged Hemingway to concern himself more with the permanent values of literature, he was actually subjecting himself to a rigid professional discipline. He was dismayed and angered, however—as he has continued to be—by too much talking in large, vague terms about writing. 'Artist, art, artistic!' he would shout. 'Can't we ever hear the last of that stuff!' While they talked about art, with the rather easy intensity of dilettantes, Hemingway talked about story markets, and about the fighters he was watching in Kid Howard's gym; and above all, his friends remembered, he talked about soldiering. . . 'You've got to see it, feel it, smell it, hear it,' he once declared to the group."

It was into the parlor of Y. K. Smith's apartment that Sherwood Anderson walked one night. A former advertising agency colleague of Smith's, Anderson lived on Division Street, not far from Smith's address at One Hundred East Chicago, and he was to become a frequent visitor during the winter of 1920. Recently returned from his first expatriate journey to Paris and already famous as the author of *Winesburg, Ohio,* Anderson commanded an instantaneous respect from the inmates of Smith's hostelry, although there remains some doubt whether he got all the respect due him from Ernest Hemingway. According to Fenton, Hemingway's co-tenants remembered that Hemingway remained distant, critical, and even hostile, despite his outward attentiveness to Anderson. In 1925, however, Hemingway himself confessed to F. Scott Fitzgerald that his first pattern of writing had been *Winesburg,* and the proof appeared in Hemingway's early short stories *Up in Michigan* and *My Old Man.* "His actual debt to Anderson was a large one," wrote Fenton. ". . . Hemingway read Anderson's work constantly. . ." At another time, however, Hemingway sent a letter to Edmund

Wilson saying: "No I don't think *My Old Man* derives from Anderson. It is about a boy and his father and race-horses. Sherwood has written about boys and horses. But very differently. It derives from boys and horses. Anderson derives from boys and horses. I don't think they're anything alike. I know I wasn't inspired by him."

Whatever Hemingway thought of Anderson, there is no doubt that Anderson was impressed with Hemingway. "Thanks for introducing me to that young fellow," Anderson told his hosts as he left the Smith apartment that first night. "I think he's going to go some place." There also is no doubt that Anderson helped Hemingway go there. And the first stop was Paris.

Anderson never claimed to be a major influence on Hemingway, although he later said it was "through my efforts" that Hemingway "first got published." "Anyway, it is sure," he wrote in his *Memoirs* twenty years later, "that if others said I had shown Hemingway the way, I myself had never said so. I thought . . . that he had his own gift, which had nothing particularly to do with me." In any event, Anderson soon was regarded as something of a sponsor to Hemingway and later, after Hemingway decided to leave for Europe, Anderson gave him letters of introduction to Gertrude Stein, Ezra Pound, and everyone else whom Anderson thought Hemingway ought to know. In return, Hemingway, on the night before his departure, packed all the leftover canned food from his apartment into a knapsack and brought it up to Anderson's place. "That was a nice idea," Anderson wrote later, "bringing thus to a fellow scribbler the food he had to abandon . . . I remember his coming up the stairs, a magnificent broad-shouldered man, shouting as he came."

III

There had been, of course, no such thing as a GI Bill when Hemingway returned from World War I. It couldn't have made any difference. "Ernest Hemingway's college . . ." as Carlos Baker later wrote in his book, *Hemingway, The Writer As Artist*, "was the continent of Europe. Besides the electives in art and literature, there were required courses in languages, people, statecraftiness, power politics, peace conferences and war." Chiefs on the faculty of Europe U. were Ezra Pound and Gertrude Stein.

An obvious pair of dissimilarities, they most certainly did not make a couple. Miss Stein, with close-cropped hair, a deep, masculine voice and a face to match, had been in Paris since 1903, holding her authoritarian seminars in her salon at Twenty-seven Rue de Fleurus, where she held, in addition, an extreme distaste for Pound. "Pound's special interests at this time ran to Japanese prints, political economy and Oriental music," wrote John Malcolm Brinnin in *The Third Rose,* his biography of Miss Stein. "Gertrude shared none of these, and there was little else about his thinking, his person or his manner that attracted her. A nervous, self-conscious young man with a high voice, a laugh described as being like the triumphant bray of a jackass, and a robust, red-blond bearing, Pound struck many people as being in perpetual motion. 'His beard, his open collar, his earring, the lopsided table he had made for himself, the coats he wore, his aggressive mannerims,' said critic Herbert Gorman, 'proclaimed to the world in the most militant way that he was continuously either lashing or thumbing his nose at the Philistines.' One of Gertrude's objections to the man was his avuncular attitude toward women; with no warrant or warning, he might kiss them on the forehead or draw them upon his knees with no concern for their wishes in the matter or their taste for such displays. Gertrude was nevertheless taken with Ezra 'in a sort of way' at first, but soon found him 'not amusing.' She felt he was a 'village explainer' (a term she had once used in describing her brother) which meant that his talk was 'excellent if you were a village, but if you were not, not.' In particular she took exception to his attempts to 'explain' to her the significance of the paintings hanging on her walls. Since they both had widely celebrated reputations as discoverers and sponsors of new talent, it was perhaps fortunate for the peace of letters that they never found themselves in contest over the same prodigy . . . The competitive air that emanated from Ezra Pound was certain to keep Gertrude at a distance, even had she been able to overlook his lack of personal charm. Any sort of competition was anathema to her, and she was continually on the alert for signs that circumstance might force her into it. Pound took exception to the pointedly cool treatment she gave him, but she was adamant in refusing him welcome to her atelier. In retaliation, Ezra advertised Gertrude as a mere parasite on the body of literature and delighted in opportunities to refer to her as 'old tub of guts.' "

Whether Miss Stein and Mr. Pound actually became rivals for the prodigious Mr. Hemingway soon developed into a debate which is still continuing. In any event, by the time Hemingway arrived in Paris Miss Stein already had established her *avant-garde* reputation with the then-daring prose of *Three Lives* and the poet Pound was busy establishing the reputation of others with his even more daring letters to magazine and book editors. Miss Stein had arrived in Paris years before Pound, but they were both, in a way, the vanguard of the expatriate American invasion that followed World War I. And as the invaders advanced up the slopes of Montparnasse, each of them established a separate command post.

Miss Stein's, at Twenty-seven Rue de Fleurus, was probably the most famous. In it, at various times, could be found Pablo Picasso, Henri Matisse, Juan Gris, Georges Braque, and later, as the Expatriate Expeditionary Force grew, T. S. Eliot, William Carlos Williams, E. E. Cummings, F. Scott Fitzgerald and Sherwood Anderson.

"Imagine a strong woman with legs like stone pillars sitting in a room hung with Picassos," Anderson wrote in his notebook after his first visit to her salon. "The woman is the very symbol of health and strength. She laughs. She smokes cigarettes. She tells stories with an American shrewdness in getting the tang and the kick into the telling."

She would sit in a high-backed Italian Renaissance chair placed strategically near a stove, with her sandaled feet dangling, unable to reach the floor. Her disciples would gather on their haunches below her, waiting for her words to fall. With her words often would fall a reputation or two.

Pound's command post, somewhat different, was at Seventy-*bis* Rue Notre-Dame-des-Champs, where, in a small sculpture-filled *pavillon*, or summer house, he played host to some of the same and other artists, edited T. S. Eliot's *Waste Land* to its surviving proportions, acted as a psychic talent scout, and devoted about one-fifth of his energy to his own work. "With the rest of his time," as Hemingway later wrote, "he tries to advance the fortunes, both material and artistic, of his friends. He defends them when they are attacked, he gets them into magazines and out of jail. He loans them money. He sells their pictures. He arranges concerts for them.

He writes articles about them. He introduces them to wealthy women. He gets publishers to take their books. He sits up all night with them when they claim to be dying and he witnesses their wills. He advances them hospital expenses and dissuades them from suicide. And in the end a few of them refrain from knifing him at the first opportunity."

There were other command posts in the expatriate invasion. At least one more, headquarters for the Dadaist ranks, was at Twelve Rue de l'Odéon, where Sylvia Beach, a Princeton clergyman's daughter who also had been an ambulance driver, established Shakespeare and Company, a bookstore where browsers could find James Joyce, André Gide, André Breton and Tristan Tzara in person as well as on book jackets. Hemingway eventually found his way to all these citadels, although it was to Twenty-seven Rue de Fleurus that he reported first. As in any invasion of which he was to become a participant, Hemingway was among the first troops to land.

He came as a newspaperman. In Y. K. Smith's Chicago apartment, he had met Hadley Richardson, a red-haired St. Louis beauty who had dropped in to visit Smith's sister. They had married in Horton's Bay, had honeymooned there in September, and then, in the late autumn of 1921, had gone to Toronto, where Hemingway had resumed work for the *Star Weekly* and the *Daily Star*. There, in an unexpected tribute to the twenty-two-year-old Hemingway's professionalism, the editor of the *Star* had offered to pay his way to Europe as a space rate correspondent. The Hemingways left in December.

"We went there with a remarkable bunch of letters of introduction, notably from Sherwood Anderson," recalled Hadley. "That's really what launched Ernest there. It really gave us our start."

Hemingway was no sooner in Paris when he was knocking at the door of Twenty-Seven Rue de Fleurus to cash in the first of the letters.

"I remember very well the impression I had of Hemingway that first afternoon," Miss Stein wrote in *The Autobiography of Alice B. Toklas*. "He was an extraordinarily good-looking young man, twenty-three years old . . . rather foreign-looking, with passionately interested, rather than interesting eyes. He sat in front of Gertrude Stein and listened and looked.

"They talked then, and more and more, a great deal together. He asked her to come and spend an evening in their

54

apartment and look at his work. Hemingway had then and has always a very good instinct for finding apartments in strange but pleasing localities and good *femmes de menage* and good food. This his first apartment was just off the Place du Tertre. We spent the evening there and he and Gertrude Stein went over all the writing he had done up to that time. He had begun the novel that it was inevitable he would begin and there were the little poems afterwards printed . . . in the Contact Edition. Gertrude Stein rather liked the poems, they were direct, Kiplingesque, but the novel she found wanting. There is a great deal of description in this, she said, and not particularly good description. Begin over again and concentrate, she said."

When Hemingway was not concentrating on *his* writing, he could often be found at Sylvia Beach's bookstore, where he concentrated on the writing of others. "A customer we liked," Miss Beach recalled later, "one who gave us no trouble, was that young man you saw almost every morning over there in a corner at Shakespeare and Company, reading the magazines or Captain Marryat or some other book. This was Ernest Hemingway . . . My 'best customer,' he called himself, a title that no one disputed with him." Again it was an Anderson letter that had introduced Hemingway to Shakespeare and Company, where he in turn was introduced to James Joyce. Still another letter sent him up the Rue Notre-Dame-des-Champs to see Pound. Before long he was conversant with almost every writer of importance on the Left Bank, although the conversation wasn't always about his or their writing. "In company with people of your own trade you ordinarily speak of other writers' books," Hemingway later told George Plimpton. "The better the writers the less they will speak about what they have written themselves. Joyce was a very great writer and he would only explain what he was doing to jerks. Other writers that he respected were supposed to be able to know what he was doing by reading it."

As Archibald MacLeish, another one of the Expatriate Expeditionary Force, wrote in *Life* magazine, "You can't converse about instincts." MacLeish told of once having dragged Hemingway to a French literary afternoon where André Gide, Jules Romains and several others of their group were sitting around Shakespeare and Company, talking "as though they had rehearsed all morning. But Hemingway, whom all of them were watching, watched the floor."

"It was too much for Gide," MacLeish wrote. "He dropped the topic, whatever it was, and drew Hemingway aside to explain how he punished his cat. He punished his cat, he said, by lifting him up by the scruff of his neck and saying PHT! in his face. Whether Hemingway restrained a desire to hit him, I don't know. I was watching the back of his head."

Malcolm Cowley, in his book *Exile's Return*, remembered meeting Hemingway at Pound's *pavillon* in Rue Notre-Dame-des-Champs in the summer of 1923. "A big young man with intent eyes and a toothbrush mustache was there when I arrived, and Pound introduced him as Ernest Hemingway; I said that I had heard about him. Hemingway gave a slow Midwestern grin. He was then working for the International News Service, but there were rumors that he had stories in manuscript and that Pound had spoken of them as being something new in American literature. He didn't talk about the stories that afternoon; he listened as if with his eyes while Pound discussed the literary world. Very soon he rose, made a date with Pound for tennis the following day and went out the door, walking on the balls of his feet like a boxer."

Hemingway eventually was to become a self-conscious part of the Left Bank's artistic world although he reacted with some emphasis to the frenzied Bohemian creativity which he found limiting itself to idle talk at sidewalk tables. "It is a strange-acting and strange-looking breed that crowd the tables of the Cafe Rotonde," he wrote in a 1922 dispatch to the *Star Weekly*. "You can find anything you are looking for at the Rotonde—except serious artists . . . They are nearly all loafers expending the energy that an artist puts into his creative work in talking about what they are going to do and condemning the work of all artists who have gained any degree of recognition. By talking about art they obtain the same satisfaction that the real artist does in his work. That is very pleasant, of course, but they insist upon posing as artists."

Even so, Hemingway himself became a customer of the Rotonde and other cafes. Often he would sit alone at a table, learning French by reading the newspapers, first an Associated Press story in an American newspaper and then the same Associated Press story in a French journal. "Finally learned to read it," he later claimed, "by reading accounts of things I had seen—*les événements sportifs*—and from that and *les crimes* it was only a jump to Dr. de Maupassant, who wrote about things I had seen or could understand." From de Maupassant, Hemingway said, he went on to Dumas, Daudet, Stendahl, Flaubert, Baudelaire, Rimbaud, Gide and Valéry. But at the beginning, at least, his *maître* was the Associated Press, and he probably had more enthusiasm than syntax. "Ernest's French was far from perfect and never got much better," Hadley said, more than three decades later. "But he could put himself over and could understand. . ." When he tired of locating accents and conjugating verbs, he would tour the bars with one or two of his literary friends, such as John Dos Passos or James Joyce.

"Once in one of those casual conversations you have when you're drinking," Hemingway later said, "Joyce said to me he was afraid his writing was too suburban and that maybe he should get around a bit and see the world. He was afraid of some things, lightning and things, but a wonderful man. He was under great discipline—his wife, his work and his bad eyes. His wife was there and she said, yes, his work was too suburban—'Jim could do with a spot of that lion hunting.' We would go out to drink and Joyce would fall into a fight. He couldn't even see the man so he'd say, 'Deal with him, Hemingway! Deal with him!'"

IV

As a Midwesterner who had received his first great revelation of style from a Ring Lardner newspaper column and whose concepts of literature had been confined largely to the demands of the English syllabus at Oak Park High, Hemingway hardly could have been classified as an intellectual among the intellectuals of the Left Bank.

"Hemingway," Miss Stein later told him, "after all, you are ninety per cent Rotarian."

"Can't you make it eighty per cent?" he said.

"No," she answered, "I can't."

Years afterward, Hemingway himself was to tell Lillian Ross: ". . . People think I'm an ignorant bastard who doesn't know the ten dollar words. I know the ten dollar words. But there are older and better words."

Nevertheless, he did not then, nor did he ever, achieve the strictly intellectual heights of some of his contemporaries. Instead, he used the "older and better words" to surpass them, forging a prose, that in Ford Madox Ford's phrase, resembled "pebbles fetched fresh from a brook." Among a Gertrude Stein, an Ezra Pound, a Pablo Picasso, an F. Scott Fitzgerald, a Sherwood Anderson, an Henri Matisse, a John Dos Passos, a William Carlos Williams, or a James Joyce, Hemingway came to be recognized as an equal, even if also as a Rotarian. "The son of a bitch's *instincts* are right," said Pound to Archibald MacLeish. Fitzgerald wrote to Maxwell Perkins: "This is to tell you about a young writer named Ernest Hemingway, who lives in Paris . . . writes for the *transatlantic review*, and has a brilliant future. I'd look him up right away. He's the real thing."

Like all genius, Hemingway's was both intuitive and irrepressible. It also was undisciplined. From Ezra Pound, however, he learned control, and from Gertrude Stein he learned language. "He studied writing as if he were studying geometry without a textbook and inventing theorems as he went along," wrote Malcolm Cowley, who also had joined the Left Bank intellectuals. "Ezra read his stories and sent them back blue-penciled, with most of the adjectives gone. Gertrude confined herself to general comments, but they were searching and sometimes merciless."

Later, Hemingway aid of his teachers: "Ezra was right half the time, and when he was wrong he was so wrong you were never in any doubt about it. Gertrude was always right."

Hemingway's friendship with Miss Stein grew to a height possibly not imagined even by Plato. "Gertrude Stein and me are just like brothers," Hemingway wrote back to Sherwood Anderson. ". . . We love Gertrude Stein." For her part, even after their eventual estrangement, Miss Stein wrote: "Yes, sure I have a weakness for Hemingway."

When Hemingway's first son, John, was born to his first wife, Hadley, he asked Miss Stein and Miss Toklas to be godmothers. "The first thing to do when they came back was, as they thought, to get the baby baptised," Miss Stein wrote in the *Autobiography of Alice B. Toklas*. ". . . We were all born of different religions and most of us were not practising any, so it was rather difficult to know in what church the baby could be baptised. We spent a great deal of time that winter, all of us, discussing the matter. Finally it was decided that it should be baptised episcopalian and episcopalian it was. Just how it was managed with the assortment of godparents I am sure I do not know, but it was baptised in the episcopalian chapel . . . In the beginning we were active god-parents, I [Alice Toklas] particularly. I embroidered a little chair and I knitted a gay coloured garment for the god-child. . ."

When Miss Stein wrote *The Making of Americans,* Hemingway was instrumental in getting it published. "Hemingway," she wrote, "came in then very excited and said that Ford [Madox Ford] wanted something of Gertrude Stein's for the next number [of the *transatlantic review*] and he, Hemingway, wanted *The Making of Americans* to be run in it as a serial and he had to have the first fifty pages at once. Gertrude Stein was of course quite overcome with her excitement at this idea, but there was no copy of the manuscript except the one we had had bound. That makes no difference, said Hemingway, I will copy it. And he did and I between us did copy it and it was printed in the next number of the *Transatlantic.* So for the first time a piece of the monumental work which was the beginning, really the beginning of modern writing, was printed, and we were very happy."

It was Miss Stein, finally, who persuaded Hemingway to "get out of journalism and write, as she said that the one would use up the juice I needed for the other. She was quite right, and that was the best advice she gave me."

Hemingway did not, however, get out of journalism post-haste. According to an anecdote told by Earl Wilson, he was dispatched on at least one occasion by cable charges. While still in Paris among the other ex-ambulance drivers and ex-patriates who had left America to escape Prohibition and to join the Left Bank, Hemingway persuaded a friend, Frank Mason, head of the Paris Bureau of the International News Service, to get him a job covering the Greco-Turkish War for the Hearst organization.

INS, it turned out, was delighted with Hemingway's cables but not with their cost. Despite orders to the contrary, he persisted in marking all his dispatches "URGENT," which cost three times as much. Finally Mason warned Hemingway that the "URGENT" might also cost him his job. By this time fascinated with cabelese, Hemingway wired back: "UPSTICK JOB ASSWARD." He marked that message "URGENT," too.

The anecdote, to use one of Hemingway's favorite words, may have been apocryphal. According to Charles A. Fenton, his relations with Hearst, became, if anything, stronger after his coverage of the Near East war, and when he journeyed to Lausanne to report on the diplomatic settling of that conflict, most of his writing was done for Universal News, the second of Hearst's two overseas news agencies, rather than for the Toronto *Star.* Cabelese, however, did fascinate him. In Lausanne, he showed Lincoln Steffens a copy of a cable he had sent about the evacuation of the Greeks from Smyrna. When Steffens praised Hemingway's writing style, Hemingway protested. *"No,"* Hemingway roared, *"read the cabelese, only the cabelese!* Isn't it a great language?"

Years later, there came a time when Gertrude Stein would entertain visitors by seizing a handkerchief, waving it at her poodle, going through the maneuverings of a matador and ordering the dog to act out the part of an enraged bull.

"Play Hemingway," she would tell the pampered white dog. "Be fierce."

For his part, Hemingway outlined the entire evolution of his opinion of Miss Stein with a single sentence in his novel, *For Whom the Bell Tolls:*

"An onion is an onion is an onion," Robert Jordan said *cheerily and, he thought, a stone is a stein is a rock is a boulder is a pebble.*

Harold Loeb, one of his Paris contemporaries, thinks that Hemingway was influenced not so much by Gertrude Stein as by Ford Madox Ford, the novelist, critic and editor who ran the *transatlantic review* while Hemingway ran its copy. Philip Young, Pennsylvania State University's Hemingway scholar, says Hemingway's clearest literary I. O. U. was to Sherwood Anderson. Returned exile Malcolm Cowley remembers that Hemingway once took instruction by giving his manuscripts to Ezra Pound to edit. Literary historian Carlos Baker traces Hemingway's debt all the way back to Gustave Flaubert's Madame Bovary. And Steward Sanderson, in an appraisal of Hemingway's Paris apprenticeship, has written:

"He had moved freely in this society, but he had also remained a little on the outside: latterly he had descended much less frequently from the apartment in the Rue Notre-Dame-des-Champs to the tables of the Rotonde or the Deux Magots. He took a nicely detached view of the playboy element on the café terraces, especially of the boys who were playing at literature. He, on the other hand, was working at it."

Hemingway himself, in his most recent pronouncement on

the subject of his influences, told George Plimpton of the *Paris Review* in 1958:

"I'm sorry but I am no good at these post-mortems. There are coroners literary and non-literary provided to deal with such matters. Miss Stein wrote at some length and with considerable inaccuracy about her influence on my work. It was necessary for her to do this after she had learned to write dialogue from a book called *The Sun Also Rises*. I was very fond of her and I thought it was splendid she had learned to write conversation. It was no new thing to me to learn from everyone I could, living or dead, and I had no idea it would affect Gertrude so violently. She already wrote very well in other ways. Ezra was extremely intelligent on the subjects he really knew. Doesn't this sort of talk bore you? This backyard literary gossip while washing out the dirty clothes of thirty-five years ago is disgusting to me. It would be different if one had tried to tell the whole truth. That would have some value. Here it is simpler and better to thank Gertrude for everything I learned from her about the abstract relationship of words, say how fond I was of her, re-affirm my loyalty to Ezra as a great poet and loyal friend. . ."

Hemingway's six expatriate years in Paris certainly were as unlike those of his literary contemporaries as they were similar. For one thing, he had a job, although the space rates paid by the Toronto *Daily Star* and *Star Weekly* weren't designed to leave much room for financial manipulation. Even so, Hemingway manipulated. Besides traveling through Spain, Switzerland, Germany and Italy, covering the 1922 Economic Conference at Genoa, filing somber dispatches about the Russo-German Treaty of Rapallo, watching the Greek retreat at Smyrna, attending the ensuing peace conference at Lausanne and interviewing Benito Mussolini, whom he discerned even then to be the chief of a "lead pipe government," Hemingway also established himself as the manager of several prize fighters, acquired the stature of an aficionado at the bull rings, skied through the best of the Alpine resorts, stayed weeks at the six day bike races, plumbed all the more famous fishing villages and spent much time at the race tracks, although he actually earned more than he spent.

For it was time, as a matter of fact, that Hemingway was trying to acquire. His plan was to continue working as a newspaperman for only as long as it might take to save the money necessary to devote himself to his creative efforts.

Whatever he could earn over the bare needs of his subsistence and the somewhat less abject needs of his pleasure went directly into the bank. As for the 1922 version of pari-mutuel tickets, Hemingway considered them an investment. In June of that year, for example, Hemingway, writing from Milan, where he said most of the races were fixed, told Gertrude Stein that he had picked seventeen winners out of twenty-one starts.

On another occasion, according to Malcolm Cowley, Hemingway made still a greater investment by befriending one Jim Winkfield, a cross-eyed Negro jockey from Cincinnati. Cowley, who said he heard the story from Evan Shipman, a poet, a trotting-horse columnist, and a good Hemingway friend, told how Winkfield, a two-time Kentucky Derby winner, had been training horses for the Pierre Wertheimer stables. "There is no outside audience when colts are training in France," Cowley wrote, "and there are no professional clockers at their time trials; every stable has its own secrets. At the Wertheimer stable the secret was Epinard, a sensationally promising colt with an unfashionable sire. Winkfield, who was seeing a lot of Hemingway, told him that Epinard was going to run his first race at Deauville that summer. Having borrowed all the money he could, Hemingway laid it on Epinard's nose." Epinard, as Hemingway's bank account later showed, won the race.

In his Paris prize fight endeavors, Hemingway managed several boxers including one Larry Gaines, a Negro heavyweight whom Hemingway had seen in Toronto and who, although he never contributed much to Hemingway's administrative coffers, later went on to knock out Max Schmeling in 1930 and take a ten-round decision from Primo Carnera in 1932. With Hemingway, Gaines' biggest year was 1923, when, according to Lemuel F. Parton, "the fighting-writing combination went on nicely—now a sonnet, now a knockout, bringing in a few hundred francs. That was the start of what are now two old established firms." Parton, a sportswriter, later told how Hemingway took him on a 1923 night to the stadium of one Monsieur Anatase in the Rue Pelleport, where Gaines was to meet Mitieu, the champion of the French Army.

"It was a medieval, open-air stadium, flanked with huge ramparts and bastions and circled with boxes with chintz curtains," wrote Parton. "The moon was shining and the crowd was sipping aperitifs and singing. At one end of the inclosure was the Academy of the *Combat du Boxe,* where a stable of whippy little boxers had lace curtains on their windows and window boxes with geraniums in them. There was a salon, where boxers danced, and then changed from their evening dress to trunks as their turn came. There was a string of fast lightweight bouts, with some very earnest socking. Around the ring were grandmothers knitting, women with babies, uncles, aunts and cousins of the fighters. *"Bis Armand!"* This was the cry when Armand landed a good smack. Hemingway's black boy, huddled in a frowsy dressing gown, looked on with bewilderment. He had never seen a prize fight like that! One could see the whites of his eyes clear across the stadium. . .

"Hemingway's immediate hopes were freighted on his black argosy. As the bouts went on he kept repeating tensely some lines of Baudelaire, which sounded like conjuring. When one fighter flattened another he, the other fighter, decorously picked the flattened one up, kissed him on each cheek, laid him down gently, bowed to the crowd and made an exit like one of John Drew's—again to the amazement and perturbation of Monsieur Gaines.

"His was the last bout, and the main event. Monsieur Mitieu came dancing out in a gold bathrobe to the frantic cheers of the crowd. He was a handsome, pink, roached, lacquered Hercules. Gaines looked worried. As they squared away he hunched and covered. The Frenchman opened himself up like the Panama Canal and sank his right clear down to his heel for a long haymaker. He put bells on it, tied it up in ribbons and then telegraphed it. It went so far afield it didn't even stir a breeze in Monsieur Gaines' vicinity. An ecstatic look of joy and relief lit up the black boy's face. Flashing an octave of shining white teeth, he unloosed two or three devastating wallops and Monsieur Mitieu took the count.

"For an instant, Gaines looked hesitatingly at the crowd. There was bewildered silence in the audience and two big smacks could be heard clear across the arena as Gaines picked up the Frenchman and kissed him on each cheek. . ."

If Hemingway didn't pick up much profit from his boxers' pugilism, he sometimes did from his own. In the absence of other activities, he occasionally would rent himself out as a sparring partner to other boxers or else spar with those in his stable, thus cutting his managerial costs. Otherwise, he simply would box for the sport of it. "I enjoyed boxing with Hem," wrote Harold Loeb, in his book, *The Way It Was*, "although I never lost a slight feeling of trepidation. Hem was some forty pounds heavier that I, but he did not fully exert his strength, and on that basis I could hold my own. One day I was able to get in my left jab when a shift in Hem's eyes signaled that a punch was coming. This checked his blows. It was a pleasant feeling, but I felt that the ground was treacherous: one hot afternoon, for no apparent reason, Hem let go on Paul Fisher. Paul got pretty well battered; Hem explained that he had just felt like 'blasting hell out of him.'" On another occasion, Hemingway even had illusions about teaching Ezra Pound to box, and he worked hard at it. Pound, of course, did not.

Wyndham Lewis, for example, recalled one of these lessons, which he discovered after walking in on Pound.

"A splendidly built young man, stript to the waist, and with a torso of dazzling white, was standing not far from me," Lewis wrote. "He was tall, handsome, and serene, and was repelling with his boxing gloves—I thought without undue exertion—a hectic assault of Ezra's. After a final swing at the dazzling solar plexus (parried effortlessly by the trousered statue) Pound fell back upon his settee. The young man was Hemingway."

In addition to Gaines, Hemingway had a sportive, if not a financial, interest in another boxer, Young Travet, a promising French welterweight. Travet was signed to fight Francis Charles, the French middleweight champion, who, for the occasion, agreed to bring his weight down from its usual one hundred and sixty-five to the welterweight limit of one hundred and forty-seven. When the two men weighed in for the match, however, Charles was still one hundred and sixty-five. He hadn't even tried to lose the required pounds.

With Charles so much heavier than Travet, the outcome of the battle was a foregone murder. Travet's manager, nevertheless, didn't even attempt to call it off and Hemingway immediately decided that Travet was the victim of a gambling plot, that French boxing was crooked and that he might as well abandon his own financial interest in it. When the match began at the *Cirque d'Hiver* that night, however, Travet fooled everyone by standing up to his heavier opponent and beating him for the first nine rounds. It wasn't until the tenth round that Travet began to weaken and Charles, whose boxing ethics always had been subject to doubt, caught Travet with his hands outside the ropes and began to kick him in his groin, jump on his body and hammer his head in what could have been a murder witnessed by several thousand cheering spectators. The referee should have stopped the fight, but it was Hemingway who did. From his newspaper correspondent's ringside seat, he drew his two hundred pounds of outrage to its six-foot height, leaped through the ropes and began smashing the champion with his fists and a water bottle until the police rushed up and dragged him away. He had saved Travet's life. Even so, Travet never recovered from Charles' beating.

V

By 1923, Hemingway's savings account was still far short of his goal and, with his wife expecting their first child, he reluctantly accepted an offer to return to Toronto to write features for the *Daily Star* at one hundred and twenty-five dollars per week, a sum which is still more than most newspapermen earn today. He left Europe for Toronto August seventeenth, 1923, with more of a feeling that he was leaving home than returning to it and with promises that he would be back in Paris as soon as he could afford it. Hemingway at first thought he would remain in Toronto for two years, or just long enough to save the money necessary to go back to his expatriate life, support his family, and do nothing but write. However, a conflict of temperaments soon led to a conflict of tempers between him and Harry Comfort Hindmarsh, then assitant managing editor of the *Daily Star*. Just at the time when the birth of Hemingway's child appeared imminent, for instance, Hindmarsh assigned Hemingway to cover the New York arrival of British Prime Minister Lloyd George. The job originally had been scheduled to go to Hemingway and two other reporters but when Hindmarsh, despite Hemingway's pleas, sent him on it alone, Hemingway took the order as a personal affront. As Hemingway later told the story, his coverage of Lloyd George was supposed to begin at the docks in the morning and end after the Prime Minister attended a Broadway play at the Music Box Theatre that night. But as soon as he saw Lloyd George enter the theater, Hemingway decided to quit early and go instead to the Charlie White-Pal Moran boxing match. What happened after Hemingway left, however, was that Sinn Fein sympathizers in the Music Box audience recognized Lloyd George and began a demonstration. It made the front pages all over the world, including the Toronto *Daily Star*, which had to get the story from a wire service.

Otherwise, Hemingway's assignments from Hindmarsh weren't of the type he might have expected at one hundred and twenty-five dollars per week. Canadian author Morley Callaghan, a staff member of the *Star* at the time, remembered one day when Hemingway was put down in the assignment book for three different cases of trivia. *"Jesus Christ!"* growled Hemingway. The last straw came when Hemingway was assigned to cover a luncheon speech by the Hungarian diplomat, Count Apponyi. Meeting Hemingway for breakfast, the Count lent him several diplomatic papers to help in the preparation of his article. Hemingway promised faithfully to return them and then sent them to Hindmarsh with a copy boy and an explanatory note. For some still unexplained reason, Hindmarsh threw the papers directly into a wastepaper basket which, in turn, led directly to the incinerator. Hemingway promptly quit the *Daily Star*. By January of 1924, after four months in Toronto, he was back in Paris.

VI

Unencumbered at last by any journalistic duties, Hemingway devoted all his time to writing fiction. But he also was unencumbered by any income. His stories kept being rejected, one after another, and, as he later wrote, "we lived on *poireaux* and drank *cahors* and water." He also said he drove a taxicab. "His wardrobe in those days was distinguished by an old beret with holes in it," wrote Earl Wilson, "and an ancient gray turtleneck sweater which was similarly but more generously ventilated." With Hadley and their son, nick-named Bumby, he lived in a flat over a sawmill at One hundred and thirteen Rue Notre-Dame-des-Champs, not too far from Ezra Pound's studio. *". . . And the sudden whine of the saw,"* he later wrote in *Green Hills of Africa, "the smell of sawdust and the chestnut tree over the roof with a mad woman downstairs . . . all of the stories back in the mail that came in through a slit in the saw-mill door, with notes of rejection that would never call them stories, but always anecdotes, sketches, contes, etc. . . . What I had to do was work. I did not care, particularly, how it all came out. I did not*

66

take my own life seriously anymore, any one else's life, yes but not mine. They all wanted something that I did not want and I would get it without wanting it, if I worked. To work was the only thing, it was the only thing that always made you feel good, and in the meantime it was my own damned life and I would lead it where and how I pleased."

Hemingway's flat was heated, on some occasions, by a recalcitrant coal stove and on other occasions Hemingway would find warmth in one of the nearby cafés. "Hemingway did not, of course, live a monastic life," wrote Carlos Baker. "The passing show eddied beneath the window, and the life of the cafés could be investigated at the close of a working day. Sometimes, in quiet seasons, he began the day in a café. He took the short cut through the Luxembourg Gardens past the bust of Flaubert which seemed both a symbol and a goal. Breakfast coffee and a brioche came to a franc or less at any of the places along the Rue Soufflot, and he could write all morning at a back corner table without expectation of prolonged disturbance. Afterwards he could rest strained eyes on the bronze-green of the fountains in the place de L'Observatoire, where the water flowed thinly over the sculptured manes and shoulders of the horses. With Dos Passos in the winter afternoons he drank hot kirsch, flavored like cherry-pits. He mixed work and play at the six-day bike races. He argued the merits of race-horses with Harold Stearns and Evan Shipman, or went to the prize-fights with Sisley Huddleston and Bill Bird. When the fights were poor, Bird used to remember the brave colored fighters of the past. He had a line modified from Villon which went, "Ou sont les nègres d'antan?' When the fights were good, like the Mascart-Ledoux battle at the Cirque de Paris, one yelled himself hoarse and stopped in at Lipp's for a midnight beer on the way home."

Although Hemingway's appearances became more frequent among the Latin Quarter cafés that once had so riled his newspaper prose, and although he began to achieve more and more respect from their Bohemian habitués, Hemingway was by no means a leader among them. Writing about Hemingway shortly after his death, Malcolm Cowley remembered that he belonged to no group of table sitters, although all claimed him. In Cowley's recollection, it was an event of the evening when Hemingway walked past the sidewalk cafés and there was heavy competition in waving and calling for his companionship.

"The occasions were charming little scenes, as if spontaneous even though repeated," said novelist Nathan Asch, who was one of Hemingway's friends of the period. "In view of the whole terrace, Hemingway would be striding toward the Montparnasse railroad station, his mind seemingly busy with the mechanics of someone's arrival or departure, and he wouldn't quite recognize whoever greeted him. Then suddenly his beautiful smile appeared that made those watching him also smile; and with a will and an eagerness he put out his hands and warmly greeted his acquaintance, who, overcome by this reception, simply glowed; and who returned with Hem to the table as if with an overwhelming prize."

VII

Despite Hemingway's meteoric reputation among his local contemporaries, he had no reputation at all among the publishers of the time. His, to them, was little more than an often repeated but hardly remembered name on a rejection slip. When, for example, Edward J. O'Brien decided to include the Hemingway short story, *My Old Man*, in his anthology, *The Best Short Stories of 1923*, Hemingway's name came out in the book as Ernest Hemenway. Today the book is a collector's item because of the error.

There were other unfortunate endings for Hemingway's unprinted poetry and prose. Another time, for example. Hemingway's wife, Hadley, set out from Paris shortly before Christmas of 1922 to join him in Switzerland, where he was covering the Lausanne Conference. In her railroad compartment in the Gare de Lyon, she placed a suitcase containing some eighteen stories, thirty poems, and an unfinished novel, almost all the manuscripts which Hemingway had written since their marriage. The material had been neatly copied and filed in dossiers and Hemingway wanted it so he could show it to Lincoln Steffens, who also was covering the conference. While the train was still in the station, however, Hadley left the compartment for a drink of water. When she returned, the suitcase was gone.

The thief, of course, had been interested only in the suitcase, although it might pay him to look up the contents of the trunk in his attic today. Unwittingly, however, the thief also accomplished what all of Gertrude Stein's persuasion had only partially done—to force Hemingway to discard his early attempts and begin with the freshness that became his style.

Actually, however, the manuscripts in the suitcase probably didn't deserve so extreme a fate. Two stories, *My Old Man* and *Up in Michigan*, survived the theft, *Up in Michigan* because it was in a drawer gathering dust and *My Old Man* because it was en route back to Hemingway with a rejection slip. And if they are any indication of what else was in the suitcase, the loss is as great to literature as it was to Hemingway.

Despite the thousands and thousands of his words that already had gotten into newsprint, Hemingway's creative writing didn't see the light of a publisher's press until May, 1922, when an *avant-garde* New Orleans magazine, the *Double Dealer*, printed a work which Hemingway described as a fable and which he entitled *A Divine Gesture*. Already a haven for literary works by Sherwood Anderson and William Faulkner, the *Double Dealer* not only liked the fable but in its next issue printed a Hemingway poem, *Ultimately*. The rewards for his first publication were not great. The *Double Dealer* did not pay for contributions and about all Hemingway could show for his first successes were copies of the magazine. It was with the same financial results that Hemingway contributed six vignettes to another *avant-garde* publication, New York's *Little Review*, which included the vignettes in a special "Exiles" issue in April, 1923.

"As the spring moved on," wrote Carlos Baker, "the prospect of a book of his own began to look brighter. William Bird, a newspaperman and a good friend of Hemingway's, was the proprietor of the Three Mountains Press company, which consisted of much patience, a supply of fine rag paper, and an ancient seventeenth-century hand press in a domed wine-vault on the Ile St. Louis. Since the summer of 1922 he and Ezra Pound had talked of bringing out some of Hemingway's short stories, perhaps a little book, well-printed on good paper and wearing boards against the weather. But the ancient hand press ground slowly, too. William Bird was doing a series of modern writers; there were some previous commitments and he was not to be rushed.

"It was different with Robert McAlmon, the 'nine hundred horse power linotype-publisher' who ran the contact Publishing Company and had his books cheaply printed for him at Dijon. By his own account he had met Hemingway at Rapallo early in the year. Before you could say 'In Our Time,' McAlmon came out with *Three Stories and Ten Poems*. The edition ran to three hundred copies and had gray-blue paper wrappers boldly lettered in black capitals. The stories were *Up in Michigan* and *My Old Man*, the survivors of the Gare de Lyon thievery, together with *Out of Season*, a new and remarkable piece of work which had been written during the spring of 1923 in the mountains of northern Italy . . . Along with youth and a burgeoning talent, that summer of 1923, Hemingway also had a first book to his credit."

Hemingway's second book was *in our time*, which William Bird finally ground out in the spring of 1924, but then Bird, after all, had taken up printing only as a hobby. For *in our time*, Hemingway added twelve vignettes to the six which had appeared in the *Little Review*, and when the book came off the seventeenth century press, a woodcut of Hemingway by his friend Henry Strater was on the frontispiece. Only one hundred and seventy copies of the book were printed, each of them on handmade Rives paper, and the cover was made up of a montage of world press headlines. Even then, the book, not unlike the fine editions printed by various small beat publishers during the late 1950s, became a collector's item. But Hemingway wasn't satisfied with it. According to a story later told to Earl Wilson, he glanced over the first copy, roared *"Oh, balls!"* and then slashed a pencil angrily through the pages. In Chapter XV, he had forgotten to insert the phrase, "the rope around his neck," a second time for repetition.

in our time, the Paris edition, soon became *In Our Time* with capital letters. By 1925, Boni and Liveright, Sherwood Anderson's publishers, had decided to sign up Hemingway as well, and the New York edition of *In Our Time*, including the eighteen vignettes and twelve short stories, came out on October fifth, 1925.

It was for this much of Hemingway's career that Anderson took credit. One of the firm's best-selling authors, he had interceded personally with Horace Liveright, the head of the company, to impress him with Hemingway's ability and especially with Hemingway's saleability. "I went to bat," he said. At the same time, however, F. Scott Fitzgerald, although he had never met Hemingway, was going to bat for him with *his* publishers, Charles Scribner's Sons. He had learned about Hemingway from critic Edmund Wilson, who had recommended some of Hemingway's early writing. As soon as Fitzgerald had read the writing, he, in turn, recommended it to Maxwell Perkins. Just as Anderson's word carried weight at Boni and Liveright, Fitzgerald's words were enriching Scribner's treasury. Consequently, Perkins, Fitzgerald's editor there, decided to write to Hemingway. That made the difference. When Boni and Liveright wanted to get in touch with Hemingway, they did it by cable.

"On February twenty-first, 1925, Perkins wrote to Hemingway expressing interest in seeing some of his work," wrote Carlos Baker. "The letter lacked a sufficient address and evidently was lost. On February twenty-sixth, Perkins obtained the correct address from John Peale Bishop and immediately sent out a follow-up letter, enclosing a copy of the first. At this date Hemingway was writing and skiing at Schruns in the Austrian Vorarlberg. The Perkins letter was held for him with other mail by Sylvia Beach in Paris. About ten days before he called for his mail in the Rue de l'Odéon, he received a cable from one of the Liveright editors offering an advance of two hundred dollars and a request for acceptance by return cable. Hemingway accepted."

Hemingway, who by this time had heard of Perkins and who had liked what he heard, would rather have signed with Scribner's. On April fifteenth of that year, however, he wrote to Perkins explaining that he already had the Boni and Liveright contract, which committed him to do *In Our Time* and two additional books for that firm. The contract, nevertheless, had one loophole. It provided that if Boni and Liveright didn't accept Hemingway's second book within sixty days, then they forfeited their rights to his third book. It was through this loophole that his literary contemporaries were to get a strange new look at Hemingway.

To have been approached by two American publishers quite naturally put a smile on the distant Hemingway's face. His name was beginning to be spelled right. But he still wasn't making any money. The rejection slips continued to pour in through the slot in the door, including several from Ray Long, the editor of *Cosmopolitan*. It was Long, incidentally, who had placed *Up in Michigan* in the return mail at the time that the thief was picking up Mrs. Hemingway's suitcase in the Gare de Lyon. Another short story that Long later decided to reject was *Fifty Grand*. "It left me cold," he said. "I couldn't see why my associate had got so excited about it." Eventually *Fifty Grand* was published in the *Atlantic Monthly*, and when Long read it there, he got excited, too. Years later, Long published an anthology of what he thought were the twenty best short stories of all time. *Fifty Grand* was the first story in the book.

VIII

Even by the fall of 1926, when *The Torrents of Spring* and *The Sun Also Rises* were already in American bookstores, Hemingway was still breakfasting on brioches. "He could not be bought," remembered John Peale Bishop, one of his friends at the time. "I happened to be with him on the day he turned down an offer from one of Mr. Hearst's editors which, had he accepted it, would have supported him handsomely for years. He was at the time living back of the Montparnasse cemetery over the studio of a friend, in a room small and bare except for a bed and table, and buying his midday meal for five sous from the street vendors of fried potatoes."

Not that Hemingway's lunches were always on fried potatoes. They were often on F. Scott Fitzgerald. Even before he met "Hemmingway," as he persisted in misspelling the name, the slender, handsome, Princeton sophisticate had developed the beginnings of what was to be his lifelong admiration for the gruff, bigger, heroic Hemingway. He felt that since he liked Hemingway's prose so much, he had to like Hemingway. Consequently, when he arrived in Paris in May of 1925, some one hundred and thirteen thousand dollars richer from the royalties of his own successes, Fitzgerald, as his first order of business, made it a point to call on Hemingway. In one way or another, he kept calling on Hemingway for the rest of his life. "I loved Scott very much. . . ," Hemingway said later. Even in their quarrels they were to remain close.

Part of their closeness was lunch once a week with Christian Gauss. Another part was to devote this lunch period to the discussion of a serious topic, as compared to their more usual topics in non-Prohibition Paris. At the end of each lunch, they would agree on the topic for the next week's meeting. They had plenty of time to think about it between bites.

". . . Fitzgerald . . . remained an earnest and competent student of the art of writing," wrote Gauss afterwards, "and this was one of the bonds between Scott and Hemingway. In other respects they were worlds apart. Hemingway was not interested in the Ritz or playboys."

In addition, Hemingway turned for friendship during his

Left Bank days toward, among others, John Dos Passos, who had married Y. K. Smith's sister Kate; Donald Ogden Stewart, the humorist who started accompanying him to the bullfights; Guy Hickok, another foreign correspondent and luncheon partner; Captain E. E. Dorman-Smith, of His Majesty's Fifth Fusiliers; and Ford Madox Ford, the fifty-one-year-old aristocrat of British literature, who reminisced about Joseph Conrad, Thomas Hardy, and Henry James through an asthmatic wheeze and beneath a walrus mustache and who thought Ezra Pound played golf and Ernest Hemingway was an ex-cowboy.

Ford began his *transatlantic review* in Paris in January of 1924 and Hemingway was soon an associate editor, occupying the tiny, cluttered quarters of the magazine at Number twenty-nine, Quai d'Anjou. "I used to go down there," Hemingway wrote, "and take a batch of [manuscripts] out on the Quai and read them. Would make an annotation of what Ford was to say in refusal. . . 'This stinks but he might write a story if he keeps trying.'" Sometimes, for practice, Hemingway would rewrite several of the rejects.

In the meantime, Hemingway permitted neither his literary activities nor his poverty to interfere with his muscular recreations. If he wasn't skiing in the Vorarlberg, he was skiing in the Dolomites, provided there was snow on the slopes. To pay his way there, he acted as a ski instructor. Or, in the spring, he might fish the Stockalper or bicycle across the Rhone valley. Once he toured the ancient Italian battlegrounds at Piombino and Orbetello, taking with him Ezra Pound. Together, they strode across the scene where the despot-general Sigismondo Malatesta, patron of artists and writers, had conducted his fifteenth century campaigns. As they made their way over the silent ground, Hemingway tried to explain to Pound how the battle must have been fought.

"Many people hate him and he plays a fine game of tennis," Hemingway later wrote of the fiery poet. "He would live much longer if he did not eat so fast. Young men in the years after the war coming over from America where Pound was a legendary person to Paris where they found him with a patchy red beard, very accessible, fond of tennis and occasionally playing the bassoon, decided there could not be anything in the Pound legend and that he was probably not a great poet after all. As the army rhyme used to say: hence criticism in America."

Hemingway was not one of those who knifed Pound at the first opportunity, or at any other. It was, rather, circumstances which cut the two friends apart. They last saw each other in Paris in 1934 after a dinner to which James Joyce, convinced that Pound was mad and saying that he was "genuinely frightened of him," insisted that Hemingway come along. Four years later, after the Spanish Civil War broke out, Pound, espousing the fascists, returned to America and told reporters: ". . . Hemingway is a good guy, but I don't suppose we'd want to meet personally." Then he added significantly: "Spain."

When, in the closing years of World War II, Pound was captured in Italy by American troops and accused of broadcasting Axis propaganda, Hemingway sent for a transcript of the broadcasts and then wielded his influence in Washington to prevent Pound from being tried on charges of treason. When Pound instead was labeled a lunatic and shut into Saint Elizabeth's Hospital for the mentally ill, Hemingway was one of his few former friends who signed a petition for his release.

"Sure I signed it," Hemingway told Leonard Lyons. "I'm against everything Ezra Pound stands for, politically, but I signed it. Pound's crazy. All poets are a bit crazy. The greatest have all been somewhat crazy. They have to be. You don't put a poet like Pound in the loony bin. For history's sake we shouldn't keep him there. If you don't have compassion, how can you judge? I'd chip in to help support Pound after he's out. And if he starts making those same speeches again, I'll give him a spanking. But he's a poet, a bit crazy and he should be let out."

IX

Hemingway's other literary estrangements were early and often. Unlike Fitzgerald, he worshipped no heroes, or at least he didn't do so with any constancy. The vagaries of his friendships eventually extended in all directions, but they especially over-extended his friendship with Gertrude Stein.

"The last time I took a 'skeered' person to see Gertrude was when Ernest Hemingway told me he wanted to make up his quarrel with her but couldn't get up the courage to go alone," wrote Sylvia Beach in her autobiography, *Shakespeare and Company.* "I encouraged him in his plan, and promised to accompany him to the Rue Christine, where Gertrude and Alice were then living. I thought it better for Hemingway to go up alone, so I took him all the way to her door and left him with my best wishes. He came to tell me afterward that it was 'fine' between them again."

At another time, the poet Allen Tate, who also was in one of the expatriate landings, remembered a similar story. "One day Ernest Hemingway came to the little *pension* where I was living and he said, 'Gertrude has taken me back into favor.' She hadn't spoken to him for some time. He said, 'She's taken me back into favor but I'm scared to go and see her alone. Won't you come along?' Well, I saw no reason why I shouldn't and so I agreed to go. By that evening Mr. Hemingway had assembled a party of friends. There were the Fitzgeralds and the Bishops and maybe one or two other persons. As usual the gentlemen were standing off to the right and the ladies in the rear and Miss Stein proceeded to give us a lecture: nothing less than a kind of synopsis of the history of American literature from Emerson to about 1930. Emerson was the great forerunner because he had a genius for abstraction. He was not particularly concerned with experience. Hawthorne was practically impossible because he was still European. Emily Dickinson was fairly good. Whitman was on the right track. Henry James was really awfully good because the design of his novels showed a genius for abstract construction; but alas, Henry James was also partly European. He was bogged down in 'experience.' The climax, of course, of the lecture on American literature was that Miss Stein was the climax. The genius for abstraction had finally realized itself in her."

For her part, Gertrude Stein never acted the woman more than when she felt she was double-crossed. By 1924, Hemingway apparently had crossed her path several times. "I arrived with the baby one day, as usual, to stop in at Gertrude and Alice's apartment and chat for a few minutes," said Hadley. "And Alice came to the door and she said, 'I'm very sorry. Gertrude can't see you today.' It was just a complete dismissal. And I know of no explanation. And I wish I did. Because it was very curious and quite sudden and increasing in ardor—ardor in the wrong direction.

"I've never been able to dig that one up. They're both as silent as the grave. I've seen Gertrude Stein a good many times since then and she was still very sardonic about him as in the *Autobiography of Alice B. Toklas*. That section where she just pokes very mysterious, undocumented fun at Hemingway I thought was quite personally disgusting and I was awfully sorry they printed it. This sort of secretive, surreptitious hinting at what a literary crook Ernest was infuriated me. I think, and I think Ernest thought—they both having talked a great deal together about how the approval and interest of the general public in your work was almost enough to send a writer to hell—that all of a sudden Ernest did win the approval and a great deal of interest. And I think it was very hard for her to take And I think Ernest thought that, too.

"But I really don't know. I *do* know that everything was fine, our son was her god-son, and all of a sudden something happened. And of course Ernest kept things to himself and I don't know what it was."

The *Autobiography of Alice B. Toklas* actually turned out to be the autobiography of Gertrude Stein. In it, she indicated that she had more than one break with Hemingway. At one point, for example, she wrote:

> So then Hemingway's career was begun. For a little while we saw less of him and then he began to come again. He used to recount to Gertrude Stein the conversations that he afterwards used in *The Sun Also Rises* and they talked endlessly about the character of Harold Loeb.

Or, at another point, she wrote:

> After this we did not see Hemingway for quite a while and then we went to see some one, just after *The Making of Americans* was printed, and Hemingway who was there came up to Gertrude Stein and began to explain why he would not be able to write a review of the book. . . Or, at another point, she wrote again:

For some years after this Gertrude Stein and Hemingway did not meet. And then we heard that he was back in Paris and telling a number of people how much he wanted to see her. Don't you come home with Hemingway on your arm, I used to say when she went out for a walk. Sure enough one day she did come back bringing him with her. They sat and talked a long time. . . After that they met quite often. Gertrude Stein always says she likes to see him, he is so wonderful. And if he could only tell his own story. In their last conversation she accused him of having killed a great many of his rivals and put them under the sod. I never, said Hemingway, seriously killed anybody but one man and he was a bad man and, he deserved it, but if I killed anybody else I did it unknowingly, and so I am not responsible.

X

There are several candidates in literature for the post of Hemingway's victim. One, of course, is Sherwood Anderson. It wasn't that Hemingway had poisoned the one hundred pounds of canned food he so thoughtfully had left in Anderson's Chicago flat. It was rather that Hemingway afterwards detected a growing sour taste in his mouth. Whether his previous deference to Anderson had been lip service or not, he now began to speak of Anderson with a tongue that was bathed in acid. And so although, in the summer of 1925, he could still tell Fitzgerald that *Winesburg, Ohio* was his early model, by November of 1925 he was able to write *The Torrents of Spring*.

Hemingway later said he wrote *The Torrents of Spring* "to cool out" after finishing the first draft of *The Sun Also Rises*. He wrote it, he said, after spending an evening with John Dos Passos in a discussion of *Dark Laughter*, one of Anderson's later books. He had gone home after the discussion, he said, and had written *The Torrents of Spring* in seven days. But for something designed to cool Hemingway out, *The Torrents of Spring* had just started to get him warm. Set in a town that was supposed to be Petoskey, Michigan, but that actually was uncomfortably close to Winesburg, the novel was about two men drawn to some surrealist self-questioning by the advent of spring. It also was about a continuum of other nonsense that might be described as playful, except that the play was with stilettos. *The Torrents of Spring* was actually a merciless lampoon of Anderson and his style.

If *The Torrents of Spring* hurt Anderson, an accompanying letter sent by Hemingway apparently did little to bandage the wound. Although the text of the message has never been made public, Anderson described it as "the most self-

77

conscious and probably the most patronizing letter ever written . . . There was something in the letter that was gigantic. It was a kind of funeral oration over my grave. . ." Anderson said the letter seemed to imply that he was a champion past his prime, knocked to the canvas and unable to get up under the count. On the other hand, Hemingway, although he usually took delight in knocking adversaries to the canvas, said what he had written to Anderson was an "all-right letter."

"I really don't understand about Ernest and that," said Hadley. "Possibly at that point he thought that Sherwood wasn't interesting. I always thought it was too bad he wrote that book because they'd been such good friends."

Most Hemingway scholars agree that Hemingway was genuinely appalled by the literary decline which Anderson showed in *Dark Laughter,* published in 1925. "You see," said Fitzgerald, writing to Maxwell Perkins, "I agree with Ernest that Anderson's last two books have let everybody down who believed in him—I think they're cheap, faked, obscurantic and awful." But there also remains conjecture that the forced, hasty and topical plot of *The Torrents of Spring* had been conceived not for a novel but to get Hemingway and *The Sun Also Rises* signed up with Fitzgerald's publisher. According to the terms of their contract, Boni and Liveright had to print *The Torrents of Spring* or leave Hemingway and *The Sun Also Rises* free to go to another publisher.

"I have known all along," Hemingway wrote to Fitzgerald in 1925, "that they could not and would not be able to publish it as it makes a bum out of their present ace and best seller Anderson. Now in tenth printing. I did not, however, have that in mind in any way when I wrote it."

Boni and Liveright did indeed decide not to publish *The Torrents of Spring,* even though the decision lost for them the eventual best-seller, *The Sun Also Rises,* which Hemingway still had only in first draft. Almost immediately, Hemingway, despite other offers, signed with Scribner's.

"Am turning down a sure thing for delay and a chance," Hemingway wrote Fitzgerald, "but feel no regret because of the impression I have formed of Maxwell Perkins through his letters and what you have told me of him. Also confidence in Scribners and would like to be lined up with you. . ."

Despite the impact of *The Torrents of Spring*, Hemingway kept insisting that there were no hard feelings between him and Anderson. On January twentieth, 1927, he even wrote Perkins: "Sherwood Anderson is in Paris and we had two fine afternoons together . . . He was not at all sore about 'Torrents' and we had a fine time." Anderson's recollection of the two fine afternoons, however, was somewhat different. He later wrote that Hemingway, despite urgings from mutual friends, didn't make any effort to see him until his last day in Paris. He was sitting on his packed bags in his hotel room, Anderson wrote, when "there was a sudden knock on the door, and there Hemingway was.

"He stood in the doorway.

" 'How about a drink,' he said, and I followed him down a stairway and across a street.

"We went into a small bar.

" 'What will you have?'

" 'Beer.'

" 'And you?'

" 'A beer.'

" 'Well, here's how.'

" 'Here's how.'

"He turned and walked rapidly away."

XI

There today is still no clear or single reason for the estrangement between Hemingway and Sherwood Anderson on the one hand or, for that matter, between Hemingway and Gertrude Stein on the other. There is only the recollection that as Hemingway's success grew, so did the gulfs between them. Years later, Miss Stein, fishing in the gulf, reeled up even more bitterness.

"Gertrude Stein and Sherwood Anderson are very funny on the subject of Hemingway," she wrote in *The Autobiography of Alice B. Toklas*. "The last time that Sherwood was in Paris they often talked about him. Hemingway had been formed by the two of them and they were both a little proud and a little ashamed of the work of their minds. Hemingway had at one moment, when he had repudiated Sherwood Anderson and all his works, written him a letter in the name of American literature which he, Hemingway, in company with his contemporaries was about to save, telling Sherwood just what he, Hemingway thought about Sherwood's work, and, that thinking, was in no sense co plimentary. When Sherwood came to Paris Hemingway naturally was afraid. Sherwood as naturally was not.

"As I say he and Gertrude Stein were endlessly amusing on the subject. They admitted that Hemingway was yellow, he is, Gertrude Stein insisted, just like the flat-boat men on the Mississippi river as described by Mark Twain. But what a book, they both agreed, would be the real story of Hemingway, not those he writes but the confessions of the real Ernest Hemingway. . .

"And then they both agreed that they have a weakness for Hemingway because he is such a good pupil. He is a rotten pupil, I [Alice B. Toklas] protested. You don't understand, they both said, it is so flattering to have a pupil who does it without understanding it, in other words he takes training and anybody who takes training is a favorite pupil. . .

"Hemingway, he looks like a modern and he smells of the museums. But what a story that of the real Hem, and one he should tell himself but alas he never will. After all, as he himself once murmured, there is the career, the career."

There is, of course, no record that Gertrude Stein ever wrote the confessions of the real Gertrude Stein or, for that matter, of the real Alice B. Toklas, either. Not *The Autobiography of Alice B. Toklas* nor anything else from Gertrude Stein's pen seem ever to have told about their inner souls. What she asked of Hemingway, she never demanded from herself.

Hemingway replied to *The Autobiography of Alice B. Toklas* in his *Green Hills of Africa*, published in 1935.

"*Yes,*" he wrote, describing a conversation between himself and his wife, "*and he doesn't have to read books written by some female he's tried to help get published saying how he's yellow.*"

"*She's just jealous and malicious. You never should have helped her. Some people never forgive that.*"

"*It's a damned shame, though, with all that talent gone to malice and nonsense and self-praise. It's a god-damned shame, really. It's a shame you never knew her before she went to pot. You know a funny thing; she never could write dialogue. It was terrible. She learned how to do it from my stuff and used it in that book. She had never written like that before. She never could forgive learning that and she was afraid people would notice it, where she'd learned it, so she had to attack me. It's a funny racket, really. But I swear she was damned nice before she got ambitious. You would have liked her then, really."*

XII

Whatever other disagreements there were between Gertrude Stein and Hemingway, there is one that will always remain on the inscription page of *The Sun Also Rises.* If, to Miss Stein, the expatriates of the Left Bank, avoiding Main Street Prohibition amid the sweet and raving drunkenness of Montparnasse cafes, shouting *F - - - Yous!* to audiences and starting riots at their own jazzed, frenzied concerts, sweeping out the atrophies of literature with little magazines like *Broom* and *transition,* rediscovering lost sex in the emerging pubic beard of Sigmund Freud, obliterating the shock of war with the shock of Dadaism, proclaiming funeral orations over the burial of a God that never was, starving in waterless garrets even at twenty-five francs to the dollar, looking for love and finding it in a new nymphomania, and laying their sad, artistic souls bare at her feet—if they were, to her, a lost generation, they were to Hemingway something else.

As he explained to Maxwell Perkins on November nineteenth, 1926, Hemingway regarded Miss Stein's garage-keeper interpretation as a piece of "splendid bombast." He placed her words—*"You are all a lost generation"*—on the inscription page of *The Sun Also Rises,* but the only reason he did so, he said, was to counter it with another inscription from *Ecclesiastes:*

"One generation passeth away, and another generation cometh; but the earth abideth forever . . . The sun also ariseth, and the sun goeth down, and hasteth to the place where he arose . . . The wind goeth toward the south, and turneth about unto the north; it whirleth about continually, and the wind returneth again according to his circuits . . . All the rivers run into the sea; yet the sea is not full; unto the place from whence the rivers come, thither they return again."

It was from this inscription page that Hemingway got his

title and his generation got its label. In trying to prove Miss Stein wrong, he gave a misunderstanding world documentation that she was right. Until his dying day, Hemingway, or at least a part of him, continued to be regarded as the author of the Lost Generation and until his dying day he continued to deny it.

"No," he told George Plimpton of the *Paris Review* in 1958, "there was no group feeling. We had respect for each other. I respected a lot of painters, some of my own age, others older—Gris, Picasso, Braque, Monet, who was still alive then—and a few writers: Joyce, Ezra, the good of Stein. . ."

To the *New York Post* in 1959, he said: "I never believed in any of these generation labels at all, and I never threw in with any generation. I've been writing since 1921 and it's now 1959 and I don't belong to any generation. I used a phrase by one writer, Gertrude Stein, who was complaining about the generation being lost. I didn't believe it was lost at all, and I countered that with a phrase out of *Ecclesiastes*. One is the opinion of a woman. The other is the opinion of a man. . .

"At the time, there was no movement . . . There was simply a lot of people who were writing, who were more or less the same age, and who had been through the war—and others who had not been through the war and who wished they had been or were delighted they hadn't. There was no promotion of a generation by the people who were involved. Nobody gave lectures. Nobody said we are such-and-such generation. Nobody did a damn thing about it except that I put the two quotations opposite each other in front of a book . . . Nobody sang to guitars and, as far as I know, no one who was at that time in what they called the Lost Generation had any consciousness of being a member of it."

In 1951, Hemingway told Carlos Baker; "I though beat-up, maybe, F - - - ed-up in many ways. But damned if we were lost except for deads, *gueules cassées*, and certified crazies. Lost, no. And Criqui, who was a real *gueule cassée*, won the featherweight championship of the world. We were a very solid generation though without education (some of us). But you could always get it."

"He told me," Baker remembers, "that Gertrude, donning

the mantle of prophetess, had picked up what this garage-keeper said and began to apply it to a whole generation, when it really only applied to a few lousy French mechanics down in the south of France."

But it was Hemingway, after all, who wrote *The Sun Also Rises.*

CHAPTER FIVE

And the Sun Goes Down

FOR THIRTY-FIVE YEARS, literary historians throughout the world have been ascribing all sorts of complex symbolisms to Ernest Hemingway's sexual incapacity as Jake Barnes, the war-maimed newspaper correspondent in *The Sun Also Rises*. It took only about thirty-five seconds, however, for the heroine of the book, a real woman, to recognize why the hero wasn't a real man.

"Hem's emasculation were his wife and child," the original Lady Brett Ashley is said to have told her friends after she first read the book. Or, as she previously had explained to the original Robert Cohn: "Even if I liked Hemingway, I wouldn't go off with him, because of Hadley and the baby —even if I wanted to I wouldn't."

There is considerable evidence that *he*, at least, wanted to go off with *her*. "Certainly it seemed so," recalled Harold Loeb, the original of the aforementioned Robert Cohn. Speaking not from the events in *The Sun Also Rises*, but from the events which led to the writing of it, Loeb said:

"I had suspected that Hem liked her. I don't really know. But I can't explain *The Sun Also Rises* except to suppose that he tried to get off with her. Did he succeed? I'm certain that he didn't."

According to the way the original Lady Brett Ashley explained *The Sun Also Rises* Hemingway translated her unwillingness to go to bed with him into an inability on his part to do so. In the book, the reason for his failure to consummate the affair became not his wife and child, but a war wound. In other words, Hemingway, self-committed to record an event "the way it was" but unwilling to record his sexual failure, preserved both his romance and his integrity with a literary rationalization. Instead of encumbering his story with Hadley and the baby, he did the more fanciful thing of encumbering Jake.

Even so, there is still the question of why the real Lady Brett exempted the convention of Hemingway's marriage from her defiance of all others. "Darling," she replied when Harold Loeb asked her that question some thirty-seven years ago, "you have such faith in what the world calls logic." In Hemingway's imagination the exemption was *her* loss as well as poor, helpless Jake's.

"Oh, Jake," Brett said, "we could have had such a damned good time together."

Ahead was a mounted policeman in khaki directing traffic. He raised his baton. The car slowed suddenly pressing Brett against me.

"Yes," I said. "Isn't it pretty to think so."

Her name, was, actually, Duff Twysden, and she was more of a woman than a Lady, a title she had acquired along with one of her own several husbands. She was tall, dark, English and thirty, with almost Oriental eyes and a sweetness of voice not yet affected by her capacity for whiskey. As she looked to Hemingway in *The Sun Also Rises*, she was *"damned good looking. She wore a slipover jersey sweater and a tweed skirt, and her hair was brushed back like a boy's. She started all that. She was built with curves like the hull of a racing yacht, and you missed none of it with the wool jersey."*

To recreate an event "the way it was" had been one of Hemingway's foremost literary preachments. In his own recollection of the events of *The Sun Also Rises*, however, Loeb has written his own book, called *The Way It Was*.

"I had first noticed Duff some months earlier at the Select Cafe, where I had often gone to work on a chapter of *Doodab*," Loeb wrote. "One afternoon, while my eyes were on the manuscript, I heard a laugh so gay and musical that it seemed to brighten the dingy room. I looked up. A group of men were concentrated on the only woman seated at the bar. A ruddy, round-faced type was telling a story. Every now and then they broke into laughter. But it was the woman's laugh which had caught my attention. Low-pitched, it had the liquid quality of the lilt of a mockingbird singing to the moon. . .

"She was not strikingly beautiful, but her features had a special appeal for me. I particularly liked the expressive eyes and the fresh complexion, and there was a grace about the way she held herself. Her clothes were of the simplest: slouch hat worn askew, soft jersey, and tweed skirt. . .

"I suppose that Duff interested me because she moved around in a muck of lost souls without losing a certain aloof splendor. She would sit at the bar drinking and talking . . . Other characters would wander in—riffraff who passed their lives drifting from bar to bar never quite sober, stray American businessmen, French sailors, schoolteachers, artists, Midwestern widows, dark-skinned noncoms of the French Army, and the queers. They would cluster around the bar talking. In a little while nasal lines deepened, jaws wobbled, lower lips dropped at one end. They became old and sloppy as you watched—all but Duff. Her color did not change. Even when her legs were unsteady, her walk flowed and her laugh rang clear. I wondered how long she could keep it up without losing her looks."

Although his mother was from the Guggenheim family and his father was from the Kuhn Loeb fortune, Loeb, after World War I, had forsaken the New York regimen of finance to open a book shop, write several novels and publish the international literary magazine *Broom,* which has now taken its place in the history of American esthetics along with such other journals as the *Little Review, transition,* and the *transatlantic review.* Even today, thirty-six years later, he thinks he deserved better than he received as Hemingway's Robert Cohn.

"Everybody in *The Sun Also Rises* is based on somebody who was in the party that went with Hem and me to the fiesta at Pamplona in 1924, and they're all distorted," Loeb said. "I think possibly Frances got off worst or maybe Cohn —it irritated me no end, obviously. Because he could have changed the background so that everybody wouldn't know who everybody was.

"But the way Hem did, he just spotted each one of us. Of course, Frances was very upset, but I don't want to say who *she* was. Duff, everybody knows, but Frances is a little more concealed. Jake, of course, as far as I know, Hemingway used Jake as *his* spokesman. Bill Gorton, he was Bill Smith—he's still alive. And Mike Campbell, the playboy, he was Pat Guthrie. I don't know what happened to him.

"We were all pretty mad over the book, although Duff didn't mind, she's a little more, well, she'd been around. She was in another book, *The Green Hat*, by Michael Arlen. If you're curious about Duff now, you would have been a lot more curious if you were there and had seen her. She was quite a woman. There were always men around her. She had a couple of good friends who were fairies, one of them with a title back in England, but Hemingway stresses that. They were rather nice people and most of us were friendly enough with them, except Hemingway, who maintained his extra-masculinity. I think that what he found was if there were any fairies around, it was somewhat of an exaggeration, but once after he had heard she had gone off with one of them, he wired me when I was supposed to meet them at the train in Spain that she was not bringing any and that I should have a band of local fairies meet her at the station carrying a daisy chain so the transition from the Latin Quarter would not be too sudden.

"I saw her again when I went back to Paris in 1927. Oh, yes, we talked about Hem's book, but I can't remember exactly what she said, it was thirty years ago. I know she didn't take it seriously. I didn't excite her much. She shrugged her shoulders at it, wasn't even upset by it. She was somewhat amused."

Whatever his characters thought of their author, the world, nevertheless, was soon fascinated by them. Although *The Sun Also Rises* sold little more than a respectable twenty-six thousand copies in the first eight months of its publication, the book soon began to have an impact on popular culture that still makes it required reading in many history courses. With Gertrude Stein's *"You are all a lost generation"* quoted inside the title page, the youth of America soon adopted the phrase as the label of their time and the characters became their model.

"You're an expatriate," Bill Gorton tells Jake Barnes on a fishing trip before they leave for the bull fights and fiesta at Pamplona. *"You've lost touch with the soil. You get precious. Fake European standards have ruined you. You drink your-self to death. You become obsessed by sex. You spend all*

your time talking, not working. You're an expatriate, see? You hang around cafes."

The effect of *The Sun Also Rises* on Hemingway's juniors of the 1920s was much the same as the effect Jack Kerouac's *On The Road* has had among latter-day youth. The effect on mass culture also was similar. Just as Kerouac's "Beat Generation" has resulted in a new word for "Bohemian," a new mystique for graduating intellectuals, a new show business for bearded entertainers, a new tourism for Main Street *voyeurs* and the appearance of mother-and-daughter beatnik outfits in high-fashion stores, so did *The Sun Also Rises* excite a nation which had shackled itself with Warren G. Harding and Calvin Coolidge. But *The Sun Also Rises*, much the same as Kerouac's book has done, also created a new artistry. In its glow, another generation of expatriates assaulted Paris, arriving with little more luggage than their typewriters. Even the time lapses were similar. After the publication of *On The Road* in 1957, an inspired portion of American youth began copying a life which Kerouac actually had lived and wrote about ten years before. When *The Sun Also Rises* was published, on October twenty-second, 1926, the tide of young people it attracted to France were seeking sad joys which already were in Hemingway's past.

"Hemingway, as Lord Byron had done a century before, gave the young people attitudes to strike and patterns of conduct to follow," wrote Malcolm Cowley. "They not only wrote like him, if they wrote, and walked with his rolling slouch, if they had seen him, but also drank like his heroes and heroines, cultivated a hard-boiled melancholy and talked in page after page of Hemingway dialogue."

The story of the book, of course, is that of the unrequited love of Brett and Jake, although she doesn't go through the book entirely unrequited. It's also the story of Robert Cohn, himself in love with Brett, and of his friendship with Jake, although their friendship never quite reaches either of them. *"Robert Cohn was once middleweight boxing champion of Princeton,"* Hemingway began his novel. *"Do not think that I am very much impressed by that as a boxing title, but it meant a lot to Cohn."* Harold Loeb has been smarting over these and Hemingway's subsequent words ever since.

The narrative of the novel takes its characters, fictional or otherwise, from Paris' sidewalk cafes and *bal musettes* to the bullfight fiesta at Pamplona, where the interpersonal relationships among Jake, Cohn, Lady Brett, and her fiance, Mike Campbell, an unsobered British playboy who in real life was patterned after the fabled Pat Guthrie, reach their drunken, regretful heights. Another character in the novel was Bill Gorton, whom Loeb said was patterned after William Smith but who, according to Carlos Baker, actually was based on humorist Donald Ogden Stewart, a close friend of Hemingway and not at all troubled by his portrait in the book. Still another figure was Pedro Romero, whom Hemingway himself later acknowledged to be a fictionalized picture of Niño de la Palma, then a heroic young bullfighter and eventually the father of Hemingway's most recent bullring hero, Antonio Ordoñez.

"One immediate cause of its [*The Sun Also Rises*'] success," Carlos Baker has written, "was that if you knew something about the Montparnassians who frequented the Dôme, the Rotonde, the Select, the Deux Magots, the Napolitain, the Dingo Bar, or Zelli's during the period 1923-1925, you were alleged to own a key which would admit the bearer to the 'real' identities of the fictional people. As Model-T jokes helped early Fords to fame, so the international guessing-game of who was who in *The Sun Also Rises* assisted with the word-of-mouth promotion of the book . . . For a time after the book was published, Paris gossip asserted that its title should have been *Six Characters in Search of an Author —With a Gun Apiece*."

Hemingway, in fact, based most of the fiesta scenes of *The Sun Also Rises* on the 1925 visit that he made to Pamplona with Hadley, Loeb, Lady Duff, Guthrie, Stewart and other friends of the time. Many of the incidents described by Hemingway in the book were approximations of actual events, and Loeb, of course, thinks they were *too* approximate. In *The Sun Also Rises*, for example, there are scenes in which Cohn knocks out Jake, swings at Mike and then beats up Pedro Romero. Actually, according to Loeb, on the night that he and Hemingway challenged each other to a fist fight, they ended up holding each other's coats. Only grins were exchanged.

From his own book, here, according to Loeb, is the way it was:

Pat kept on yapping. I didn't mind Pat's not liking me;

I didn't like him either. But it hurt to have Hem taking Pat's side.

"Look here," said Pat. "I may be dumb. I may be useless. But I know enough to stay away when I'm not wanted."

"Is that how you got through school?" I asked.

"You lay off Pat," said Hem grimly. "You've done enough to spoil this party."

I gripped the table hard.

"Why don't you get out?" Pat said. "I don't want you here. Hem doesn't want you here. Nobody wants you here, though some may be too decent to say so."

"Get out?"

"Get out!" said Pat.

"I will," I said, "the instant Duff wants it."

In the silence that followed, Duff dropped the pretense of talking to Hadley and turned her head slowly. "You know," she said, looking directly at me, "that I do *not* want you to go."

"You lousy bastard," said Hemingway. "Running to a woman."

I got up unsteadily. Struggling to keep my voice calm, I said to Hem, "Do you mind stepping out for a moment."

"Oh, willingly, willingly," he said.

Hem got up and followed me. The square was full of light, though most of the celebrants were now seated at tables. There was an unlit corner diagonally across from us. The street beyond the plaza would be dark and empty. I started toward it, not across the square, but down one side on the covered pavement behind the columns. Hem walked beside me.

I was scared—not shaken or panicky, but just plain scared. . .

We walked in silence. Out of the corner of my eye I could see Hem against the shop windows. His features were fixed, his expression grim. . .

We reached the last cafe, the last illuminated shop front. We went down a few steps. Now there were only street lamps. The small street carried on in semi-darkness.

I took my glasses off and, after considering the safest place, put them in the side pocket of my jacket. Then I stopped, faced Hem, and took my jacket off.

90

"My glasses," I said, "are in the side pocket. If they're broken I couldn't get them fixed here."

Feeling ridiculous, I looked around for someplace to put my jacket.

"Shall I hold it for you?" he asked.

I smiled. There was just enough light for me to see that Hem was smiling too, the boyish, contagious, smile that made it so hard not to like him.

"If I may hold yours," I said.

We stood hesitantly looking at each other.

"I don't want to hit you," I said.

"Me either," said Hem.

We put on our jackets and started back.

Loeb recalled that the next day Hemingway sent him a letter of apology which explained that he had been drunk, that he wished he could erase the meanness of what he had said and that he was ashamed of what had happened. "Of course, I had boxed with Hem before," Loeb said, recalling the incident thirty-six years later. "He wasn't too good a boxer. Well, naturally not. He had one eye that wasn't quite right. He had forty pounds on me, but I could get in a lick occasionally."

According to Loeb, *The Sun Also Rises* was filled with other approximations of the way it was. But the most puzzling approximations to literary historians remains this: although Hemingway actually went to the fiesta with his wife Hadley, Jake was accompanied only by his emasculation.

"It was quite a hectic party," Hadley, who later became Mrs. Paul Scott Mowrer, remembered in the weeks after Hemingway's death. "All mixed up with street music and dancing and what-not. Loeb? Well, he had a chip on his shoulder and Ernest had a chip on his. I don't think they were really terribly congenial fellows. They were thrown together a bit. . .

"Duff? She was lovely, a very fine lady, and very much of a man's woman. She was very, very popular, and very nice to women, too. She was fair and square. Well, you know there were lots of awfully rowdy people that we met up with in the course of our careers but she was really, truly a lady—who had gone very tough, I must admit—but she really was a lady and nothing could stop that.

"I think Ernest met her in one of the cafes around Montparnasse—the Dôme or the Select or the Rotonde. You just automatically went out, sat around. That's the way you met people. I don't know if they had an affair. I think it's perfectly possible but I don't know it for a fact. That isn't the kind of a thing a husband talks to his wife about too much, don't you agree? I think there were quite a number of things, but largely I think the women were crazy about *him*. I think Duff was very keen on Ernest. . .

"After all these years, I don't know what to say about the Duff Twysden thing because I think they didn't actually have an affair. But I just think it. What can a poor wife do? But I do think they were awfully crazy about each other."

Hemingway, who dedicated *The Sun Also Rises* to Hadley, also dedicated the royalties from it to her. But when, in the weeks after his death, she felt a desire to reread it, she found she didn't even have a copy.

"I think I lent my own inscribed copy to somebody and they thought it was a good thing," she said. "I don't know when it disappeared, but I didn't want to ask Ernest for another, so I haven't got any. The inscription was nothing long or philosophical—probably, 'To a Feather Cat,' or something like that. It was one of my names. We must have talked about the book when he was writing it, but I don't remember. It was something I didn't mind very much. You know, I wasn't in it at all. Did I feel left out? No, I don't think so. I don't mind it *now*, anyway. I can't remember my feelings so far back."

Loeb's feelings, of course, never changed. Still searching for the reasons why Hemingway turned on him, he seemed to become somewhat self-conscious about the prospects of going through eternity as a literary villain. In his book, however, are several implied theories. One is that Hemingway turned him into Robert Cohn out of jealousy for the fact that Hemingway's romance with Lady Duff was not consummated, Loeb's romance with her was.

"It was a small room and messy, not at all the kind of place I would have chosen," Loeb wrote. "Clothes were strewn about, and a dirty towel lay across the back of the only chair. The wallpaper was stained above the basin. A wrinkled coverlet lay across the bed.

"We sat beside each other holding hands and the room and everything in it departed quietly. I kissed her.

"After a time Duff drew away and stood before me as if

in a trance. Quietly she began to undress. I did not look at her while her clothes were coming off. When I looked up I saw that she was lovely. . ."

In love with Lady Duff himself, Loeb stole away with her for several days at St.-Jean-de-Luz, a French resort. It was there that she told him she liked Hemingway. "Yes," she said, "a good chap." Later, when they all were to meet at Pamplona, she wrote Loeb that "Hem has promised to be good. . ." At the time Loeb wondered why she had found it necessary to extract such a promise from Hemingway. Then he concluded that Hemingway had become involved with Duff.

In *The Sun Also Rises,* it was Lady Brett herself who told Jake that she had gone away with Cohn. According to *The Way It Was,* Hemingway learned of Loeb's affair with Duff from someone else:

"Hem seems to be bitter about something," I said to Bill. "Do you know what it is? You've known him longer than I have."

"It's that *wagon-lit!*"

"What?"

"You should have seen his face," said Bill, "when Jo Bennett told him you and Duff had gone off in a *wagon-lit.*"

"How did she get into the act?"

"He was sure to hear from someone. He went off muttering the foulest string of curses I ever heard. 'In a *wagon-lit,*' he said at every other step."

"But why should that upset him?"

"Hem has a mean streak," said Bill. "I guess *wagon-lits* bring it out."

"You mean he's in love with Duff?"

"I didn't say that," said Bill.

Duff Twysden had been born in a small village in Scotland. She came from a tradition of mist, heather and neighbors in for tea. In her childhood, she had sat in a hiding place and dreamed of sailing to far-away places. As soon as she could, she had gotten married. Her husband was an English baronet many times older than she.

On her second wedding day she had eloped with the best man. He had been a naval officer who had given her a child and then had gone away to sea. When, later, he had come home between voyages, it was to get drunk. She lost the memory of seeing him sober.

" 'I don't believe she would marry anybody she didn't love,' " wrote Hemingway in *The Sun Also Rises*.

" 'Well,' I said, 'She's done it twice.' "

Like her fiance, Pat Guthrie, Lady Duff lived on an allowance from her family, or, rather, hers or one of her husbands'. The allowance came to about ten or twenty British pounds per month, but it did not come with any regularity. Sometimes she received several months' allowance in one sum. And sometimes, Guthrie's, too, came with accumulated caprice. "But when a check arrived," wrote Loeb, "they moved to the Ritz. Everyone knew them there. She would get out her white gloves and evening gowns; he'd have his dinner jacket pressed. They'd have champagne and caviar and a wonderful time until their money gave out. Then they'd pack up their things and move back to the Quarter and poverty. Often they did not have enough to eat. But there was always someone to buy drinks."

In a similar manner, when the Pamplona fiesta was over and Hemingway had completed gathering his material, the prototypes of the Lost Generation promptly disbanded. Ironically, Hemingway hardly ever saw them again.

"He and Hadley went to Madrid," recalled Loeb, "and Duff and Pat and Bill Smith and I left for St.-Jean-de-Luz. I was pretty mad and I didn't see Hem afterwards. Oh, I'd see him at a distance and sort of wave or something. Before the book was out I ran into him in Paris and we had dinner. Today I look back and I remember the charm and pleasure I had for years with him, but I still think that he could have done a little switching around in his book without pointing out the people so clearly."

Despite Loeb's disappointment in both Hemingway and his book, Loeb has not failed to see the historicity of them. He has seemed, in fact, proud of his connection with Hemingway and even of the place in literature which Hemingway has assured for him. Although his interest turned, after the 1929 stock market crash, toward economics and he later became director of the National Survey of Potential Product Capacity, Loeb has continued to write. *The Way It Was* was meant to be as much an aid to literary historians as a self-explanation. In addition, Loeb has given his letters from

Hemingway to Princeton University, his alma mater. He has made plans to give his other letters to Princeton after his death. They are his letters from Duff.

Describing his own experience with *The Sun Also Rises*, Hemingway has had other considerations. *"The Sun Also Rises,"* he told George Plimpton of the *Paris Review*, "I started in Valencia on my birthday, July twenty-first. Hadley, my wife, and I had gone to Valencia early to get good tickets for the Feriá there which started twenty-fourth of July. Everybody my age had written a novel and I was still having a difficult time writing a paragraph. So I started the book on my birthday, wrote all through the Feria, in bed in the morning, went on to Madrid and wrote there.

"There was no Feria there, so we had a room with a table and I wrote in great luxury on the table and around the corner from the hotel in a beer place in the Pasaje Alvarez where it was cool. It finally got too hot to write and we went to Hendaye. There was a small cheap hotel there on the big long lovely beach and I worked very well there and then went up to Paris and finished the first draft in the apartment over the sawmill at one hundred and thirteen Rue Notre-Dame-des-Champs six weeks from the day I started it.

"I showed the first draft to Nathan Asch, the novelist, who then had quite a strong accent and he said 'Hem vaht do you mean saying you wrote a novel? A novel huh. Hem you are riding a travhel büch.' I was not too discouraged by Nathan and rewrote the book. . ."

In his interview with Hemingway, Plimpton asked: ". . . One of the advisory staff editors wonders about a parallel he feels he's found in *The Sun Also Rises* between the dramatis personae of the bull ring and the character of the novel itself. He points out that the first sentence of the book tells us Robert Cohn is a boxer; later, during the *desencajonada,* the bull is described as using his horns like a boxer, hooking and jabbing. And just as the bull is attracted and pacified by the presence of a steer, Robert Cohn defers to Jake who is emasculated precisely as a steer. He sees Mike as the picador, baiting Cohn repeatedly. The editor's thesis goes on, but he wondered if it was your conscious intention to inform the novel with the tragic structure of the bullfight ritual."

"It sounds as though the advistory staff editor was a little bit screwy," answered Hemingway. "Who ever said Jake was 'emasculated precisely as is a steer?' Actually he had been wounded in quite a different way and his testicles were intact and not damaged. Thus he was capable of all normal feelings as a *man* but incapable of consummating them. The important distinction is that his wound was physical and not psychological and that he was not emasculated."

What Hemingway meant was that Jake's penis had been shot away, which is still a proper definition for emasculation. How Hemingway got the idea for such a wound, however, is still as obscure as the advisory staff editor's thesis. In 1926, Guy Hickok once asked Hemingway:

"Why did you have Jake wounded like that?"

"Oh," Hemingway replied, "I saw a ward full of men wounded that way. I got to wondering what might become of some of them."

In another possible explanation, Carlos Baker reports once hearing a story, still undocumented, that the Austrian trench-mortar which exploded near Hemingway during World War I actually blew fragments of his uniform into the skin of his genitalia, necessitating removal by tweezers. And then, too, after the publication of *The Sun Also Rises* there was a widespread belief that Hemingway himself had suffered a wound as serious as Jake's. Or at least that he was impotent.

"Well," said Hadley, "I have heard hints from other people that they probably thought Ernest was not very powerful in those directions, but if you would see his sons you would know differently. And women have been enthusiastic."

Hemingway has left other *pronunciamentos* concerning *The Sun Also Rises*. To F. Scott Fitzgerald, he wrote:

If you are worried [*The Sun Also Rises*] is *not* a series of anecdotes—nor is it written very much like either Manhattan Transfer nor Dark Laughter . . . The hero, like Gatsby, is a Lake Superior Salmon Fisherman. (There are no salmon in Lake Superior.) The action all takes place in Newport, R. I. and the heroine is a girl named Sophie Irene Loeb who kills her mother. The scene in which Sophie gives birth to twins in the death house at Sing Sing where she is waiting to be electrocuted for the murder of the father and sister of her, as then, unborn children I got from Dreiser but practically everything else in the book is either my own or yours. I know you'll be glad to see it. The Sun Also Rises comes from Sophie's statement as she is strapped into the chair as the current mounts.

Actually, Hemingway's first and truest thoughts about *The Sun Also Rises* probably were contained in a letter to Maxwell Perkins dated November nineteenth, 1926. The point of the book for him, he told Perkins, was "that the earth abideth forever." He had "a great deal of fondness and admiration for the earth, and not a hell of a lot for my generation." The book, he said, was not meant to be "a hollow or bitter satire, but a damn tragedy with the earth abiding forever as the hero."

Duff and Hemingway never saw each other again. According to Loeb, she eventually married an American, a Texan. "The family didn't approve and they lived a pretty tough life for a while," Loeb remembered. Afterwards, she moved to New York City, New York.

"I can recall meeting her at a party there," remembered a New York newspaper editor. "Somebody whispered into my ear that she was the original Lady Brett Ashley. I was twenty-two at the time and like every other twenty-two-year-old man I had been in love with Brett. All I can tell you is that it was a terrible letdown for a young man to see what she looked like by the time I saw her. I was quite disillusioned."

Later, Lady Duff Twysden moved to Santa Fe, New Mexico. She died in Saint Vincent's Hospital there on June twenty-seventh, 1938, of tuberculosis. She was forty-three years old. She is buried in Santa Fe.

CHAPTER SIX

The Champion

PERHAPS it began that July night on the Piave riverbank in the brilliance of an exploding mortar shell. As he was carried back on a blood-soaked stretcher, someone said he hadn't been handing out chocolate bars after all but had borrowed an Italian rifle to keep his wing shot in practice, using Austrian targets. He had been wounded, the story went, the moment after he put his eye to the sights, but that didn't stop him when he saw an Italian soldier hanging on the barbed wire in no-man's land. He had crawled from his dugout, wound and all, to rescue the Italian and then the trench-mortar had exploded. That was the rumor which came back from the front along with him and his pulpy legs, and, among the fifty or so men who had been his companions in Section IV of the American Red Cross ambulance corps, Ernest Hemingway became a legend even then. It didn't matter that the truth was legendary enough. They told their friends about him.

Or perhaps it began in another July, this one in Pamplona, where, with John Dos Passos, Robert McAlmon, and Donald Ogden Stewart, he had gone to the fiesta to participate in the running of the bulls. On their second day there, one of the animals tossed Stewart several feet but, unhurt, he quickly got up and bet Hemingway that he could mount the same bull, ride it, blow smoke in its eyes, wrestle with it and throw it. As he was about to launch this enterprise, a matador presented him with a red cape and Stewart turned to shake hands. Behind his back, the bull charged again, lifting him on its horns, rolling him over and hurling him into the air. When he crashed to the ground, he had two broken ribs. Unable to move, Stewart lay helpless while the bull turned to gore him once more. Without hesitation, Hemingway ran to Stewart's aid and took the bull's charge himself. He suffered only a few painful bruises, but the story got into the newspapers.

Or perhaps it began that 1928 day when, with F. Scott Fitzgerald acting as timekeeper, he engaged Morley Callaghan in a boxing match at which Fitzgerald was also the audience. The fight was an interesting one, so interesting that Fitzgerald became too busy watching it to watch the clock. According to one version, Callaghan knocked Hemingway down, but, without the bell, Hemingway had to stand up and take some more. According to another version, it was as energetic a match for Callaghan as it was for Hemingway. Either way, Hemingway and Fitzgerald argued about it and Callaghan wrote a public denial. He also succumbed to interviews entitled, "I Never Knocked Out Ernest Hemingway."

Or perhaps it began when, from 1930 until 1931, his autograph, or what was purported to be his autograph, started appearing on book contracts, hotel registers and even a speakeasy deed, signed by a man whose true identity remains unknown to this day. In one commitment, the imposter pledged Hemingway to ghost-write the life story of a man he chanced to meet in a tavern. In another, he enlisted Hemingway as a press agent for the USSR. The impostor even introduced himself as Hemingway in explorers' clubs, cocktail parties and bars throughout Europe and America, displaying manuscripts of works in progress, giving away first editions of his books and suitably inscribing their title pages with long, friendly prose. Finally, federal authorities raided the "Hemingway" speakeasy in New York and cabled Hemingway in Paris for an explanation.

"After all," Hemingway said later, "one has enough to defend as a writer without having someone get you out of bed with the command to come down to the foyer and finish 'that biography of me as a brick salesman' . . ."

Or perhaps it began when, in expatriate Paris, he pulled the wrong chain in his garret lavatory and the skylight came crashing down on his head. There are still pictures of him, taken by Dadaist photographer Man Ray, showing him with bandages beneath a tyrolean hat. The accident cut his forehead open, leaving fierce, manly scars over his left eye. They added to his appearance.

Or perhaps it began when Hemingway, after ten years of chasing bulls and being chased by them, publicly decided that matadoring had become too formalized and he went on a three-month safari into Tanganyika to chase lions instead. "Lions, are fine animals," he told newspaper reporters. "They can cover a hundred yards in three seconds. They are upon you before there is any time to act."

Or perhaps it began when *A Farewell to Arms* was banned from the 1929 newsstands of Boston, the cradle of liberty and best-sellers. Or when, while on a 1930 hunting trip with John Dos Passos near Billings, Montana, he was blinded by approaching headlights and nearly lost an arm in an automobile accident. Or when, fishing off Bimini in the Bahamas, he hooked a specimen never catalogued by man before. He sent the fish to a friend, Henry Weed Fowler, chief ichthyologist at the Philadelphia Academy of Natural Sciences, who promptly named the newly discovered species neomerinthe hemingwayi.

Or perhaps Ernest Hemingway's legend began with himself. His greatness, after all, was in the art of storytelling.

"I looked up," wrote Sylvia Beach, telling about her 1921 introduction to him in her autobiography, *Shakespeare And Company*, "and saw a tall, dark young fellow with a small mustache, and heard him say, in a deep, deep voice, that he was Ernest Hemingway. I invited him to sit down, and, drawing him out, I learned that he was from Chicago originally. I also learned that he had spent two years in a military hospital, getting back the use of his leg. What had happened to his leg? Well, he told me apologetically, like a boy confessing he had been in a scrap, he had got wounded in the knee, fighting in Italy. Would I care to see it? Of course I would. So business at Shakespeare and Company was suspended while he removed his shoe and sock, and showed me the dreadful scars covering his leg and foot . . . In the hospital, they had thought he was done for; there was even some question of administering the last sacraments. But this was changed, with his feeble consent to baptism—'just in case they were right.' . . .

"Hemingway confided to me that before he was out of high school, when he was still 'a boy in short pants,' his father had died suddenly and in tragic circumstances, leaving him a gun as a sole legacy. He found himself the head of a family, his mother and brothers and sister dependent on him. He had to leave school and begin making a living. He earned his first money in a boxing match, but, from what I gathered, didn't linger in this career. He spoke rather bitterly of his boyhood.

"He didn't tell me much about his life after he left school. He earned his living at various jobs, including newspaper work, I believe, then went over to Canada and enlisted in the armed forces. He was so young he had to fake his age to be accepted. . ."

In his lifetime, Hemingway has faked other facts about himself. "Well," said his first wife, Hadley, laughing with nostalgic heartiness at the inaccuracies that Sylvia Beach had compounded, "he was a good story writer, too." Or, as Carlos Baker has on other occasions remarked: "If Hemingway told you something about himself, I guess you could trust it about fifty per cent." On the other hand, so much more has been faked *about* Hemingway. In the last years of his life, he complained frequently about the great body of inaccuracies and trivia that had grown with his age and stature. There was too much, in fact, for him even to contend with. If he sat down, he said, to contradict all the errors about himself with the same rapidity that they appeared, he wouldn't have any time left for his own writing.

II

In the yellow, faded, brittle, crumbling memorabilia and memories which remain of his life, there are many moments when the great legend of him might have had its conception. It was a legend that grew apart from his books, although the bond between them is inescapable. He lived his life according to the same code by which he forced his heroes to live. In Spanish, they had *cojones*. In English, they had *guts*. Hemingway had both in either language, or, for that matter, in any of the other four which he spoke with varying success. In his own language, of course, the word was *balls*. "Survival, with honor, that outmoded and all-important word, is as difficult as ever and as all important to a writer," he said. He believed that to live well was to know how to die well, and his legend grew with that belief. It seems, today, inconceivable that so affirmative a statement of it should end with a question mark.

The probability is that the Hemingway legend began to

spread even before the first popularity of his literary heroes. In 1924, for example, Malcolm Cowley, back in New York, learned just that—"that Hemingway was becoming a legendary figure."

"In the hidden saloons which are patronized by the returning exiles, by the repatriated expatriates; in the little noisy bars which take the place of the Dome and the Jockey, I began to hear his name," Cowley wrote. "I would meet an acquaintance lately returned from Paris. 'Hello, Dick,' I would say, 'How's Montparnasse?'

" 'Swell. You can bet I was sorry to leave . . . And say, did you hear what Hemingway did last?' "

According to Cowley, the Hemingway legend had one of its strongest foundations in that expatriate night in Paris when Hemingway, outraged because the middleweight champion of France had started fighting dirty against a boxer twenty pounds lighter, had leaped into the ring and had begun hitting the champion with his fists and a water bottle. Hemingway had saved the challenger's life, but it took a dozen police to save the champion's.

" 'Did you hear how old Hem knocked out the middleweight champion of France?' " Cowley later wrote. "I must have been asked the question twenty times, in speakeasies where the returning exiles used to gather, and it was followed by twenty different versions of the real story."

Hemingway himself never bothered to document the report, although later, when someone asked him about the incident, he replied: "Any sane person knows that writers do not knock out middleweight champions, unless the writer's name happens to be Gene Tunney."

Another factor in the early propagandization of Hemingway's exploits was his friendship with Guy Hickok, who, eking out a space-rate existence as the Paris correspondent for the now-defunct *Brooklyn Eagle*, first helped broadcast Hemingway's bravery to the American rear echelon. In 1925, even before Hemingway's fame came over the horizon with *The Sun Also Rises*, Hickok was sending back long dispatches full of stories about Hemingway and also full of Hickok's idolatry of him. In one, for example, Hickok devoted an entire *Brooklyn Eagle* page to describing some of Hemingway's war experiences coupled with some of the incidents of his honeymoon:

During the war a succession of accidents made him quite

by surprise a temporary officer without command in the Italian army. He had been sent to Italy to show the American uniform, to show that America was in the war. Then there was a historic rout. And he found himself with Italian soldiers at night on the bank of the Piave.

An Austrian searchlight on the opposite bank spotted them. A little later Hemingway lurched up a sunken road away from the river with a wounded Italian soldier on his back. The searchlight followed him. He couldn't climb out of the ditch. There was nothing behind which he could hide. And shells followed the light with disconcerting accuracy. One exploded just behind him and damaged him in a dozen places, left him a stiffened knee and peppered him with vaccination scars.

With this account, printed in the *Brooklyn Eagle* of May seventeenth, 1925, Hickok also told how Hemingway and Hadley had suffered attacks of ptomaine poisoning and the flu during their honeymoon in Horton's Bay. He told how Hemingway, in need of supplies, one day walked into town, met a bootlegger friend and got drunk. Unwilling, or unable, to walk back to the Hemingway summer cabin, Hemingway instead borrowed a motorboat. When he reached the opposite shore, however, he realized that the cabin lacked a landing. Still several hundred feet away, he called to Hadley. Then he picked up the bundle of provisions, which happened to include his old army uniform, his tin helmet and a four-pound beefsteak, and he tossed it at his bride. Unprepared, Hadley caught the missile not in her hands but on her nose. It knocked her out, or that's how the story went.

"Ernest *did* make up a good story, didn't he?" said Hadley thirty-four years later. "I never even knew that Guy had printed such an article. In the first place, there *was* a dock there. I think Ernest probably talked to Guy, of whom he was very fond, the same way he talked to Sylvia Beach. You know making up stories was the way Ernest made his living. But I certainly never got hit on the nose."

By 1928, the legend of Ernest Hemingway had grown to such proportions that Hickok, although one of those most responsible for it, was able to report that Hemingway no longer could lead a private life in his Paris retreat. With *The Sun Also Rises* already making its impact on America, tourists would tip Left Bank waiters to point out the tall, muscular, mustachioed author to them and, lacking Hemingway, the waiters would motion toward any habitue who happened to be handy.

"Nobody tries harder to live a private life than Hemingway in Paris," Hickok wrote on March fourth of that year. "He buries himself away in an old, narrow street near the Church of Saint Sulpice, runs away to Germany to escape being a guest of honor at literary dinners, hunts out hard-to-get-at places in Spain (Pamplona having turned tourist resort after the success of *The Sun Also Rises*), and goes off to small Swiss villages when the snow gets deep enough to ski.

"He denies his publishers the intimate details that they need for modern publicity. He answers few letters and accords no interviews.

"The result is that he has a whole series of wilder private lives than he could possibly live.

"Clipping services bring them back to him. It seems from the clippings that anybody who has spent any time in the Paris Latin Quarter is expected to know Hemingway, and all about him. And the visitors who like to shine in the reflected glory of wild notables they have met love to please.

" 'Hemingway is a tall, sad, pale, bald-headed young man who goes about alone bareheaded, always with his finger in a book,' said one of them. 'He is always thinking. He never talks to anybody. He just walks about Paris in golf pants with his finger in a book.' "

The *Brooklyn Eagle* wasn't the only North American newspaper to specialize in accounts of Hemingway's activities in Europe. Hemingway, who attended the weekly lunches of the Paris press association and who lunched more frequently with Hickok and the International News Service's Frank Mason, knew just about all the foreign correspondents in Europe and was a good friend of many of them. In addition, his alma maters, the Toronto and the Kansas City *Star*, were particularly concerned with chronicling his exploits just as the Chicago papers were particularly concerned with items about any hometown boy. And when, for instance, he slugged it out with Morley Callaghan, it was the *Denver Post* which first printed the story of his knockout. Callaghan, at Hemingway's insistence, eventually wrote his denial for the *New York Herald Tribune*. By 1929, the *New Yorker* magazine had chosen Hemingway as the subject for a profile and Dorothy Parker was able to babble:

I have heard of him, both at various times and all in one great bunch, that he is so hard-boiled he makes a daily practice of busting his widowed mother in the nose; that he dictates his stories because he can't write, and has them read to him because he can't read; that he is expatriate to such a degree that he tears down any American flag he sees flying in France; that no woman within half-a-mile of him is a safe woman; that he not only commands enormous prices for his short stories, but insists, additionally, on taking the right eye out of the editor's face; that he has been a tramp, a safe-cracker, and a stockyard attendant; that he is the Pet of the Left Bank, and may be found at any hour of the day or night sitting at a little table at the Select, rubbing absinthe into his gums; that he really hates all forms of sport, and only skis, hunts, fishes, and fights bulls in order to be cute; that a wound he sustained in the Great War was of a whimsical, inconvenient, and inevitably laughable description; and that he also writes under the name of Morley Callaghan.

III

It was probably the Morley Callaghan incident that Gertrude Stein referred to when, in 1933, she wrote in *The Autobiography of Alice B. Toklas:* "In these days Hemingway was teaching some young chap how to box. The boy did not know how, but by accident he knocked Hemingway out. I believe this sometimes happens. At any rate in these days Hemingway although a sportsman was easily tired. He used to get quite worn out walking from his house to ours. But then he had been worn by the war. Even now he is . . . fragile. Recently a robust friend of his said: Ernest is very fragile, whenever he does anything sporting something breaks, his arm, his leg, or his head."

Although his reply was limited to a passage in *Green Hills of Africa,* Hemingway probably was more wounded by Gertrude Stein's barb than by any opponent's boxing glove. "I get the feeling," says Hemingway's son John, "that Miss Stein knew how to hurt him. And that she knew the way to get to him was to say something like this. But that he was fragile is not exactly the case. I'm kind of rough, but he was *awful* rough . . . You see, to say he was accident-prone is the wrong kind of thing. Accident-prone things are where people trip and fall and do things of that nature. But as for Papa, I would say that he did a lot of *active* things, and if you do a lot of active things long enough a lot of other things are going to happen to you."

Accident-prone or prone for any other reason, Hemingway always seemed to rise to his feet again. Even today, the pugs he came to spar with at Charlie Brown's gym at West Fifty-Seventh Street in New York, or the fishermen who later bantered him with baseball gossip on the docks at Cojimar in Cuba, or the bartenders who would pour *Papa* his roja at Chicote's in Madrid or all the others he came to know in the roughhouse of his world would express probably only a minimum of surprise, in addition to their maximum of pleasure, if Hemingway just happened to materialize again.

Hemingway, of course, had amazed Miss Stein no less than the others in the expatriate American colony with his derring-do and with his boastfulness of it. "Like a child showing off before an only half-attentive parent, he was . . . continually calling her attention to his exploits in boxing, bullfighting, skiing and fishing. . . ," wrote John Malcolm Brinnin. To his fellow artists, in fact, his masculinity seemed to be the schizophrenic side of him. "Hemingway was a type not easy to size up," said his friend, novelist Robert McAlmon. "At times he was deliberately hard-boiled and case-hardened; again he appeared deliberately innocent, sentimental, the hurt, soft, but fairly sensitive boy trying to conceal hurt, wanting to be brave, not bitter or cynical but being somewhat both, and somehow on the defensive, suspicions lurking in his peering analytic glances at a person with whom he was talking. He approached a cafe with a small-boy, tough-guy swagger, and before strangers of whom he was doubtful a potential snarl of scorn played on his large-lipped, rather loose mouth." Said Margaret Anderson, editor of the *Little Review:* "Hemingway is so soft-hearted that it must be as much as he can bear to beat a punching-bag." And Jane Heap, Margaret Anderson's co-editor, said that if Hemingway had an animal prototype it would be a rabbit, "pink and white face, soft brown eyes that look at you without blinking. As for his love for boxing and bull-fighting—all that is thrashing up the ground with his hind legs." In a less bitter and more serious appraisal of Hemingway's heroics, Miss Stein herself later told novelist John Hyde Preston:

". . . When I first met Hemingway he had a truly sensitive

capacity for emotion, and that was the stuff of the first stories; but he was shy of himself and he began to develop, as a shield, a big Kansas City-boy brutality about it, and so he was 'touchy' because he was really sensitive and ashamed that he was . . .

"He went the way so many other Americans have gone before, the way they are still going. He became obsessed with sex and violent death . . . Now you will mistake me. Sex and death are the springs of the most valid of human emotions. But they are not all; they are not even all emotion. But for Hemingway everything became multiplied by and subtracted from sex and death. . ."

Hemingway, obsessed with actualities and "the way it was," didn't always agree with Miss Stein's analyses, and especially of him. The truth of the matter, according to a 1942 introduction he wrote for a *Men at War* anthology, was that it was a World War I British officer who, quoting Shakespeare's *Henry IV*, taught Hemingway his precepts of courage. "I was very ignorant at nineteen," he wrote, "and had read little and I remember the sudden happiness and the feeling of having a permanent talisman when a young British officer I met when in the hospital first wrote out for me, so that I could remember them, these lines." The British officer was Captain E. E. Dorman-Smith, later a general, and the lines were the same which Hemingway later incorporated into his story, *The Short Happy Life of Francis Macomber*:

"By my troth, I care not; a man can die but once; we owe God a death . . . and let it go which way it will he that dies this year is quit for the next."

IV

The Hemingway legend was geometrically enhanced by the publication of *A Farewell to Arms*, which came out in 1929 following a short delay caused by the literary tastes of a friend's dog. The dog chewed up Hemingway's copy of the galley proofs. An even longer delay, however, had been experienced by Hemingway in his creation of the novel. "I remember feeling so awful about the first war," he later told Lillian Ross, "that I couldn't write about it for ten years."

A Farewell to Arms was based, largely, on Hemingway's experiences on the Italian front, and if there was anyone left in the United States who hadn't heard of Hemingway's war heroism, the book soon apprised him of it. Even without actual knowledge of Hemingway's personal history, the mass of readers began, through the pages, to make up their own versions of it. They could not know, for example, that Hemingway's description of the Italian retreat at Caporetto, which he did *not* witness, was actually based in large measure on the Greek retreat at Smyrna, which he *did* witness. He had arrived at the World War I Italian battlefront too late for the Caporetto disaster but had listened for many hours to its victims' stories about it. Later, with his continuing interest in the manly art of violence, he had gone over the battlefield and had studied military maps and histories of the action. *A Farewell to Arms*, nevertheless, turned out to be something more and something less than a war story.

"I was always embarrassed," he wrote in the book, *"by the words sacred, glorious, and sacrifice and the expression in vain. We had heard them, sometimes standing in the rain almost out of ear-shot, so that only the shouted words came through, and had read them, on proclamations that were slapped up by billposters over other proclamations, now for a long time, and I had seen nothing sacred, and the things that were glorious had no glory and the sacrifices were like the stockyards at Chicago if nothing was done with the meat except to bury it. There were many words that you could not stand to hear and finally only the names of places had any dignity. Certain numbers were the same way and certain dates and these with the names of places were all you could say and have them mean anything. Abstract words such as glory, honor, courage or hallow were obscene beside the concrete names of villages, the numbers of roads, the names of rivers, the numbers of regiments and the dates."*

Although it did not have the high and wide cultural impact of *The Sun Also Rises*, the story of Catherine Barkley and Lieutenant Frederick Henry was a far greater financial success. In the first four months after its publication, *A Farewell to Arms* sold almost eighty thousand copies, and not only did the public like it but the book reviewers did, too. *A Farewell to Arms*, they said, proved Hemingway's competence as a novelist. It also proved that he was not subject to the same jinx which seemed to prevent so many other writers from producing successful second books in the wake of outstanding first ones.

Hemingway himself referred to the story of the love affair as "my Romeo and Juliet." Consequent with his work on it, he had been having his own romantic emergencies. In 1927 he had divorced Hadley to marry his second wife, Pauline Pfeiffer. "During the time I was writing the first draft," he remembered in 1948, "my second son Patrick was delivered in Kansas City by Caesarean section, and while I was re-writing my father killed himself in Oak Park, Illinois. . . I remember all these things happening and all the places we lived in and the fine times and the bad times we had in that year. But much more vividly I remember living in the book and making up what happened in it every day. Making the country and the people and the things that happened I was happier than I had ever been. Each day I read the book through from the beginning to the point where I went on writing and each day I stopped when I was still going good and when I knew what would happen next. The fact that the book was a tragic one did not make me unhappy since I believed that life was a tragedy and knew it could only have one end. But finding you were able to make something up; to create truly enough so that it made you happy to read it; and to do this every day you worked was something that gave a greater pleasure than any I had ever known. Beside it nothing else mattered."

Paramount bought the movie rights. Helen Hayes played Catherine Barkley and Gary Cooper played Lieutenant Henry. The film was released in 1932 and Mussolini promptly banned its showing in Italy. Hemingway, too, felt compelled to complain. He told his publisher that the movie's press agents were trying "to build me into a glamorous personality like Floyd Gibbons or Tom Mix's horse, Tony." It was true, Hemingway admitted, that he had been in Italy during the war, but "it was only because a man was notoriously less liable to be killed there than in France." In the meantime, Hemingway had reached a new audience.

V

With his income growing at the same rate as his legend, Hemingway, by 1928, had ensconced himself in a large, white, stucco villa in Key West, where the Chamber of Commerce soon listed the Hemingway residence in the city guide book as a point of interest for tourists.

"It was during the Key West years," wrote Malcolm Cowley in *Life* magazine, "that he earned his reputation as a fisherman, a big-game hunter, a boxer and an all-round sportsman. . . In 1933 he caught his first giant, a marlin weighing four hundred and sixty-eight pounds, which he brought to gaff in sixty-five minutes without using a harness. 'It jumped like in the Apocalypse,' he said. He became known for fighting his fish and boating them fast, before the sharks had time to mutilate them. After his return from Africa in 1934—with a fine collection of mounted heads and with material for his least satisfactory book, *Green Hills of Africa*—he had a fishing boat, the Pilar, built to his design at a Brooklyn shipyard. He had taught himself navigation and soon was taking the Pilar on cruises through the Bahamas. At Bimini he boated the first unmutilated tuna—a 310 pounder—ever caught in those waters on rod and reel. That was in the summer of 1935, the big season at Bimini when he caught so many marlin and won the fishing tournament. There was ill-feeling that year between the islanders and the visiting fishermen, and Hemingway tried to pacify the locals by giving them a chance to fight. He offered two hundred dollars to any one who could stay four rounds in the ring with him and several of the locals tried it, but none lasted four rounds.

"Tom Heeney, the British Empire heavyweight champion, was in Bimini early that summer before the ring was built and he boxed with Hemingway on the beach, with the whole island watching. At last Tom said, 'Let's cut this out. We're doing this for nothing and we ought to be paid for it.'"

It was also while he was living in Key West that Hemingway decided to go back into the fight managing business. One of his proteges was John Hadley Nicanor Hemingway, his first son.

"I was fourteen and I weighed about one hundred and seventy pounds," said John. "And the only reason I was allowed to be a sparring partner is that I was bigger than all the fighters. There were a bunch of these tough colored boys down in Key West, tough kids around town who wanted to box, and most of them, whenever they got into any kind of a bout, they'd get beat pretty bad by the real pros. Papa had them and they'd come into the back yard and we'd spar with them and he had a few of them going pretty well.

"So, I would spar with these guys and after we were through we would put on kind of a little exhibition, Papa and I. He'd take it real easy on me, but the only trouble was he taught me to throw a pretty good left and I cut his eye.

And he didn't know it at the time and it got infected. So it was out for a while.

"Now about him offering two hundred dollars to any one who could stay four rounds with him, what he actually was doing was trying to develop some fighters. And there were some good boys, too. Among them were the Butler brothers. There was a Louis, pretty good, and there was a very tough, sort of bully type guy called Jaime Butler. Well this Jaime Butler was actually either the uncle or the oldest brother, twenty-five years removed, of this new boxer Yama Bahama. Jaime and Papa, they had a real good fight. The fight with Tom Heeney was a real good fight, too, kind of rough. But you must remember, Tom wasn't British Empire heavyweight champ any more, so he wasn't in his prime. He owned a bar in Miami Beach.

"Papa used to live or try to live a quiet life, particularly when he was working. When you say that he had prize fighters and matadors and generals and jockeys and people like that as friends, it wasn't a case of him seeking them out so much as they sought him out. Down in Key West, for instance, it was very tough for him to work, because everybody would just show up and Papa was the kind of a guy who couldn't say no to them. When somebody would come in, he'd stop work just to be nice and have a drink with them."

The quiet life that Hemingway tried to live continued to get into the newspapers. "Hell," he told Leonard Lyons after an array of headlines about one night club boxing match, "down in Key West everyone has at least three or four fights a day—and we just call that ordinary exercise." Other ordinary exercise was aboard his cabin cruiser. Hemingway chose Key West for his home, as he would later choose Cuba, because he liked to fish in the Gulf Stream, where the giants of the sea, marlin, tuna and other varieties, made *their* home. In 1935, he was elected vice president of the Salt Water Anglers of America. Fishing in the Gulf Stream, Hemingway found his own angles.

Once, for example, while fishing off Bimini with Floyd Gibbons and Jed Kiley, Hemingway helped reel in a five-hundred-pound tuna. By the time the fish was aboard the boat, however, sharks had taken a pair of fifty-pound bites from the catch. Hemingway was furious.

"No use fishing around here any more," he said. "But I'll

show you landlubbers some real sport. We will go back and get the tools. We've got five hundred pounds of bait."

Hemingway ordered the boat back and, as author Ki'ey later wrote the story:

"I began to catch on when the natives hooked a wooden raft on the stern of our boat and started wiring our tuna to the raft. Then I saw what Papa meant by tools. One was a sawed-off repeating shotgun that looked like a howitzer. Instead of buckshot each shell was loaded with ten or t velve big steel ball-bearings about the size of a forty-five slug. It had once belonged to gangsters and you only had to g t hit by one of those pellets to get your name in the papers. The muzzle of the thing looked like the entrance to the Hudson Tunnel.

"The second tool was a Thompson submachinegun. The Tommygun had also been taken away from gangsters in a certain town and presented to a certain person by the police."

With the raft following on a twenty-foot tow line, Hemingway's boat returned to the scene of the sharks' crime. The blood from the tuna kept dripping into the sea, and Hemingway explained to his companions that it was an invitation to dinner to other sharks

"Half a bottle out," wrote Kiley, "the sharks started picking up the scent. You could see their dorsal fins coming up on all sides." Kiley, armed with a Colt automatic, sat below in the stern fishing-chair. Gibbons, with the sawed-off shotgun, and Hemingway, carrying the submachinegun, climbed to the top deck.

"Don't stand up," Hemingway warned Kiley. "And don't shoot till they start to jump."

The captain slowed the boat to a walk and Hemingway and his fellow fishermen waited. They didn't have to wait lo g.

". . . A big shark suddenly speeded up and jumped," wrote Kiley. "From where I sat he looked like a flying freight car coming out of the water. I had never been hunting on the ocean before and this guy was so big I got buck-fever. Shook like a cocktail shaker and forgot to shoot. Guess Gibbons did, too—didn't hear his cannon go off. But Papa was shooting—rat-tat-tat-tat-tat-tat—you could see the tracers going into the shark's body. At the top of his arc he seemed to hang for an instant in the air and then fell like a pile driver on the raft. The heavy log raft shivered under the impact and almost turned over and you could see the blood shooting out of the bullet holes in the shark's sides.

"While that wounded shark was still flopping and very much alive the others forgot all about the tuna and turned on him. They tore him to pieces before our eyes. Hemingway kept on shooting and the sharks kept on biting each other until you couldn't tell who was eating who."

Kiley soon began shooting, too, and despite Hemingway's warning he leaped to his feet to get a better aim. This, unfortunately, put his head in line of fire of Gibbon's shotgun. When Kiley recovered consciousness, everyone was standing over him on the deck of the boat with Gibbons almost crying in remorse.

"But Hemingway was enjoying it," Kiley wrote. "He ran his big hands through my hair, and he laughed until the tears rolled down his cheeks. 'Never touched him,' Papa said. 'Concussion just blew his hat off.'"

VI

Otherwise, Hemingway did his hunting on land. Although his boyhood preserves were confined to the Northern Michigan Walloon Lake country, he later expanded them, once he could afford the traveling expenses, to include the Wyoming and Montana hills, where he shot bighorn antelope, or Venice, where he went duck-hunting, or Africa, where he massacred lions, kudu, and other prey. Once, later, when he was asked to supply *Sports Illustrated* with a recipe for lion steak, he began it: "Catch your lion and skin it. . ." Still later he discovered that bird-shooting in Sun Valley, Idaho, was also extremely to his taste. But wherever he happened to be, Hemingway's hunting routines were similar.

"We'd go around through the canals and jump-shoot," Hemingway once told Lillian Ross in a description of an expedition to Torcello, an island in the lagoon northeast of Venice, "and I'd walk the prairies at low tide for snipe. It was a big fly route for ducks that came all the way down from the Pripet Marshes. I shot good and thus became a respected local character. They have some sort of little bird that comes through, after eating grapes in the north, on his way to eat grapes in the south. The local characters sometimes shot them sitting and I occasionally shot them flying. Once, I shot two high doubles, rights and lefts, in a row, and the gardener cried with emotion. Coming home, I shot a high duck against the rising moon and dropped him in the canal. That precipitated an emotional crisis I thought I would never get him out of but did, with about a pint of Chianti. We each took a pint out with us. I drank mine to keep warm coming home. He drank his when overcome by emotion."

Hemingway didn't always drink Chianti, but he always drank. Whether on land or sea or in the air or a night club, he inevitably had a bottle handy, even when someone might not think a bottle available for miles. Leonard Lyons remembered that once Hemingway tried to teach Lyons' sons how to shoot and took them out to a field where rows and rows of empty liquor bottles had been set up as targets. "How do you get so many empty bottles?" the youngest boy asked. Hemingway smiled. Another time, at Toots Shor's restaurant, Hemingway ordered vodka and the waiter said no vodka was left. "No vodka?" Hemingway said. "I'll make some. Just bring me a potato and a lamp." Hemingway, referring to some then unpublished references to his private life, told Lyons: "You know, I never ran as a saint. I just try to be a good boy all the time, and bat around three hundred at it."

It was in the public darkness of night clubs that Hemingway did a lot of his private batting, with friends such as Lyons and, later, Earl Wilson handy to chronicle it. That the stories gained something in their retelling wasn't always his fault or their's, but often a single incident would result in many versions and the many versions would become many incidents. Probably the most famous was the one in which Wall Street lawyer Edward Chapman approached Hemingway in New York's Stork Club one 1939 night while Hemingway was sitting with Quentin Reynolds, Toots Shor and sports columnist Bill Corum.

"The funny part is," said Reynolds shortly after the brawl, "we were sober, and I don't care whether this staggers the imagination or not. This big guy came blooping over to our table about two-thirty a.m. and announced he was going to sit down. He squatted with a grunt. Then he looked at Ernest, who is a mild guy, and said, 'So you're Hemingway? Tough, huh?' Without another word the guy reached over and pushed Ernest in the face. Ernest doesn't like having his face pushed, even if it isn't much of a face. So he said to me, 'I think I'll have to do something; what should I do?' I said, 'Ernest, this calls for maybe a mild massacre.' Toots Shor said, 'Don't be too intemperate, Ernest. I don't think the guy should suffer more than a slight loss of life.' Then Ernest said, 'Well, I think I will tap him easy, but I will be careful not to draw blood.' So Ernest just tapped the guy and surprisingly the guy fell over on his—he went right down. It really wasn't what you'd call a fight; not even an unpleasantness."

The story, on top of all the others which had been printed about Hemingway, not only gained him additional and unnecessary stature but also additional challenges. Deluged with them, he eventually was to tell Leonard Lyons: "If I hit someone, I'd make him famous. Besides, nowadays they sue you, and I can't afford to give up my writing time to defend a law suit. I'm too rich to go around hitting people. But the day I go broke, they'd better watch out." In the meantime, Hemingway continued his preparations for come-what-may. It was just about the time of his exchange with the Wall Street lawyer, for example, that he started coming around to George Brown's gym on West Fifty-Seventh Street.

"He was as hard as a rock, had fantastic endurance," said Jimmy Devlin, a former professional lightweight in both England and America with a record of fifty wins, four losses and two draws. Devlin was a boxing instructor at George Brown's gym and knew Hemingway only as Ernie. From then on, whenever Hemingway was in New York, he would try to knock Devlin out three or four times a week.

"He'd go three rounds with George, a fine boxing teacher from Philadelphia Jack O'Brien's old place and a big man," Devlin later told Lester Bromberg of the *New York World Telegram and Sun*. "Then he'd take me on for speed, two, three rounds. He always boxed barefoot. He loved to hit and kept coming at you out of a bob and weave. His favorite punch was a right hand to the body, a three-quarters hook. He nailed me under the heart with it every now and then and I tell you it hurt. . . He flattened many a fresh guy in his time. Once I recall Pat DeCicco, a six-foot-four guy who used to come around to the gym, hit a bellhop in a hotel. When he heard about it, he boiled, he wanted to get DeCicco to box with him but DeCicco would never go for it. . . He didn't like the speed bag in the gym. Too tricky and not enough to hit at for him. Mr. Hemingway gave me twenty dollars every time we boxed, every Christmas there was a C note in an envelope for me."

According to Toots Shor, Hemingway had other areas of toughness. Once, Shor said, John O'Hara told Hemingway that no man alive could break a shillelagh. Hemingway bet O'Hara fifty dollars that he could, then picked one up, brought it down on top of his own head and snapped it in two. "Oh," said Hemingway's son John on hearing the anecdote, "you don't believe *that*, do you?" Another, better documented story told by Shor concerned Hemingway in his later years, when he had moved to Cuba. The Brooklyn Dodgers at the time were using the island as their spring training camp and Hemingway, a lifelong baseball fan, joined several members of the team in their training at a Havana bar. On the way home, according to Shor, Hemingway made a bet with Dodger pitcher Kirby Higbe to see who could hit harder. In the open doorway where they happened to be standing, they started the contest.

"Each blow was an absolute knockdown," Shor said. "Finally, Higbe couldn't get up on his feet any longer so Ernie was declared the winner. But you know each punch had been so clean that there was no blood or even so much as a loosened tooth. It's just like Ernie always says about these kind of scraps, 'Spittin' teeth is for suckers.' "

VII

Proud of his physical fitness and diligent in maintaining it, Hemingway derived great inner pleasure from these moments of exertion. They weren't just meaningless bravado to him, despite their often drunken origins. They were to him, more and more, what he stood for, and he trained his body so that he could stand a great deal. They were an unavoidable part of his mystique, which, incidentally, did not exclude long hours of writing and even longer hours of reading. His reading ranged from the daily columns of Leonard Lyons and Earl Wilson to the everlasting classics of history, but he also exacted, typically of himself, great pleasure from reading military histories—Maurice de Saxe, Clausewitz, Frederick the Great, Ulysses S. Grant and Colonel De Picq. Under his grandfather's tutelage, he had begun reading them when he was ten. "I remember my grandfather telling me you could always get a good answer out of Grant if you could wake him up," Hemingway said. Under his tutelage, his sons began reading them. "His favorite was the *Memoires* of General Marbot," said his son John. "He made me read it, too." But just as typically, he also made John learn how to box. What it all added up to was that he was a walking mixture of a meta-

116

phor of himself. He was like the Ring Lardner sports stories he so often would imitate in his high school newspaper, and he even talked with the same metaphorical aberrations. To *The New Yorker's* Lillian Ross, for example, he would tell about fighting a draw with Stendahl and not getting into the ring with Tolstoy, but Flaubert he described as someone "who always threw them perfectly straight, hard, high, and inside." Or, as Lillian Ross' *New Yorker* profile continued:

> Then Mr. Baudelaire, that I learned my knuckle ball from, and Mr. Rimbaud, who never threw a fast ball in his life. Mr. Gide and Mr. Valery I couldn't learn from. I think Mr. Valery was too smart for me. Like Jack Britton and Benny Leonard."
>
> Jack Britton, he continued, was a fighter he admired very much. "Jack Britton kept on his toes and moved around and never let them hit him solid," he said. "I like to keep on my toes and never let them hit me solid. Never lead against a hitter unless you can outhit him. Crowd a boxer," he said, assuming a boxing stance and holding his right hand, which was grasping the champagne glass, close to his chest. With his left hand, he punched at the air, saying, "Remember. Duck a swing. Block a hook. And counter a jab with everything you own." . . .

Hemingway in other words was his own version of the multi-purpose Renaissance man. If reading was an intellectual stimulation, reading Clausewitz was a manly one. Trading blows with Kirby Higbe in a Havana doorway could be as much a form of entertainment to Hemingway as a look at El Greco's Toledo. Both experiences reached his intellect, unless Higbe happened to throw a punch below the belt. To Hemingway, keeping his physique in shape and using it were equal parts of his code. The mark of a Renaissance man was that he was a braggart, too. Here, for example, is Lillian Ross' *New Yorker* verion of Hemingway buying a belt at Abercrombie and Fitch in 1950. This profile, incidentally, the second which *The New Yorker* printed about him, was another rock in the public's stonewall picture of him:

> "Will you show Mr. Hemingway a belt?" the first clerk said, and stepped back and thoughtfully watched Hemingway.

The second clerk took a tape measure from his pocket, saying he thought Hemingway was a size forty-four or forty-six.

"Wanna bet?" Hemingway asked. He took the clerk's hand and punched himself in the stomach with it.

"Gee, he's got a hard tummy," the belt clerk said. He measured Hemingway's waistline. "Thirty-eight!" he reported. "Small waist for your size. What do you do—a lot of exercise?"

Hemingway hunched his shoulders, feinted, laughed, and looked happy for the first time since we'd left the hotel. He punched himself in the stomach with his own fist.

Hemingway's waist eventually did measure forty and his chest forty-eight. A favorite pastime for him not only to have clerks at Abercrombie and Fitch punch him in the stomach but anybody who happened to drop by the house or the Stork Club. It was, for Hemingway, again getting fun out of his body. "Punch as hard as you can!" he would order, whether in barrooms or at parties, and it usually turned out to be less damaging to Hemingway than to his playmates. "Howard Hawks, the director," reported Leonard Lyons, "broke his wrist punching Papa's stomach."

VIII

His literary assailants, however, didn't break their wrists punching Papa. As his legendary stature grew, there seemed to be more of him that was vulnerable. Hemingway began to feel the blows. "I want to run as a writer," he found it necessary to say in 1950, "not as a man who has been to the wars; nor a barroom fighter; nor a shooter; nor a horseplayer; nor a drinker. What difference does it make if you live in a picturesque little outhouse surrounded by three hundred feeble-minded goats and your faithful dog Black Dog? The question is: can you write?"

Hemingway, of course, thought he had been answering that question all along. In 1932, he published *Death in the Afternoon*, a treatise on bullfighting which really was a recapitulation of his code. In 1935, he published *Green Hills of Africa*, still another recapitulation, this time with different animals. He also contributed a flow of articles and short stories to *Esquire, Cosmopolitan* and other magazines, although the articles mostly concerned him and the very activities which were enshrining him in the public's awe. It was this fact—that not only was he living the Hemingway legend but he also was writing it—which began to turn literary critics, intellectuals and other esthetes against Hemingway, an estrangement which was to endure more or less, until his death. As Carlos Baker appraised the situation:

When the Depression reaffirmed for American society the connection between literature on the one hand and politics and economics on the other, the minority fashion of the late twenties became the majority fashion of the early thirties. As often happens in such a situation, some of the true artists suffered for remaining true to their esthetic convictions. Writers began to be judged according to a politico-economic scale of values. A left-of-center man could often get an A for effort even while he committed all the literary sins known to human society. A rightist or a middle-of-the-roâder, deeply committed to serious authorship, would find his best work rewarded with an E for Escapism, or possibly an F, for failure to include some account of the latest streetcar strike in Waban, Massachusetts. Reviewers had a new measuring-stick, although, happily, many of them clung to sounder standards.

To certain members of the new Marxist clan, Hemingway began to look unfashionable in the early 1930's. *Death in the Afternoon* came out in the dead vast and bottom of the Depression. And how could he have the temerity to publish a manual of the bullfight while Americans were selling apples on street-corners, fighting over restaurant garbage cans for food, or being laid off in wholesale lots?

Hemingway's own position on politics was interspersed among travelogues, marlin tips and advice to kudu shooters which he wrote in the form of twenty-five letters to *Esquire.* As a veteran newspaperman who had interviewed Mussolini, Clemenceau, Lloyd George, Tchitcherin and other statesmen presiding over the post-war political materialism of Europe, and as a veteran who had been personally blown apart by previous diplomacy, Hemingway declared outright that "no history is written honestly." In an *Esquire* piece called *Old Newsman Writes,* Hemingway said: "It is not enough to have a big heart, a pretty good head, a charm of personality, baggy pants, and a facility with a typewriter to know how the world is run; and who is making the assists, the put-outs, and the errors; and who are merely the players and who are the owners . . . You have to keep in touch with it at the time, and you can depend on just as much as you have actually seen and followed."

It wasn't that Hemingway necessarily lacked idealism. What he lacked was the conviction that art and marxism or, for that matter, art, marxism and freudianism were necessary in combination to produce art. And yet, from the other point of view, Hemingway on safari in Africa was bound to have a somewhat vapid effect in an intellectual climate where the only safaris were to soup kitchens. When *Death in the Afternoon* came out, it sold, despite the depths of the Depression, for ten dollars a copy. When the banks closed in 1933, Hemingway had thirty thousand dollars in his pocket. When he offered some of it to Dorothy Parker and Robert Benchley, they thought it was stage money. "Never yet sold a share of stock I bought," he was to tell Leonard Lyons. "Never had to. I can ride out any depression as long as they put me in a chair and give me pen and paper." That, in effect, is what Hemingway's critics thought he was doing with his letters to *Esquire*. Even if Hemingway's critics hadn't been leftist-oriented, as they may no longer be today, they at least had the charge that Hemingway had lowered his literary standards to earn good money in journalism. He was doing nothing, they said, but publicizing himself.

Not that Hemingway, in the resort luxury of Key West, was immune from the impact of the Depression. Not far away, on Matecumbe Key, were the work-camps which the Roosevelt Administration had set up to house otherwise jobless veterans assigned to FERA projects building roads and bridges between Key West and Miami. On pay days, a number of the veterans would journey into Key West to frequent the tavern of Captain Joe Russell, owner of the charter-boat that Hemingway used for fishing expeditions. There, Hemingway would mix with them, often in his usual two-fisted manner. As Carlos Baker pointed out, a number of the scenes he witnessed at Joe Russell's were later to appear in his *To Have and Have Not*. But the tragedy of the Depression was not to be brought home to Hemingway stronger than it was on September third, 1935, when a hurricane cut through the Florida Keys, destroying the Matecumbe work-camps and drowning more than two hundred of the veterans.

A rescue party including Hemingway was the first to reach Camp Five on Matecumbe Key in the wake of the disaster. Afterwards he told how horrified and angry he was at the failure of the camp administration to evacuate the veterans when there was still opportunity. He also said he saw more dead in one place at one time than he had seen since his war action on the lower Piave in 1918. Hemingway, in fact, was so angry that he complied with a request by *The New Masses* to wire a twenty-eight hundred word dispatch even though he considered the magazine a leftist, "puerile house-organ." The article, entitled "Who Murdered the Vets?", was an indictment of the administration, which Hemingway accused of sending the veterans to the Florida Keys to be drowned. "You're dead now, brother," he wrote, "but who left you there in the hurricane months on the Keys where a thousand men died before you in the hurricane months when they were building the road that's now washed out? Who left you there? And what's the punishment for manslaughter now?" Hemingway refused to be paid for the article. He said he didn't believe in making money out of murder.

IX

As he indicated, Hemingway otherwise had little trouble making money, even in misfortune. When he went, in 1933, on his four-month safari to Tanganyika, for example, he was stricken with amoebic dysentery, probably the result of improper sanitation on the French ship he had taken through the Red Sea and the Indian Ocean. Hemingway, as usual, ignored the illness as long as he could, continuing his hunt on every day but two. Finally his condition became so serious that he was forced to leave the motorized expedition and seek medical treatment. He was flown from the safari camp on the Serengetti Plain in a small two-seater that took him four hundred miles past the Ngorongoro Crater, the Rift Escarpment and Mount Kilimanjaro to Nairobi. There, he recuperated. From his experience he was to write *The Snows of Kilimanjaro*, the story of a writer dying on the African plain, which was printed in *Esquire* in 1936 and which has since earned more money than any short story in history.

By 1960, its sales including those of its movie rights, had accumulated two hundred thousand dollars for Hemingway.

Probably the most expert and concise analysis of the Hemingway legend has been written by literary biographer Philip Young in his book, *Ernest Hemingway.*

"The Heroic Hemingway and the Public Hemingway have somehow conspired to produce a Mythical or Legendary Hemingway," Young wrote. "This is an imaginary person who departs from the actual person at some point that is very difficult to determine. He is partly the product of a branch of myth known as hero worship, which tries to make a man familiar to us by elaborating actual details of his life and career while at the same time exaggerating unusual or colorful traits in order to make the man seem very special, and a little more than human. This figure is also the product of Hemingway himself, who seems at times to be both creating and imitating his hero. When this romanticized and rather Byronic legend began to catch on, there were plenty of other people who were willing to contribute to it.

"Thus we have the man who administered a very bad beating to a boxer who had fought a dirty fight, who spectacularly rescued John Dos Passos from an afternoon death on the horns of a bull, and so on. Very often, the stories turn out to have been true. Years ago, Hemingway did (with a water bottle) beat up a prizefighter who had nearly succeeded in killing a lighter boxer. The writer is himself modest about his own exploits, of an extraliterary sort. But even when the stories about him are factual, they have an air of having been gone over by a press agent, as though everyone who has come in contact with him must respond extravagantly. This Hemingway is the 'gossip columnist's delight,' whose activities are regularly reported in the newspapers and news magazines. Whenever he is in New York, the Broadway columns are given over in large part to accounts of what he said, did, looked like, and was drinking. His name is forever cropping up on such lists as enumerate the ten most 'Fascinating Men I Ever Met,' or 'Distinguished Heads (or Stimulating Faces) I Ever Saw.' One comes across his picture—either bearded or bandaged—more often than one sees pictures of, say, Faulkner, Dos Passos and Steinbeck combined.

"It is very had to know the facts about a man whom

journalists have taken over in this way, and his adoption by the photographers has resulted in no great clarification. Pictures of Hemingway show first a round-faced but stalwart youngster with bangs and a Dutch cut. Later they present a thin, shy adolescent with a large frame not grown into, and then a lean soldier with sensitive, clean-shaven face. In the twenties the face takes on a dark, full mustache, and a pleasant yet grimacing grin. The legend was beginning to develop, now, and in the thirties it was full-blown. There were pictures of a quite handsome figure squatting with gun beside the corpse or head of some large beast, or with rod beside some enormous, strung-up fish. In the forties there were pictures of a man coarsely dressed in a not-quite-regulation field uniform, with pensive, tactical eyes, and a pair of binoculars hanging carelessly from a pair of massive shoulders. (It was at this point that Edmund Wilson noted an ominous resemblance to Clark Gable; and shortly thereafter Hollywood offered the novelist a part in a móvie.) Later there were pictures of a tremendous beard, opening in broad smiles beneath steel-rimmed G. I. spectacles; these framed grinning eyes that looked up from a typewriter or a bomber. Most recently the photographs have seemed to offer the head of some fuzzy, great-jowled lion, much given to riding in boats and swimming, and still rather handsome when occasionally shaved and down to fighting weight. Far from presenting the literal records of a life which might counteract the legend, the photogenic Hemingway has vastly confused the record by glamourizing it further.

"Once in a while the confusion breaks noisily into the open. A few years ago, for instance, the author was sitting quietly in a night club when a broker named Chapman came up to him, sneered, 'So you're Hemingway . . . tough guy, huh?' and pushed him in the face. Mr. Chapman was guilty of the oversimplified notion that the myth was all false, and he suffered severely for it. Max Eastman made the notorious charge that the chest hair was faked, too. Ever since Gertrude Stein published to the world the opinion that the man is yellow people have quite regularly been swinging at him. They have all lived to regret it, as far as is known, and at least one of them had to repair for several days to a hospital, for like all legends this one has taken off from facts and is nourished by them."

123

The Max Eastman incident has become an integral part of the Hemingway legend, although its details, like so many others in Hemingway's life, will always border on the myth. If it wasn't the battle of the century, it was a literary fight of amazing proportions, both large and small. At least it was a divertisement while it lasted.

Hemingway had met Eastman while they both were covering the Genoa Economic Conference 1922, Hemingway for the Toronto *Daily Star* and Eastman for the *Liberator*. Eastman by that time was a man of some influence in New York literary circles and Hemingway wasted no time in showing him what Eastman later recalled to be "a sheaf" of short stories and other creative attempts. In Eastman's words, the two of them "batted around Genoa together quite a lot." When, for example, Eastman and George Slocombe of the *London Daily Herald* drove out to Rapallo to visit Max Beerbohm, Hemingway accompanied them. On the way home, Eastman began writing down notes about what Beerbohm had said but Hemingway merely smiled, tapped his forehead and remarked: "I have every word of it in here."

Afterwards, Hemingway and Eastman saw each other in Paris, but there is evidence of friction between them even then. At a party given by Ford Madox Ford in a *bal musette* —a party, incidentally, not unlike the one at the beginning of *The Sun Also Rises*—Eastman, according to Harold Loeb, made a date to meet Hemingway at twelve o'clock. Hemingway, however, taking his wife Hadley home to relieve the baby sitter, was late. When he returned, Eastman noticed that one of Hemingway's trouser front buttons was open.

"One o'clock," said Eastman, using an expression which was then conventional in such emergencies.

Thinking Eastman was accusing him of being late, Hemingway answered:

"It's only twelve-fifteen."

Without smiling, Eastman remarked:

"It's nearer two-fifteen."

According to Loeb, Hemingway became so angry that he nearly swung at Eastman even then.

What type of swing Hemingway eventually did take at Eastman is one of the questions still unanswered from their later encounter. In any event, by 1933, Eastman, reviewing

Death in the Afternoon for *The New Republic,* had decided that Hemingway's display of masculinity had become overbearing as well as overgrown. In an essay entitled *Bull in the Afternoon,* Eastman wrote, among other things:

> Why does our iron advocate of straight talk about what things are, our full-sized man, our ferocious realist, go blind and wrap himself in clouds of juvenile romanticism the moment he crosses the border of Spain on the way to a bullfight? It is of course a commonplace that Hemingway lacks the serene confidence that he *is* a full-sized man. Most of us too delicately organized babies who grow up to be artists suffer at times from that small inward doubt. But some circumstance seems to have laid upon Hemingway a continual sense of the obligation to put forth evidences of red-blooded masculinity. . . . This trait of his character has been strong enough to form the nucleus of a new flavor in English literature, and it has moreover begotten a veritable school of fiction writers—a literary style, you might say, of wearing false hair on the chest.

Finally, also in the essay, Eastman added:
"Come out from behind that false hair on your chest, Ernest. We all know you."

It took four years for Hemingway, Eastman and the remark to catch up with one another, but when they did they made a crowd. There were as many versions of what happened as there were newspapers in New York, but when it was over Eastman, as he had done at Rapallo, took notes and Hemingway kept it in his head.

It seems that Eastman was sitting in Maxwell Perkins' office at Scribner's one August day of 1937 when Hemingway happened to walk in. According to Eastman's notes this is what happened:

"Hello, you great big son-of-a-bitch," Hemingway greeted Eastman.

Hemingway smiled, or at least Eastman chose to think so. Eastman answered:

"Hello, Ernest! Big? Why you're twice as big as you used to be."

Eastman then felt Hemingway's arm to see if it was still as hard as it had been in the Paris days.

"What are you doing here?" Eastman asked. "Where are you going?"

"Over to Spain to see what your P. O. U. M. is doing," Hemingway answered. "Is that your outfit, the P.O.U.M.?"

The P.O.U.M. was a group of Trotskyite revolutionists then involved in a struggle within the Loyalist ranks during the Spanish Civil War. Eastman, who had translated some of Leon Trotsky's works, was himself considered a Trotskyite and Hemingway seemed to resent it.

"I haven't any outfit, Ernest," Eastman answered. "I merely try to tell the truth."

"Uh-huh," Hemingway said.

"You aren't really running with that Stalin gang, are you?" Eastman asked.

"NO!" answered Hemingway.

"I'm mightly glad to hear it," said Eastman. "I was sorry I missed you last winter in Key West. I enjoyed meeting your wife and seeing your house and children."

Hemingway answered with what Eastman thought was pleasing sincerity:

"Yes, I was very sorry, too."

But then, as if he had just remembered something he meant to do, Hemingway came closer to Eastman and said: "I want to show you something." Then Hemingway opened a button of his shirt and displayed what Eastman later called some rather coarse and surprisingly dark hair on his chest.

"Is that false hair?" Hemingway asked, and he brushed his fingers through it. Then Hemingway opened a button of Eastman's shirt and, as Hemingway, Eastman and Perkins all started laughing, Eastman said: "Well I guess you've got me there." Eastman, it seemed, didn't have any hair on his chest.

The laughing continued and suddenly Hemingway's laugh died. "Look here," he said, "what did you say I was sexually impotent for?"

Eastman was surprised.

"Ernest," he said, "you know damn well I didn't say that or anything like it. You ought to be ashamed of yourself. We've been friends long enough for you to know I don't deal in dirty innuendoes."

"Yes you did," Hemingway replied, "and you played right into the hands of the gang that were saying it."

"I never heard it said," said Eastman. "I never dreamed

anybody said it." Then Eastman asked if Hemingway hadn't gotten his letter explaining his *Bull in the Afternoon* essay.

"Yes," Hemingway replied, "and I thought that was nasty, too. Moreover, you tried to kiss my wife in a taxicab in Paris."

"I never was in a taxicab with your wife," said Eastman, "and never had an impulse to kiss her."

"Yes, you did," said Hemingway, "and you go around saying things behind my back. If I had your essay here, I'd show you what you said."

Eastman's essay had long since been included in a book of his other essays, *Art and the Life of Action,* and the book happened to be lying on Maxwell Perkins' desk.

"Here it is," Eastman said, "show me—show Max, and let him judge whether I said or insinuated that you are impotent."

Hemingway took the book and leafed through the pages, finding the place.

"You've taken it out," he muttered. Then he said, "Here it is, I'll show you."

"Show it to Max," Eastman said.

"No I won't," Hemingway said, "I'll show it to you. Listen to this," and he began reading the previously-quoted passage. "What does that mean, 'some circumstance'?" Hemingway asked.

"It means I haven't any idea what the circumstance is," Eastman said. "That it does not mean sexual impotence is shown by what I say in my very first paragraph: 'Hemingway is a full-sized man whom I greatly admire.' "

"Never mind that," Hemingway said. "I'm talking about this right here."

According to Eastman, Hemingway had been growing more and more truculent and Eastman, as he later said, was not entirely surprised when Hemingway suddenly burst out:

"You know damn well what you meant!"

Then Hemingway pushed the open book in Eastman's face.

As Eastman later wrote, Hemingway apparently only meant to insult him and didn't push the book hard enough to hurt. "My response," Eastman said, "although angry and instantaneous, was circumspect. I knew that Ernest could knock me out in a half-second in a boxing match, but I can wrestle. I grappled with him, clinging so close he couldn't hit me. After some swaying and grunting I threw him on his back across Max Perkins' desk, and down on his head on the floor. My fingers were at his throat and I had some vague idea, although by that time no wish, to do him violence. More accurately, I think I was wondering how much my 'honor' demanded that I should do. I forgot all about the necessity, if that is what it was, of hitting him in the face with a book."

Hemingway, according to Eastman, solved his problem by looking up at him, smiling in a friendly way and patting his shoulder. At the time, Eastman told reporters: "I don't understand that gesture. It expressed some emotion, or some code that I am not familiar with. To me it served only to restore my natural world, a world in which fighting is unpleasant and friends try to understand each other." But in 1959, Eastman remembered Hemingway's gesture to mean: "Well, you're not as soft as I thought you were." Or, perhaps: "Okay, both my shoulders are on the floor."

With Perkins, joined by Charles Scribner and Whitney Darrow Sr., exhorting both men to get up, Eastman and Hemingway scrambled to their feet and began restoring the pencils, books, blotters and other items they had knocked from Perkins' desk.

"You don't need to pick up those things, boys," Perkins said. "The girls can do that."

"I'm glad," said Eastman, "because I'm winded," and he sat down.

At the same time, Hemingway came over to him and, still smiling the same smile, patted him on the shoulder again. But then, as if he suddenly remembered the reason for the wrestling match, Hemingway once more began shouting insults.

"I hit you in the face with your own book," Hemingway said. "I let you off easy too, see?"

On reflection, Eastman said he thought Hemingway was still talking for the benefit of the audience of heads in the doorway. But at the time, Eastman said, he thought Hemingway's shift in moods the "conduct of a madman."

"Ernest," he said, "I think you're a lunatic."

At this, according to Eastman, Hemingway's rage increased and he shouted an obscenity that Eastman interpreted as another challenge. Instead of answering the challenge, however, Eastman turned toward Perkins and said: "Max, who is calling on you here, Ernest or I?"

Perkins looked embarrassed and Eastman repeated the question. Then Hemingway, adjusting his collar and tie, said: "All right. I know. I'll get out."

And Hemingway left, grumbling.

Or at least that was Eastman's version of what happened. Another account by Hemingway, who was about to leave as a correspondent in Spain, was given out several days later in a press conference in Perkins' office. For the occasion, Hemingway displayed a book with a smudge in it and said the smudge was Eastman's noseprint. He also claimed that Eastman had violated an agreement not to speak about the incident. The *New York Times* version of Hemingway's press conference went like this:

"We were just fooling around in a way," Mr. Hemingway said yesterday. "But when I looked at him and I thought about the book, I got sore. I tried to get him to read to me, in person, some of the stuff he had written about me. He wouldn't do it. So that's when I socked him with the book."

"Was he in a chair or standing up?"

"He was standing over there," pointing to a window seat in Mr. Perkins's office. "I didn't really sock him. If I had I might have knocked him through that window and out into Fifth Avenue. That would be fine, wouldn't it? That would have got me in wrong with my boss, and he might have had me arrested. So, though I was sore, I just slapped him. That knocked him down."

"But how about throwing you over the desk?" Mr. Hemingway was asked, "and standing you on your head in a corner?"

"He didn't throw anybody anywhere. He jumped at me like a woman—clawing, you know, with his open hands. I just held him off. I didn't want to hurt him. He is ten years older than I am. . ."

Still another version, in the *New York Herald Tribune*, had Eastman tottering backward, collapsing on the window seat and trembling there with rage. The other versions, of course, had other embellishments. Out of all of them there is one certainty. The hair on Hemingway's chest wasn't false.

CHAPTER SEVEN

Four in the Afternoon

On August sixteenth, 1929, matador Sidney Franklin, having killed two bulls across the street, was confronted by another in a cafe opposite the old ring in Madrid.

"This big hulk of a brute, unshaven and unkempt, with dirty pants and bedroom slippers, comes over to me and asks if I'm Sidney Franklin," the Brooklyn-born Franklin later recalled. "Automatically, I reached into my pocket, thinking the poor devil wanted a handout. But he sits down and orders Pernod. . .

"He got to talking and the first thing I knew he asked me if I'd mind him going around the country watching me work at the different fairs. Knowing what a tremendously expensive thing that was, I sort of looked at him—his clothes, his looks and so forth—and it didn't seem to me that he could afford such a thing. But when I told him that it would be rather an expensive proposition he said, well, he'd manage to take care of that.

"I said, 'What do you do for a living?' He said, 'Well, I write. I'm an author.' I said. 'You're an author? Do you make a living at it?' 'Well,' he said, 'I manage to get along.' But he didn't say it in a way that could have given me any indication at all of who he, was or what he was.

"Then I invited him home for lunch and while at lunch he started pressing me again. Would I mind if he went around the country. I said, 'Look I can't stop anyone from going around the country and seeing me fight. Therefore, if

130

you've got the price to pay for admission you can get in any time, but I doubt if you're going to be able to, because as soon as my name goes up on a card there are no seats to be had at any price.'

"While we were eating, which lasted about five hours all through the afternoon, I was mulling the thing over and over; from his looks, truly, I didn't believe that the man was anything. But I suddenly decided I'd try to help him out. We were traveling in about twenty or twenty-five cars at the time and I felt that we'd always have room for one more if he wanted to squeeze in.

"When we finally decided on that, then I said, 'I'll tell you another thing—if you come along and if you're not scared, I might make a place for you to go into the ring with my troop, not in the procession, but to come in when my swordsman and the valet come in with the swords and capes and things like that, and you just stand behind one of the bluffers there.'

"Well, I thought he was going to break down and cry at the time . . . I didn't know him . . . I called him 'you' most of the time. He said would I really consider a thing like that? That would be great, better than anything he could think of.

"So we made the rounds and it wasn't until I got back to Madrid after that trip, which lasted about twenty-five days, that one of the secretaries from the embassy was waiting at the house for me. She said I had been traveling around the country with Ernest Hemingway, and that the ambassador would let me name my own ticket if I would bring Ernest Hemingway to tea that afternoon. Why he was the world's greatest living author, didn't I know that?"

Eventually, of course, Franklin began to travel with Hemingway rather than Hemingway with Franklin. Hemingway's manner of ingratiating himself to others seemed inevitably to end with them ingratiating themselves to him. By 1937, when Hemingway returned to Madrid as a correspondent during the Spanish Civil War, Franklin was with him as an errand boy and, in Josephine Herbst's terms, "a sort of *valet de chambre.*" Even so, Hemingway's 1929 bullfight tour with Franklin turned out to be as much an enlightenment for the one as the other. By that time, after all, Hemingway had been spilling his own guts at bullfights for six years.

A number of persons, including Pablo Picasso, have

claimed the honor of introducing Hemingway to the bullfight. Probably the strongest claim, however, has been filed by Alice B. Toklas, Gertrude Stein's roommate, who entranced Hemingway with tales, posters and photographs of the matadors and who urged him to go on the very trips to Pamplona which resulted in the writing of *The Sun Also Rises*.

"From the first time that he witnessed a bullfight Hemingway looked upon boxing as 'paler and paler,' as he wrote on a postcard from Spain, and was obviously well on his way toward becoming the *aficionado* author of *Death in the Afternoon*," wrote John Malcolm Brinnin in his biography of Gertrude Stein, *The Third Rose*.

"Some of his friends suspected that his response was less love at first sight for the sport than it was a need to love the art of the bullfight because Gertrude had praised it to him. At any rate, between brief stays in Paris and excursions about the Continent, there was always a trip to Spain to catch the performance of some sensational new *torero*.

"Bullfighting had become an obsession. It was too late for him to do anything about it, he said with a straight face, but there was 'Bumby,' the kid, and when eventually they would have to move back to Canada, Ernest was going to buy him a bull calf to practice *veronicas* with."

Whether he was obsessed with bullfighting or with the need to be obsessed with it, Hemingway soon became an expert—at watching, of course. Even after his first visits to the Spanish ring, as opposed to the pugilistic ones, he was able to write an especially perceptive dispatch on the mechanics of bullfighting for the Toronto *Star Weekly*. What was more significant about the dispatch, however, was that it showed, as early as October twentieth, 1923, that Hemingway already had begun to evolve his philosophy of bullfighting and to equate it with his philosophy of life.

"I am not going to apologize for bullfighting," the article said. "It is a survival of the days of the Roman Coliseum. But it does need some explanation. Bullfighting is not a sport. It was never supposed to be. It is a tragedy. A very great tragedy. The tragedy is the death of the bull. . ."

That he understood the tragedy earned for him, at a comparatively early date, as much the respect of the Spanish people as his respect for Spain. For example, as he would later write in *Death in the Afternoon*: "Someone with English blood has written: 'Life is real; life is earnest, and the grave is not its goal.' And where did they bury him? and what became of the reality and the earnestness? The people of Castile have great common sense. They could not produce a poet who would write a line like that. They know death is the unescapable reality, the one thing any man may be sure of; the only security; that it transcends all modern comforts and that with it you do not need a bathtub in every American home, nor, when you have it, do you need the radio. They think a great deal about death and when they have a religion they have one which believes that life is much shorter than death." Life to Hemingway, as he said so many times, was a tragedy, and in the three acts of the bullfight he found life. To the culture which had nourished him, the practice of baiting a bull and killing it was a disgusting thing, but Hemingway could see it as a beautiful one.

"The Anglo-Saxons came to the subject loaded with a number of prejudices born of sport, fair play, love of animals, and so forth," wrote the exiled Spanish historian and novelist Salvador de Madariaga, shortly after Hemingway's death. "Few among them realize that bullfighting (the very phase is a misnomer; we call it bull running) is not a sport but a spectacle, something uniting many arts: painting, sculpture, ballet, and tragedy. Hemingway realized it from the outset and may well have been the non-Spaniard who of all time has come closest to the core of this strange form of Spanish life.

"Without his meaning it, Hemingway thus revealed to his country and to the world many Iberian aspects until then badly misunderstood, which he was able to do possibly because of his familiarity and almost obsession with those essentials of the Spanish ethos: love, death, and eternity. . ."

Love, death and eternity were, as his books show, what Hemingway was writing about from the beginning. *Death in the Afternoon*, although meant to be as thorough an explanation of the mechanics of bullfighting as has ever been written in the English language, was also essentially an elaboration of these themes. Because *Death in the Afternoon* meant just that. "In sixteen fights I saw there were only two in which there was no one badly hurt," Hemingway wrote way back in 1923. In bullfighting he found the exactitudes of his code. In bullfighters he found men living up to them. His description, for example, of Maera, one of the first great *toreros* to gain his attention, sounds like it might fit any one of the heroes of his literary creation:

"He was generous, proud, bitter, foul-mouthed and a great drinker. He neither sucked after intellectuals nor married money. He loved to kill bulls and lived with much passion and enjoyment although the last six months of his life he was very bitter. He knew he had tuberculosis and took absolutely no care of himself; having no fear of death he preferred to burn out, not as an act of bravado, but from choice."

Like any real sports fan, although he insisted it wasn't a sport, Hemingway had a number of enthusiasms among the players. His first great passion was for Nicanor Villalta, whose name he added to those of his first son, John Hadley Nicanor Hemingway. But he soon lost interest in Nicanor after watching the prowess of, as Hemingway called him, the young messiah of bullfighting, Cayetano Ordoñez, who was billed on the posters as Niño de la Palma. Cayetano, a full-fledged matador at sixteen, was the prototype for Pedro Romero, the bullfighter of *The Sun Also Rises*. "He was sincerity and purity of style itself," Hemingway wrote. "Cayetano Ordoñez looked like a bullfighter, he acted like a bullfighter and for one season he was a bullfighter." But at the end of that season, Cayetano was gored in the thigh near the femoral artery and afterwards became a false messiah to Hemingway. "If you see Niño de la Palma," Hemingway wrote only a few short years after *The Sun Also Rises*, "the chances are you will see cowardice in its least attractive form; its fat rumpled, prematurely bald form using hair fixatives, prematurely senile form."

And so, years later, when he returned to watching bullfights and saw another young bullfighter, Antonio Ordoñez, Niño de la Palma's son, he would write: "I had known their fathers, some of them very well, but after some of them died and others lost out to fear or other causes I had resolved never to have a bullfighter for a friend again because I suffered too much for them and with them when they could not cope with the bull from fear or the incapacity that fear brings."

Hemingway eventually did, of course, become Antonio Ordoñez's inseparable friend, but in the meantime his Babe Ruth and Lou Gehrig of the bullring were Juan Belmonte and Maera, whose real name was Manuel Garcia. For the rest of his life, Hemingway would mix references of Belmonte with those of Jack Britton, Scott Fitzgerald, Turgenev and anybody else whom Hemingway admired. "The man I know who talks best about his own trade and has the pleasantest and most wicked tongue," Hemingway would say, "is Juan Belmonte, the matador." It was Belmonte, Hemingway explained, who taught him that courage is in one's nose, or the length of it. Which might have been one of the reasons why Hemingway admired Sidney Franklin.

"Franklin," Hemingway wrote in *Death in the Afternoon*, "is brave with a cold, serene, and intelligent valor . . . he is one of the most skillful, graceful, and slow manipulators of a cape fighting today. His repertoire with the cape is enormous but he does not attempt by a varied repertoire to escape from the performance of the *veronica* as the base of his cape work and his *veronicas* are classical, very emotional, and beautifully timed and executed. You will find no Spaniard who ever saw him fight who will deny his artistry and excellence with the cape."

Actually, the way for Hemingway's meeting with Franklin had been paved by Guy Hickok, who sent Franklin a wire saying that Hemingway wanted to meet him. "Who the hell is Hemingway?" Franklin asked. He asked some of his fans. They didn't know. He asked some other bullfighters. They didn't know either. So, he said, he forgot about it. As far as Hemingway was concerned, Franklin forgot about how they met, too. Their recollections did not completely coincide.

"I met Sidney by speaking to him over the *barrera*, after he had killed his second bull on August fifteenth, 1929, in the old ring at Madrid," Hemingway told Lillian Ross. "I made an appointment to meet him at a cafe the next day . . . I saw no reason to tell him I had written any books. I was with him at many of his fights and during much of his training, and we passed many weeks in different parts of Spain together. Someone finally told him that I was a novelist, and he found it very hard to believe. This I took as a compliment."

Franklin and Hemingway, of course, became close friends. One summer Franklin even took Hemingway's three sons to Mexico and began to teach them cape work. Any similar experiments with their father proved to be unsuccessful, however. Hemingway's experiences with the bulls were mostly limited to the amateur fights, when townspeople were allowed to crowd into the arena and be tossed about by horns especially padded for the occasion. Hemingway, in fact, has written with some remorse of his ineptitude with the *banderillas* and the *muleta*. In *Death in the Afternoon,* for instance, there is the following passage:

Old lady: . . . How is it, young man, that you talk so much and write so long about these bullfights and yet are not a bullfighter yourself. Why did you not take up this profession if you liked it so and think you know so much about it?

Madame, I tried it in its simplest phases but without success. I was too old, too heavy and too awkward. Also my figure was the wrong shape, being thick in all the places where it should be lithe and in the ring I served as little else than target or punching dummy for the bulls.

Old lady: Did they not wound you in horrible fashion? Why are you alive today?

Madame, the tips of their horns were covered or blunted or I should have been opened up like a sewing basket.

Old lady: So you fought bulls with covered horns. I had thought better of you.

Fought is an exaggeration, Madame. I did not fight them but was merely tossed about.

Old lady: Did you ever have experience with bulls with naked horns? Did they not wound you grievously?

I have been in the ring with such bulls and was unwounded though much bruised since when I had compromised myself through awkwardness, I would fall onto the bull's muzzle clinging to his horns as the figure clings to the old picture of the Rock of Ages and with equal passion. This caused great hilarity among the spectators.

Old lady: What did the bull do then?

If he were of sufficient force he threw me some distance. If this did not occur I rode a distance on his head, he tossing all the while, until the other amateurs had seized his tail.

Old lady: Were there witnesses to these feats you tell of? Or do you just invent them as a writer?

There are thousands of witnesses, although many may have died since from injuries to their diaphragms or other inner parts caused by immoderate laughter.

Old lady: Was it this that decided you against bullfighting as a profession?

My decision was reached on a consideration of my physical ineptitudes, on the welcome advice of my friends and from the fact that it became increasingly harder as I grew older to enter the ring happily except after drinking three or four absinthes which, while they inflamed my courage, slightly distorted my reflexes.

Old lady: Then I may take it that you have abandoned the bull ring even as an amateur?

Madame, no decision is irrevocable, but as age comes on I feel I must devote myself more and more to the practice of letters. . .

"He was the first American who spoke to me intelligently about bullfighting," Franklin told Lillian Ross in *The New Yorker*, referring to their 1929 sojourn. "Other Americans tried to tell me they knew more about the business than I did. Ernest let me do the talking. I found we both thought the same. Our minds ran along the same track . . . He used to stand behind the *barrera* and watch me fight. I would fight for Ernest, to solve the problems for his bullfight book —*Death in the Afternoon*. When I was on tour, he doubled up in a room with me, and we'd spend the whole night talking about fights, techniques, styles, and bulls. He'd tell me things I didn't know myself.

"For example, years ago bullfighters showed utter disregard for danger. They had such precision in their movements they'd let a handkerchief stick out of their breast pocket, then let the bull's horn pass so close that the bull would take the handkerchief out of the pocket on its horn. If you misjudged this trick by a fraction of an inch, you'd get your side torn out. Ernest showed me how to do it.

"I didn't know what I was doing. I just followed advice that Ernest gave me. We developed a set of signals. Apparently I'd be looking into the stands, but really I'd be spotting him, and he'd give me the high sign, to show me how to work the animal. It was his guidance, his knowledge of the business, that got me to do the impossible without my knowing what I was doing."

Hemingway's reaction to this tribute from Franklin was somewhat immodest.

"Obscenity!" he said, as quoted by Lillian Ross. "Do I look like the kind of guy who would make that suggestion? The only thing I told Sidney was to dramatize his killing. He made it look too easy. He'd just go in, and wham! I told him not to make it look too easy."

The bullfight begins at four in the afternoon. "The three absolute acts of the tragedy are first the entry of the bull when the *picadores* receive the shock of his attacks and attempt to protect their horses with their lances," Hemingway wrote in his first long Toronto *Star Weekly* article on bullfighting. "Then the horses go out and the second act is the planting of the *banderillos*. This is one of the most interesting and difficult parts but among the easiest for a new bull fight fan to appreciate in technique. The *banderillos* are three foot, gaily colored darts with a small fish hook prong in the end. The man who is going to plant them walks out into the arena alone with the bull. He lifts the *banderillos* at arm's length and points them toward the bull. Then he calls, '*Toro! Toro!*' The bull charges and the *banderillo* rises to his toes, bends in a curve forward and just as the bull is about to hit him drops the darts into the bull's hump just back of his horns . . . Last is the death of the bull, which is in the hands of the *matador* . . . Each matador has two bulls in the afternoon. The death of the bull is most formal. . ."

He had written about boxing. *Fifty Grand* was probably one of the best boxing stories of all time. He also could have written about football. "Football," he said, "I knew too much about and it did not interest me really and I have never written a line about it." But what he meant was that he knew to much about football to regard Frank Merriwell and other such heroes as living according to a code which was something less than his. "*Nobody ever lives their life all the way up except bullfighters,*" says Jake Barnes, in *The Sun Also Rises.* In *Death in the Afternoon,* Hemingway used other terminology:

"The only place where you could see life and death, *i.e.* violent death, now that the wars were over, was in the bull ring and I wanted very much to go to Spain where I could study it. I was trying to learn to write, commencing with the simplest things, and one of the simplest things of all and the most fundamental is violent death."

As it turned out, Hemingway, in Spain, was to find much more violent death outside the bull ring.

CHAPTER EIGHT

The Spanish Earth

I

ONE DAY during 1937, while Ernest Hemingway was spending his bank account and the summer's heat editing a documentary film on behalf of the Spanish Republican cause, a volunteer assistant, Prudencio de Pereda, turned to him and asked:

"Ernest, how come you give forty thousand dollars of your own money to help the poor people of Spain, you call everybody 'comrade' and still you go to the Stork Club every night?"

"Oh," replied Hemingway with a quiet humility which will always be de Pereda's picture of him, "I'm a celebrity. I get a celebrity privilege there. It only costs me a dollar to drink all night."

Hemingway, of course, was never a Robin Hood who took from Sherman Billingsley and gave to the poor. His devotion to the masses was actually a devotion to the mass of his contradictions, and he often would pick up everyone else's tab at the Stork Club, too. There would come a time when he would pay liquor bills running into four figures, but if his involvement as a celebrity was close to his ego, his involvement with Spain was closer to his soul.

"France is always strange and different," he once said, "but in Spain you feel as if you were born there."

He was, in fact, en route to France when he first experienced that often-to-be-repeated birth. "You ought to see the Spanish Coast," he wrote Sherwood Anderson in 1921. "Big, brown mountains looking like tired dinosaurs slumped down into the sea." Hemingway at the time was with his bride, Hadley, and on his way toward his debut as a foreign correspondent. "We sailed on an absolutely rotten old steamer," Hadley recalled. "I can't remember the name of it but it has been completely dismembered since. We stopped on Vigo to refuel, a small port on the west coast of Spain near the Bay of Biscay. We were very tired but we spent a couple of hours in the fish market there which was absolutely marvelous." If Spain's first perfume for Hemingway was to cause this casual flirtation, there would be other odors for their love affair. In Spain, he found what were to become the essentials of his writing, not only smells, but people, sounds, tastes, sights and "the way the weather was," all framed in the sun-blanched clarity that also was to become his style. Here, for example, are some parts of his famous love-letter to Spain, the epilogue of *Death in the Afternoon*:

"*. . . The Prado, looking like some big American college building, with sprinklers watering the grass early in the bright Madrid summer morning; the bare white mud hills looking across toward Carabanchel; days on the trains in August with the blinds pulled down on the side against the sun and the wind blowing them; chaff blown against the car in the wind from the hard earthen threshing floors; the odor of grain and the stone windmills. . .*

"*. . . the change in the country as you came down out of the mountains and into Valencia in the dusk on the train holding a rooster for a woman who was bringing it to her sister; . . . the wooden ring at Alciras where they dragged the dead horses out in the field and you had to pick your way over them; and the noise in the streets in Madrid after midnight, and the fair that goes on all night long, in June, and walking home on Sundays from the ring. . .*"

"*. . . clouds come fast in shadows moving over wheat and the small, careful stepping horses; the smell of olive oil; the feel of leather; rope soled shoes; the loops of twisted garlics; earthen pots; saddle bags carried across the shoulder; wine skins; the pitchforks made of natural wood (the tines were branches); the early morning smells, the cold mountain nights and long hot days of summer, with always trees and shade under the trees. . .*"

In Spain too, he found the bullfights, courage, and death in the afternoon.

If Spain, from the moment of their first heady embrace in the fish markets of Vigo, was to become Hemingway's beloved country, it also was to give him the grief that seems to accompany any great romance. At the very moment that he was watching the dinosaurs of its coastline drinking up the sea, the Spanish Foreign Legion was suffering a series of humiliating defeats at the hands of the Riffs in the Spanish North African colony of Morocco. In the country itself, the Anarchists, fueled by a government that for centuries had never been anything but tyrannical and corrupt, had enlisted one million recruits who soon would be marching defiantly in the streets of Barcelona and Madrid. And politically oriented intellectuals were meeting in the secret corners of dark cafes along the Ramblas, vehemently debating ways to bring Spain into the Twentieth Century. When Hemingway first set foot into the country, Spain literally was still a part of Africa.

By 1931, when King Alfonso XIII abdicated, leaving the country to a people which had been clamoring for his demise, the figure of Ernest Hemingway already was a familiar and respected one to those intellectuals along the Ramblas. Spanish Republican leaders such as Pio Baroja, Ortega y Gasset and Perez de Ayala had hailed *The Sun Also Rises* and some had become close friends with its author. Not only had Hemingway put Pamplona on the English-speaking map, but he understood Spain.

"Before he came," wrote Salvador de Madariaga in the *Saturday Review*, "Spain's image of the American was in the main, and save for a small elite, shaped and conditioned by the memories of the Spanish-American War, the last wrench at the Spanish empire from the growing talons of the New World eagle. 'What are they but meatpackers without history?' That is what the average Spaniard would say about Americans (Yankees he would call them) throughout pre-Hemingway Twentieth Century.

"Then this debonair giant turned up. He brought with him a combination of geniality, virility, and esthetic sensibility which for most Spaniards was a revelation. He was no longer the gaping tourist, the go-getter businessman, the Protestant ever ready to frown at Catholic superstition, the progressive commiserating on backward Spain. He was that rare thing, a human being; open-eyed, open-handed, open-hearted, open-minded, a man ready to learn, to understand, to appreciate, to see beneath the surface."

And what had been beneath the surface was rapidly coming to the Spanish top. The events preceding the formation of the new Spanish Republic were as precarious as the new Republic itself would prove to be. In January of 1930, the dictatorship of General Primo de Rivera tottered, hung for a few dangerous days on the brink of full-scale revolution and fell. The dictator issued his last communique: "And now for a little rest, after two thousand, three hundred and twenty-six days of continuous uneasiness, responsibility and labor." He then went to Paris, leaving King Alfonso to himself and the Spanish masses. The King agreed to hold elections. Their returns showed him out of the country.

The first democratic constitution in the history of Spain was written on a back table in the Buffet Italiano on Madrid's Carrera de San Jeronimo, which happened to be one of Hemingway's favorite drinking places. He was there, in fact, on the night that the Republican leaders wrote it. The advent of the Republic, however, did not necessarily mean an end to Spain's ills. Under the new constitution, the government stopped paying state salaries to priests, banished the Jesuits, confiscated a half-billion dollars' worth of Catholic church property, allowed divorces, provided for the confiscation of all unused farmlands of more than fifty-six acres and demanded an oath of loyalty to the Republic from the nineteen thousand, nine hundred and six Army officers who had been sinecured to command only two hundred and seven thousand enlisted men. The triumvirate of the Church, the landowners and the Army, which was then and still is a *picador* of Spaniards rather than a defender of their borders, fought back. In 1933, the church forced the election of a new, more conservative government and the Republican reforms were revoked. The trade unions immediately began long and bloody strikes and Army officers who had been allowed to resign at full pay began to use the Republic's money to plot against it. With churches being ransacked and burned by the hundreds, political leaders being shot down on the street, newspapers being ripped apart by angry and paid mobs and parties indulging in open, violent warfare, the Army tried to take over the country in 1934. The coup, however, failed. "Spain," wrote Hemingway, "is an open

142

wound in the right arm that cannot heal because the dust gets in . . . The tragedy is very close."

The tragedy, in fact, was no further than Spanish Morocco, across the Gibraltar straits. On July seventeenth, 1936, the garrison at Melilla rebelled. Within minutes, other garrisons in North Africa joined the insurrection. By nightfall, the rebelling generals had all of Morocco in the grip of their Spanish Foreign Legion mercenaries. The next day, two hundred Moorish regulars landed in Cadiz on the Spanish mainland and the long agony that was to take one million lives had begun. Meanwhile, in the Canary Islands, where he had been banished, a short, swarthy soldier named Francisco Franco took off for Morocco. In Madrid, people filled the streets asking for arms to defend the Republic. It was three days before the government would give them any.

III

"I've got a lot of friends fighting on both sides," Hemingway said, after it became apparent that the civil war had begun. "I don't know whether they are still my friends. Most of my writing friends are on the Madrid side, and the bullfighters with General Franco. But people are still human beings, even when they stop looking like it by fighting over their politics. . ." It was a time for picking sides, however, and there was no doubt for Hemingway which side was his. He chose his friends from the Buffet Italiano. "We're in for fifty years of undeclared wars," he would write, "and I've signed up for the duration."

Literary critics such as Carlos Baker and Stewart Sanderson have labeled Hemingway's decision as a "re-enlistment in the ranks of society." For the Anarchists, Stalinists, Trotskyites, and other leftist splinter groups which kept getting under one another's skin, Hemingway's induction into the so-called "Popular Front" of the 1930s was indeed a conquest. After his early years of expatriate devotion to art and his later years of affluence as a Key West sportsman, Hemingway, they told one another, finally had discovered he had a political conscience. It was a new discovery for an explorer who had devoted his time to pulling in big ones from the Gulf Stream and chasing kudu across Africa. "In those years and a long time afterwards, he certainly used and knew the meaning, in its true sense, of the word 'comrade,'" said

Prudencio de Pereda. As for Hemingway, he later wrote Carlos Baker:

"There are at least five parties in the Spanish Civil War on the Republican side. I tried to understand and evaluate all five (very difficult) and belonged to none . . . I had no party but a deep interest in and love for the Republic . . . In Spain I had, and have, many friends on the other side. I tried to write truly about them, too. Politically, I was always on the side of the Republic from the day it was declared and for a long time before."

Hemingway's first reaction to the outbreak of the war was to obtain a forty-thousand-dollar pawn ticket on his literary future so he could buy twenty-four ambulances and other medical supplies for the Loyalists. By January of 1937, he had helped form the Ambulance Committee, Medical Bureau, American Friends for Spanish Democracy, although he found it necessary at the time to deny that, as a former ambulance driver, he would be at the wheel of one of the vehicles himself. "I'd like to send a lot of ambulances," he said, "because you can't have a war without people getting hurt. If people help the Loyalists, others charge them right away with being Communists. I can't see any other reason why the American Red Cross has not sent help. It's like a guy lying hurt in the middle of the street with lots of nice people walking by and refusing to help him pick himself up because they're afraid of being sued."

Instead of going as an ambulance driver, Hemingway went to this war for the North American Newspaper Alliance. He was a correspondent once again, although this time at a dollar a word, filing five hundred words a day, and more than twice as much on Sundays. He sailed for Spain on February twenty-seventh, 1937, and promptly found himself against the stone wall of his own country's indifference to the struggle, as exemplified by that eternal barrier against international understanding, the U. S. State Department. From Toulouse, France, he wrote: "On the day on which the American State Department, following its policy of strictest neutrality, refused Sidney Franklin permission to accompany me to Spain as a war correspondent, fearing he may engage in bullfighting, twelve thousand Italian troops were landed at Malaga and Cadiz. . ." Franklin, of course, wasn't entirely necessary to Hemingway's activities but he proved invaluable. He knew his way around Spain by many paths other than the bullfighting circuit and he still retained much of his popular following on both sides of the fighting line.

"Pauline, Ernest's wife, wouldn't let him go alone," Franklin later told Lillian Ross, describing the scene in Key West before Hemingway's departure. "She insisted she would rather have a live husband than a dead war correspondent. When I told her I'd go along with him, she said, 'All right. In that case you can protect each other.'"

Hemingway, with his NANA accreditation, had no difficulty entering Spain. But after the State Department refusal to issue Franklin the necessary papers, Hemingway advised him to turn back, saying he might be asking for trouble.

"You really need me?" Franklin asked.

The answer was yes.

"Then to hell with getting into trouble," Franklin said. And so, instead, Franklin got into Spain.

For many Americans, Hemingway's early dispatches were the first clear look they had of the ominous events of the Civil War.

"They say you never hear the one that hits you," he cabled in 1937 from his headquarters at Madrid Hotel Florida. "That's true of bullets, because, if you hear them, they are already past. But your correspondent heard the last shell that hit his hotel. He heard it start from the battery, then come with a whistling incoming roar like a subway train to crash against the cornice and shower the room with broken glass and plaster. And while the glass still tinkled down and you listened for the next one to start, you realized that now finally you were back in Madrid."

But later, as the Loyalist tide ebbed and flowed along with Spain's blood, Hemingway became more outspoken and less objective. Finally, he was to break with Franklin.

"I weighed Ernest in the balance and found him wanting," Franklin told Lillian Ross. "When he began coloring his dispatches about the war, I felt it was time for me to back out of the deal."

Hemingway's reply to this, according to Miss Ross, was: "Obscenity!"

IV

When Hemingway arrived in Spain in March of 1937, flying from Toulouse to Barcelona and then across Valencia to Alicante, he found the Loyalists celebrating their victory over the Italians at Brihuega. Hemingway, getting up at his customary dawn hour, immediately drove to the scene of the triumph to find it littered with the bodies of the sons of men at whose side he might have fought nineteen years before. It was, as he said later, a bitter experience for him and yet he could not help sharing the elation of the victory. "The period of fighting when we thought that the Republic could win was the happiest period of our lives," he said in 1940.

Aside from his donation of ambulances and his activities as a newspaper correspondent, Hemingway joined the war in other manners, many of them unofficial and illegal. One of his enterprises was the production of a documentary propaganda film, *The Spanish Earth*, which he undertook along with John Dos Passos, Lillian Hellman, Archibald MacLeish and several others in a group that called itself *Contemporary Historians*. Turning down a Hollywood offer to write movies at forty-five hundred dollars per week, Hemingway instead spent some of his own funds on *The Spanish Earth*. He might also have spent his life. In April of 1937 he joined the young Dutch director Joris Ivens in filming war scenes near then besieged Madrid. Dressed usually in a Basque beret, a windbreaker and heavy field boots, he would act as guide for Ivens and his cameraman, John Ferno, who set up an observation post where they could watch patrol sallies in a depression below the city. Or else often he would lead the two men out into the hills of Morata de Tajuna to get pictures of tanks and infantry in action.

"Ivens and Ferno sometimes distressed their companion by unrealistically exposing themselves to enemy fire," wrote Carlos Baker of these sorties. "Hemingway cabled MacLeish that there was some doubt about Ivens' survival because he was taking the daily risks of a regular infantry officer. In his turn, Hemingway distressed his companions by carrying strong Spanish onions in the pockets of his field-jacket as a means of assuaging hunger. For battle-thirst, the trio carried a large flat silver flask of whiskey. It was always empty by four in the afternoon until they discovered the wisdom of bringing along an auxiliary bottle."

What Hemingway didn't tell MacLeish was about his own dim chances of survival. Hemingway not only took the same risks that Ivens and Ferno did but he apparently took more. After the Battle of Guadalajara in March of 1937, Hemingway, as Hugh Thomas wrote in his book, *The Spanish Civil*

146

War, "took an active part in the war on the Republican side, exceeding the duties of a mere reporter by, for instance, instructing young Spaniards in the use of rifles. The first visit of Hemingway to the Twelfth International Brigade was a great occasion, the Hungarian General Lukacz sending a message to the nearby village for all its girls to attend the banquet he was giving."

At the party, held May first, 1937, Lukacz was a good, gay companion, playing a tune on a pencil held against his teeth, Hemingway remembered. But in the Twelfth Brigade, Hemingway found many good, gay companions. He made the Twelfth his center of activities, although he also paid a number of friendly visits to the Eleventh, consisting of a group of anti-Nazi Germans who, he said, were mostly Communists and "a little serious to spend much time with." In the Twelfth, Hemingway found Communists also, but the Twelfth actually was a more politically integrated group. One friend in the Twelfth was Werner Heilbrun, the medical officer, who always could be counted on for transport, a meal and medicinal alcohol. He was later killed in a strafing attack at Huesca. Another friend was Gustav Regler, a calm, able infantry officer who also was the author of *The Great Crusade,* for which Hemingway wrote a preface. Regler later was crippled by a pound and a half of steel shrapnel, which uncovered his kidneys and exposed his spinal cord. Although he survived the wound, he ended up in a French concentration camp when the war was over. As for General Lukacz, he, too, was killed a short time after the party.

By May nineteenth, Hemingway was back in the United States, where he worked at editing *The Spanish Earth* to movie house proportions. He also wrote the narration and later, when he became dissatisfied with Orson Welles' recital of it, he junked the Welles sound track to recite the narration himself. The film had its debut in the White House on July eighth on the invitation of President and Mrs. Franklin D. Roosevelt. After its public release it brought in thousands of dollars in voluntary contributions to the Republican cause. Subsequently, Hemingway extracted the narration and published it as a pamphlet. He signed over its royalties to Werner Heilbrun's widow.

V

Hemingway made four trips to Spain during the three-year

war, taking out enough time between two of the voyages to finish *To Have and Have Not*, which he used to pay off the personal notes he had signed for the ambulances. Apparently, however, he didn't take out enough time. What was described by others as Hemingway's "great proletarian novel" was to him his least satisfactory one.

"The thing wrong with *To Have and Have Not*," he wrote afterwards, "is that it is made of short stories. I wrote one, then another when I was in Spain, then I came back and saw Harry Morgan again and that gave me the idea for a third. It came out as a new novel, but it was short stories, and there is a hell of a lot of difference."

To Have and Have Not had its inspiration in Hemingway's involvement in charter-boat fishing and with the human driftwood in and around Depression Key West. The book, too, was a part of his social reawakening, if it must be called that, and he was working on it when the Spanish Civil War broke out. The first section, called *One Trip Across*, was printed as a short story in *Cosmopolitan* in 1934 and the second section, *The Tradesman's Return*, ran in *Esquire* in 1936. In the meantime, Hemingway's desires to turn it into a novel clashed with his anxiety to get to Spain. When he left for his assignment as a war correspondent he was still dissatisfied with his first draft of *To Have and Have Not* and thought he would revise it upon his return. His return, however, was taken up with editing *The Spanish Earth* and accomplishing other errands and so he didn't have much time to apply the polish he wanted. *To Have and Have Not* nevertheless, includes some of Hemingway's finest writing, and it earned him a number of left-handed compliments, at least from the people of the left. They were, after all, to be Hemingway's colleagues for the next several years.

The Harry Morgan that Hemingway talked about is the hero of the novel, which also chronicles the activities of one Richard Gordon, a writer who has traded his talent for everything it can buy. It was the contrast of the two characters which raised so much applause from literary radicals because, the critics said, Richard Gordon was a true definition of the decay of capitalist culture and Harry Morgan exemplified what he said with his dying words:

"A man," Harry Morgan said, looking at them both. "One man alone ain't got. No man alone now." He stopped. "No matter how a man alone ain't got no bloody fucking chance."

148

One of the errands which kept Hemingway from a stronger effort on *To Have and Have Not* was his appearance at the Second American Writers' Congress in Carnegie Hall on June fourth, 1937. The congress, a sort of rally for Republican Spain, was sold out three days in advance and although John Dos Passos, Donald Ogden Stewart, Archibald MacLeish and Earl Browder also were to speak, Hemingway obviously was the star attraction. Hemingway's speech was the first and last political one he ever made, but he gave much happiness to popular front intellectuals by sitting on the dais with Browder, then secretary of the American Communist Party. The *Daily Worker* afterwards wrote in jubilant tones about Hemingway's "conversion." What Hemingway had to say, however, was hardly Marxist dialectics:

"A writer's problem does not change. It is always how to write truly and having found out what is true to project it in such a way that it becomes a part of the experience of the person who reads it . . . There is only one form of government that cannot produce good writers, and that system is fascism. For fascism is a lie told by bullies. A writer who will not lie cannot live and work under fascism."

Still another errand that kept Hemingway busy before his second trip to Civil War Spain was his how-do-you-do to Max Eastman. A day or so after the Eastman incident exploded in the newspapers and the very day before Hemingway was to leave New York he attended a party in the home of *Esquire* publisher David Smart. Besides being on every front page, Eastman was on everyone's lips.

"You could tell that Ernest was very ill at ease about it," recalled Prudencio de Pereda, who had been helping Hemingway on *The Spanish Earth* and whom Hemingway later helped as a novelist. "Every time someone came in, Mr. Smart would ask Ernest to go through the whole thing once more. And Ernest would smile and he would do it, but you could see it was upsetting him. There were some very influential people at the party whom he was trying to get to contribute a lot of money to the Loyalists, and so he swallowed his pride and acted quite humble. Then someone rang the doorbell and someone else said, 'It's Max!' And David Smart immediately put up his fists as if it were Max Eastman. But it was Max Perkins."

At the party, Hemingway made a gift of the book with Eastman's alleged nose print in it to Arnold Gingrich, the

Esquire editor who later took over as publisher. Still later, the book was offered for seventy-five dollars in the catalogue of the House of Books, Ltd., which described it as damaged on Page Ninety-five by a spot caused, the catalogue said, by contact "with Mr. Eastman's nose when Mr. Hemingway struck him with it in a gesture of disapproval of the critical essay, 'Bull in the Afternoon.'" In the lower right hand corner was an inscription:

"For Arnold from Papa."

The inscription was witnessed by the signature of Maxwell Perkins, August twelfth, 1937.

VI

The battle of Guadalajara was one of the last Loyalist victories, and during the few weeks before German and Italian reinforcements started pouring in, Hemingway felt that the Spanish Republic had a chance of winning the war. "It was bright and clear in the red hills north of Guadalajara as we stood on the rocky edge of a plateau, where a white road slanted down into a deep valley," he cabled from Madrid, "and watched the Fascist troops on a tableland that rose sheer across the narrow valley . . . This correspondent has been studying the battle for four days, going over the ground with the commanders who directed it and the officers who fought in it, checking the positions and following the tank trails, and he states flatly that the battle will take place in military history with the other decisive battles of the world . . . You may not like it and wish to believe it is propaganda, but I have seen the battlefield, the booty, the prisoners and the dead."

But despite the booty, the prisoners and the dead, the Loyalists were soon on the defensive. The Luftwaffe began its experiments in extermination at Guernica. The siege at Madrid tightened and the daily bombardments grew worse. And at the Hotel Florida, guests often had their choice of horsemeat. It was at the Hotel Florida, during the siege, that Hemingway wrote *The Fifth Column* and it was the Hotel Florida which was the setting for it. Hemingway's only play, *The Fifth Column* took its title from Fascist General Mola's 1936 boast that he had four columns moving on Madrid from the outside and a fifth from within. Neither Mola's nor Hemingway's proved at the time, however, to be successful.

"While I was writing the play, the Hotel Florida, where

we lived and worked, was struck by more than thirty high-explosive shells," Hemingway wrote in the preface. "So if it is not a good play perhaps that is what is the matter with it. If it is a good play, perhaps those thirty some shells helped write it."

There were, of course, other correspondents in the Florida, although Hemingway's shadow seems to have all but hidden them. One, Josephine Herbst, remembered Hemingway with an improvised khaki uniform, high polished boots and a two-room suite that was kept well-provisioned with ham, bacon, eggs, coffee and even marmalade, the fruits, she explained of *valet de chambre* Sidney Franklin's pre-war exploits in the Spanish bullring.

"He threw his arms around me and gave me a big kiss," Miss Herbst wrote, in *The Noble Savage*, describing her meeting with Hemingway. " 'How are you, Josie? I'll never forgive you for letting that sixty-pound king off your line.' . . . Hemingway was at home, if I wasn't, and that was something."

In the mornings, she wrote, "the odor of ham and coffee would slowly penetrate to our level and from the fourth floor Hemingway would lean down and call inviting us to breakfast. It was a terrible temptation. Everybody was hungry all the time and smells incited to gluttony . . . Gas was very limited and it was hard to get a ride to any place. Hemingway had two cars for his use, with gas allowance, but then he was undertaking the movie *Spanish Earth* and needed to be going back and forth to this village. It didn't make for good feeling among some other correspondents, particularly those who were not on regular assignments . . . He was a real friend to the Spanish . . . But in annexing new realms of experience, Hemingway was entering into some areas that were better known to people like Dos Passos, or even myself. He seemed to be naively embracing on the simpler levels the current ideologies at the very moment when Dos Passos was urgently questioning them . . . Now and then the divine odor of cooking would seep through the hallways, and Hemingway, bursting with vigor, would bustle around and confide in me that he had shot a hare and a partridge and that the good Spanish maid on our floor was cooking them for him. . ."

To Josephine Herbst, Hemingway "had answered a definite

call when he came to Spain. He wanted to be *the* war writer of his age and he knew it and went toward it. . ."

Another visitor to Madrid during the bombardment was Lillian Hellman, one of Hemingway's colleagues in *Contemporary Historians*. Although she remains highly reticent about the incident, witnesses to it remember her first night in Madrid when Hemingway, leaving notes for her all over the city, invited her to dinner at the apartment of a British correspondent. Miss Hellman had just spent eight weeks in Valencia on a diet of vegetables and air raids and Hemingway, with his connections at bullrings and other slaughter houses, provided a roast for the occasion. For dessert there was the nightly bombardment.

Scheduled to make a special short-wave radio broadcast to America that night, Miss Hellman began to view the bombardment with increasing alarm. Hemingway, however, reveling in the echoes of the explosions, suggested that she view it instead from the balcony, where the view was fine.

"Come on out and see it," he said.

"No," she answered, "I don't want to. It's dangerous. I'm scared."

Her reply seemed to stun Hemingway. He stared at her coldly.

The others at the dinner party soon joined Hemingway on the balcony, including Martha Gellhorn who also was, later, to join him in marriage. While Miss Hellman sat in an apparent paralysis of fright in the parlor, Miss Gellhorn would return from the balcony from time to time to urge her once more to come out and watch.

"How beautiful it is," Miss Gellhorn told Miss Hellman. Or: "Do you plan to go to the front? Well, how will you be able to go to the front if you're afraid to watch the bombardment here?"

Meanwhile, as the hour for Miss Hellman's broadcast grew closer, so did the explosions. Finally, it was nearly time for her to leave when the radio station telephoned.

"You must not come!" an official warned her. "It's very dangerous. It is a big bombardment tonight. You would be right in the line of fire. We've already had a minor hit. We sent a car out for you before we realized it was so bad, so we can't call the car back, but when he gets to you, just call down to the driver and tell him to go home. Don't tell him to come back here, it's too dangerous."

"All right," answered Miss Hellman. "I guess you're right."

"It's really tough luck," the radio station official added. "Because we probably won't be able to get on the air to America again. They only give us time to broadcast our side when we have someone famous like yourself."

Miss Hellman hesitated.

"Well, then," she said. "Never mind. I'll come," and she hung up.

Immediately, she grabbed her purse and, without saying goodby, started down the steps. Hemingway came running after her.

"Where are you going?" he said.

"I'm going to the radio station," she answered.

"You can't go to the radio station," Hemingway said. "They're being hit. It's directly in the line of the bombardment."

"No," she answered, "I'm going." Then, laughing, she added: "Goodby."

Hemingway leaned over the balustrade.

"Well, Lillian," he said after her, "I guess you have *cojones* after all."

Miss Hellman, by this time screaming with laughter, looked back at him as she hurried down the stairs.

"F - - - you, Ernest," she said.

VII

Although his romance with Spain would never end, Hemingway's flirtation with the Communists and other extreme leftists was to grow bitter. In their effort to defeat Franco, the Loyalist factions soon began trying harder to defeat one another. At one point there was even a revolution within the Republican ranks at Barcelona. Barricades were thrown up in the street. Hemingway, disgusted, preached that it was more important to win the war. But when the war was over, he went back to being a writer. He was going to tell what he had seen.

He had helped lift the shelled, dismembered bodies of women going to market from the pock-marked streets of Madrid. He had acted the father to the little girls with shorn hair whose own fathers had been killed. He had spent time talking kindly to the wounded soulders.

"They tell me Dos Passos and Sinclair Lewis are coming over too."

"*Yes,*" Hemingway replied at a soldier's bedside. The soldier wanted to become a writer. "*And when they come I'll bring them up to see you.*"

"*Goodby, Ernest. You don't mind if I call you Ernest.*"

"*Hell, NO!*"

Twenty-five years later, Hemingway would write: "I had quit praying for myself during the Spanish Civil War, when I saw the terrible things that happened to other people and I felt that to pray for one's self was selfish and egotistical."

His friends remember him telling them at the time: "I'm going to write about this after the war is over. I'm going to *try* to write about it."

He wrote about it in *For Whom the Bell Tolls,* which was his novel of Spain and, according to Malcolm Cowley, his favorite among his novels. "But it wasn't just the Civil War I put into it," Hemingway said later. "It was everything I had learned about Spain for eighteen years." The story of *For Whom the Bell Tolls* is, of course, about Robert Jordan, an American volunteer in Spain who joins a band of Loyalist guerillas entrusted with the task of blowing up a bridge. Neither the adventure nor Hemingway's narration of it are, however, that simple. In the book, Hemingway explains once and for all, his politics of the Spanish Civil War.

"*Here in Spain the Communists offered the best discipline,*" Robert Jordan thinks to himself. "*He accepted their discipline for the duration of the war because, in the conduct of the war, they were the only party whose program he could respect. What were his politics then? He had none now, he told himself.*"

For a long time after the war, nevertheless, Hemingway continued to support any cause, Communist-tinged or not, which might have had something to do with the Loyalists. For example, even while the Abraham Lincoln Brigade was denouncing him as a liar, a traitor and, worse yet, a "recidivist," Hemingway was writing forewards to pamphlets urging contributions to help free veterans of the unit from internment at Ellis Island. He also gave money to continue the publication of the *New Masses,* of which, at the time, he was a favorite target, and, still later, reportedly contributed funds to the Hollywood Ten.

The Abraham Lincoln Brigade's offensive against Hemingway was the result of what its members thought to be Hemingway's retreat in *For Whom The Bell Tolls.* "In one of their meetings," recalls Earl Wilson, who happened to be one of the reporters covering it, "I heard them denounce Hemingway as a liar and worse. He ate and slept with them and shook his fists at the Fascists and shouted, 'We'll get those guys yet,' they said. As a result, they let him join their secret councils. He asked them to submit material for his book, and they did. And then when the book came out, they said Hemingway didn't understand the war, that he had seen all he needed to see, but that he had got it all cockeyed."

In the book, Robert Jordan carried a sleeping bag, but the brigade members said they had never seen any such cumbersome refinement of civilization in Spain. In the book, the guerillas lived in caves, but the brigade members said no guerillas they knew had ever had so fortunate a roof. In the book, Robert Jordan dynamited a bridge, but the brigade members said that an entire army would be needed to carry enough dynamite. Even so, *For Whom The Bell Tolls* eventually was used as a textbook for guerilla fighting by both the American and Russian armies during World War II. Actually, the major complaint of the Abraham Lincoln Brigade was that Hemingway used his book to denounce the factionalism of the brigade's organizer, Andri Marty. Meanwhile, copies of *For Whom the Bell Tolls* continued to be displayed prominently in party bookshops in New York.

As Philip Young has pointed out, the Hemingway who wrote *For Whom the Bell Tolls* had come a long way from the Hemingway who could write that words such as sacred, glorious and sacrifice were obscene. But if *For Whom the Bell Tolls* was Hemingway's political, or rather non-political, manifesto, it also was a best-seller. More than one million English language copies were bought at book stores and it also earned him one hundred and fifty thousand dollars for its movie rights.

"Donald Friede was his agent in the sale of the movie rights," wrote Leonard Lyons. "Friede delivered the first installment check, for one hundred thousand dollars, to Hemingway during the intermission of the mad Olsen and Johnson show the author was attending that night. Everyone thought it was an Olsen and Johnson gag . . . Later that night we were in the Stork Club celebrating, when Hemingway called for his bill. He offered the one hundred thousand dollar check in payment and asked for the change. Owner Sherman Billingsley glanced at the sum and apologized: 'It's only twelve-thirty. Can you wait until four a.m., when we close and our cash registers are full?'"

VIII

Despite his self-contradictions and those of the Communists, Hemingway never wavered in his early allegiance to the Spanish Republic. As recently as October, 1959, he told a group of Catholic school children: "I had seen the Republic start. I was there when King Alfonso left and I watched the people write their constitution. That was the last Republic that had started in Europe and I believed in it. I believe the Republican side could have won the war and there would have been an okay Republic in Spain today. Everybody mixed into that war. But knowing Spaniards I believe the Republic would have gotten rid of all non-Spaniards when the war was over. They don't want any other people trying to run them."

In 1958, when *Esquire* sought to reprint three Hemingway short stories which, in 1938, might have seemed violently pro-Loyalist, his attorney, Alfred Rice, filed suit to prevent the publication, explaining that times and politics had changed and implying that a reprinting of the stories might make Hemingway look like a Communist. Hemingway, however, entertaining former revolutionaries, Loyalist scholars and Spanish grandees alike at *Finca Vigia* in Cuba, was furious. He insisted that his lawyer's reasons were wrong.

"That stuff is shit," he said, referring to Rice's legal prose. "Did the language in that suit sound like me? Not only was it not my style but it was not my thinking. I gave him hell for it. I don't change my politics." The only cause he had for stopping publication, he explained, was so he could insert dirty words where he once had used euphemisms. He was just as Loyalist as ever.

When Madrid fell in 1939, Hemingway was one of the last correspondents to cross the Ebro after the final disastrous battle of the war. He had made an agreement with Andre Malraux, who had flown for the Loyalist air force, that they would divide the war between them, with Malraux writing about everything up to the battle of Guadalajara in 1937 and Hemingway writing about everything after it. Malraux wrote *Man's Hope*. Hemingway took the rest and wrote *For Whom the Bell Tolls*. On the day the book was published Hemingway sat in a hotel room in New York with Gustavo Duran, a former pianist and composer who had become one of the most brilliant military commanders of the war on the Loyalist side. "The war in Spain will have to be fought again," Hemingway said.

One war and thirteen years later, Hemingway went home to Spain again. He had been assured that all his friends on both sides were out of jail. And in *The Dangerous Summer* he wrote that a *matador* had dedicated a bull to him, "thus making me respectable again, since no man you dedicate a bull to in spain can really be a true red (since a true red would not be at the bullring since it is against his religion). . ."

"It was strange going back to Spain again," he wrote. "I had never expected to be allowed to return to the country that I loved more than any other except my own. . ."

CHAPTER NINE

The Daughter Image

I

ERNEST HEMINGWAY never got the girl he wanted. The girl he wanted was the daughter he never had.

"*Why?*" an acquaintance once asked him. "*Why do you want a daughter so much?*"

"*Oh, I don't know,*" Hemingway replied. "*I guess I'm just sentimental.*"

It was a sentimentality which crept often into his literature as well as into his love, although part of Hemingway's art was that he continued to keep both of them in a constant embrace. In a sense, all of Hemingway's literary heroines were his daughters just as, in a sense, they also were daughters that any good Papa might have wanted to give a good spanking to.

"He is a romantic by nature and he falls in love like a big hemlock tree crashing down through the underbrush," Malcolm Cowley once wrote. "Also he has a puritanical streak that keeps him from being a cocktail party flirt. When he falls in love he wants to get married and stay married, and he regards the end of a marriage as a personal defeat."

Or, as his friend, magazine writer Sam Boal later said: "You and I may do one thing to our women, but Ernest married them."

By consequence, Hemingway never really married the kind of women he wrote about, although he invariably tried to write about the women he married. His first, second and third wives are part of the weave of a great deal of his writing. Although they are more recognizable as his wives than his heroines are as women. With the exception of Lady Brett Ashley, who has become one of the greatest women of literature, Hemingway's heroines have been condemned, by critic Stewart Sanderson, for example, as "the romantic vision of an adolescent's erotic day-dream" or by *New York Post* columnist Murray Kempton as "idealized camp followers." In *For Whom the Bell Tolls*, a good part of which he set in a sleeping bag, Hemingway himself recognized the limitations of the heroine, Maria.

"Maybe it is like the dreams you have when someone you have seen in the cinema comes to your bed at night and is so kind and lovely," thinks Robert Jordan, the hero. *". . . Such things don't happen."*

Whether they happened to Hemingway remains a part of his private departed life, although the secrets of a great man, like his genius, eventually will out. In his boyhood, there was perhaps a Trudy, who, as he wrote in *Fathers and Sons*, *"folded her brown legs together happily and rubbed against him. . . ."*

. . . Billy said:
"You want Trudy again?"
"You want to?"
"Un Huh."
"Come on."
"No, here."
"But Billy—"
"I no mind Billy. He my brother."

Or perhaps there was a Liz Coates, who, as he wrote in *Up In Michigan*, had breasts that *"felt plump and firm and the nipples were erect under his hands."*

One of Jim's hands went inside her dress and stroked over her breast and the other hand was in her lap. She was very frightened and didn't know how he was going to go about things but she snuggled close to him. Then the hand that felt so big in her lap went away and was on her leg and started to move up it.
"Don't, Jim," Liz said. Jim slid the hand further up.
"You musn't, Jim. You mustn't." Neither Jim nor Jim's big hand paid any attention to her.

*The boards were hard. Jim had her dress up and was
trying to do something to her. She was frightened but she
wanted it. She had to have it but it frightened her.*

"You mustn't do it, Jim. You mustn't."

"I got to. I'm going to. You know we got to."

*"No we haven't, Jim. We ain't got to. Oh, it isn't right.
Oh, it's so big and it hurts so. You can't. Oh, Jim. Jim. Oh."*

As long ago as 1923, during his Paris expatriation, Hemingway apparently was having trouble casting his girls. Sitting
one rainy night in an oyster bar on the Boulevard Montparnasse, Hemingway began to grumble to Harold Loeb about
his lack of success selling stories.

"What you've got to do," said Loeb, "is bring in women.
People like to read about women and violence. You've got
plenty of violence in your stories. Now all you need is
women."

"Women?" said Hemingway.

"It's your good luck to have married happily right off the
bat," Loeb explained. "It must be wonderful. But a happily
married man misses so much."

"Such as what?" Hemingway said.

"Oh," Loeb said, "such as misery."

Hemingway's face darkened. He grimaced so that his teeth
showed.

"So I haven't had misery?" he said. "So that's what you
think?"

Loeb smiled. As he later recalled, he didn't want to argue.

"How about another," Loeb said, emptying the bottle that
was still on the table. "It's raining. To hell with misery!"

"You think I haven't had misery?" Hemingway repeated.
"That I'm still a Midwestern—?"

"I thought you were a little luckier than some," Loeb said.

Years later, Loeb still had a stark recollection of the scene.
As Loeb wrote in his biography, *The Way It was*, Hemingway suddenly stopped listening to him and started talking.
"He was describing a girl," wrote Loeb. "She was an English
girl who had served in the Red Cross in Italy. She had taken
care of him when he was brought to the hospital. They had
fallen in love. It hadn't worked out. She had left him, gone
away. But he still couldn't rid himself of her memory. In
short words—Hem didn't like the long ones—he described her

160

hair, her breasts, her body. He described the parts of this haunting girl with an explicitness. . .

"I was quite convinced. Of nothing was I more convinced than that Hem had suffered because of this girl . . ."

The girl, or at least some of those parts of her, later appeared, of course, as Catherine Barkley, the heroine of *A Farewell to Arms*, but all of Hemingway's misery didn't prevent critic Edmund Wilson from finding her "unconvincing." Hemingway, nevertheless, continued to restrict the dimensions of his female figures to those seen only through a man's eye. And if she was making mistakes with his imaginary daughters, he also was making mistakes with his real wives. In the end, after all, he had gone through three divorces.

I have loved but three women and have lost them thrice," Hemingway wrote, interpreting the thoughts of his hero, Colonel Cantwell, in *Across the River and Into the Trees. "You lose them the same way you lose a battalion; by errors of judgment; orders that are impossible to fulfill, and through impossible conditions. Also through brutality."*

II

His first wife was Hadley Richardson, a beautiful, red-haired St. Louis woman who was a gifted pianist and who was eight years older than Hemingway. "I met Ernest in about 1919, or was it 1920," she said. "I had gone to school at Mary Institute in St. Louis with Katherine Smith, who later married Dos Passos, and she was working in Chicago at this time. Her brother was Kenley Smith, although everyone called him Y.K., and when my mother died, she asked me up to take my mind off the strain I'd been through. Katherine lived at the Three Arts Club but she said she wanted me to stay with Kenley and his wife. They had a big apartment and she wanted me to meet some of her friends, most of them from Horton's Bay. Among the other people there were Bill Smith, whom I knew before, Bill Horne, who had been an ambulance driver in the war, and Ernest Hemingway. He was very handsome and looked awfully young. We had a very nice time there—there was a whole gang at Kenley's. And then it seems to me that almost immediately after I went back to St. Louis, Bill Horne and Ernest came down to visit me and then I went up to visit them. And then, gradually, Ernest and I got engaged."

They married in September, 1921, at Horton's Bay. In the wedding party were Hemingway's oldest and best friends —Carl Edgar, Bill Smith, Theodore Brumback and Katherine Smith. "We spent our honeymoon in the Hemingway summer cabin at Horton's Bay," Hadley said. "It was an *awful* honeymoon. We both got food poisoning and we both got influenza, and we were both just absolutely overpowered with th bug, whatever it was. There were nice things about it, but we were both miserable, absolutely miserable. The nice things? Well, we went to town together. We went out on that motorboat together. There *was* a motorboat. . ."

In Hadley, Hemingway found understanding for his restlessness. It was with her that he journeyed to Paris in 1921 for his debut as a foreign correspondent. "In Paris," she said, "we lived in a little hotel in the Rue de l'Universite, down in the old part of town near St.-Germain-des-Pres. It was called Hotel Jacob et D'Angletere—Hotel Jacob and of England. I don't know how they started out, but I can smell it now. You know, old carpets on the stairs and everything . . . We finally found a little apartment over a *bal musette*—that's where you dance and have beer and wine and accordion music and sit at tables and people tap your foot under the table, and then you get up and dance with them and pay a coin or something. It was a lot of fun. We used to take some of the big 'buds' who would come and visit with us occasionally and take them down there and they loved it. This was up above the Luxembourg Gardens in the back of St. Genevieve's Church and a very crowded kind of marketing area, very kind of *hoi-polloi* and lots of fun. You see, Gertrude Stein was wrong when she said we first lived in the Place du Tertre. It was the Place de la Contrescarpe, and very, very crowded and slummy, and Ernest got to know everybody in the neighborhood.

"And we got a very good maid who was afterwards called Marie Cocotte, a Britany woman. A *cocotte* is supposed to be a rather naughty person, but she got the name from Jack, our son, who used to go out to Britany to their farm when Ernest and I would go to Spain. Jack heard her calling the chickens, *cocotte, cocotte, cocotte,* so we all called her Marie Cocotte and still do. And she took care of us until Jack was coming along. She'd come in for two, three hours a day and was a wonderful cook. You see, a maid didn't cost just anything in Paris in those days, but she wasn't a maid. She came in and gave us so many hours a day and she marketed for us when we didn't want to do it and she polished everything and we were living on very little and paying next to nothing for that apartment and next to nothing for her. There was a good rate of exchange and anyone who had dollars was really in fine shape. Not that we ever bought any clothes or anything. We just waited for people to give them to us. It was lots more fun than going and picking them out yourself.

"As you probably know, we had all these letters of introduction, notably from Sherwood Anderson. For Gertrude Stein, Ezra Pound, Sylvia Beach, and Adrienne Monnier, Sylvia's friend, who ran the book shop across the street from Shakespeare and Company, and who knew all the authors of the day of importance. Ernest, of course, found all of them interesting, and they got very much interested in him, too."

While they were in Europe, using Paris as their headquarters and journeying from city to country for Hemingway's newspaper and athletic activities, Hadley became pregnant. According to Gertrude Stein, writing in *The Autobiography of Alice B. Toklas*, Hemingway wasn't overjoyed. "He and his wife went away on a trip and shortly after Hemingway turned up alone," Miss Stein wrote. "He came to the house about ten o'clock in the morning and he stayed, he stayed for lunch, he stayed all afternoon, he stayed for dinner and he stayed until about ten o'clock at night and then all of a sudden he announced that his wife was *enceinte* and then with great bitterness, and I, I am too young to be a father. We consoled him as best we could and sent him on his way."

For the birth of the child, Hadley returned with Hemingway to Toronto, where they lived in a sparsely furnished apartment in the northern section of the city and where he worked on the *Daily Star* and *Star Weekly*. The child, John, was born October tenth, 1923, two weeks prematurely, while Hemingway was aboard a train en route home from his Lloyd George assignment in New York. Despite Miss Stein's bitter recollections and despite Hemingway's shell of insensitive masculinity, he was not unlike the usual nervous, tender and near-tearful father, and he welcomed the baby. When, after, he took his family back to Paris and baptized John, Hemingway became "Beery-Poppa," the family man, calling his wife "Feather Cat" or "Feather Kitty" and his son "Bumby." For a while, they lived in a cold-water flat, except that it didn't even have cold water. There was no toilet and

163

for a bed they spread a mattress on the floor. For Bumby, however, Hemingway provided the finest baby carriage obtainable.

"We saw James Joyce occasionally and Ford Madox Ford," said Hadley. "We would see a number of the other writers at Sylvia Beach's and Adrienne Monnier's. I didn't know Joyce very well, although I met all the family. He was a very retiring person at a party, but he and Ernest were interested in each other. Then there was Scott Fitzgerald. I remember once we went down to visit Gerald and Sara Murphy at Antibes—they had just discovered Ernest and were crazy about him and asked us down with our son, Jack, to play with their children. We stayed in an awfully cute little guest house they had, but Jack got the whooping cough. He was very small and very cute, but the whooping cough scared the Murphys, who had three children, and they were very, very particular about the least germ. So, though perfectly wonderful hosts, they said they couldn't let us stay, because we wouldn't be able to keep the children apart. At that point Scott Fitzgerald came forward. He had a villa at Juan-les-Pins, just down the beach, and Scott, just out of the goodness of his heart, gave us his villa. He said that he had another villa that he was going to move into shortly when the rental of the one we took was over. So he moved ahead of time and gave us this place. And all of them would come over yardarm time and sit in their cars outside an iron grille fence and we would be up on this little, tiny porch, and we'd all have drinks together, at a respectable distance, of course. And each empty bottle was put on a spike on the fence, and we really decorated the place in the course of a couple weeks. Scott was certainly very kind to us, and he and Ernest always had a lot to talk about. Each could think of all sorts of things the other should do a different way.

"It was, in fact, while we were quarantined with the whooping cough in our midst that Pauline—Pauline Pfeiffer—came over and took the quarantine. Well, she was crazy about Ernest. So we were all quarantined there together, and that's the only time I ever played bridge. Ernest had met Pauline and her sister, Jinny, in Paris the same time I did, and I enjoyed those two sisters very much. We went on a trip to the chateau country together and had a fine time. But there wasn't anything like a race between Pauline and me that caused me and Ernest to break up. It was, oh, well, just high time on both sides—in spite of having had a very interesting and exciting life together.

"To start with, we were growing apart, growing in different directions. And there was that eight years' difference in our ages. Fundamentally, that was the start, and then someone, Pauline, came along who was growing in the same direction. Ernest didn't want to break up, he just wanted to have his friendship. But I was ready to break up because I couldn't keep up the pace with him. I was just *tired* all the time, and I think that really was the main reason. In time, you lose interest a little bit, you know. It was a slow break and Ernest felt very badly about it. He felt things very deeply. He felt this was very unfair, but I always wanted it. We've always remained very fond of each other and very friendly. It just was that way."

Pauline, too, was from St. Louis, where she had attended Visitation Academy and the University of Missouri. The daughter of a wealthy family from Piggott, Arkansas, she had dark hair, worked as a fashion writer in the Paris office of *Vogue* magazine and, as Hemingway later told a friend, "she moved in on me." He didn't particularly mind. As the petals fell from his blossoming marriage to Hadley, he fell in love with Pauline like Malcolm Cowley's hemlock tree. During that Juan-les-Pins summer of 1925, he already had told F. Scott Fitzgerald about his marital troubles. By the fall, Hemingway and his first wife no longer were living together. They were divorced in Paris on January twenty-seventh, 1927 and a short time later Hemingway married Pauline.

III

Hemingway's second wedding occasioned several alterations in Hemingway's activities. For one thing, Pauline was a devoted Catholic and she insisted that Hemingway share that devotion, although he never really was to assume his full share. For another thing, the immensity of the Pfeiffer family wealth provided a lengthy appendix to Hemingway's own increasing royalties, paving the way to his stucco villa in Key West. At one point, he even joined Sidney Franklin in a fruitless scheme to operate a combination bullring and baseball field in Havana.

There is one story, reportedly told by Hemingway to Maxwell Perkins, that Hemingway had his first near-miss with

Catholicism in the form of artillery shell explosion on the Piave battlefield in 1918. Learning Italian from his Italian comrades, Hemingway also learned their prayers. When, several nights before he was wounded, he found himself caught in a fierce bombardment, Hemingway began promising under his breath that if the Italians' God spared him, then he would take that God as his own. He wasn't wounded, or he wasn't, that is, until several days later, and so he considered himself bound by his oath. Later, when he returned to Oak Park after World War I, he told his father about his battlefield vow and asked if he should keep it. Although Hemingway's mother was one of the most prominent members of the Congregational church only several blocks down the street, his father advised him that he should keep his word and become a Catholic. Or that's how the story goes.

In any event, Hemingway didn't convert until shortly before his marriage to Pauline and, despite his marital tangle, has been considered at least nominally a Catholic ever since. "It has become a critical truism to describe Hemingway's muse as Catholic," wrote Charles A. Brady in the Catholic magazine *America* shortly after Hemingway's death. ". . . Hemingway's habit of imagery is ritually Catholic. So is his sense of limits. So is his admiration for the Spanish thing, even for the Jesuit mystique, as we note in a reference to 'the same town where Loyola got his wound that made him think.'"

Those who knew Hemingway well, however, apparently thought more often of his Catholicism than he did. Earl Wilson, for example, has told how friends would dine with Hemingway on Fridays, order steaks for him and then, halfway through the meal, remind him what day it was. On one of these occasions, Hemingway angrily threw down his knife and fork and cried out: "Why did you have to tell me that?" Then he began figuring out how he could justify continuing the meal.

"If I were a bullfighter I could do it," he muttered. "They have permission."

"But you're not a bullfighter," his companion said.

"If I were a Spaniard, I could, too," he said. "They have a dispensation because they drove the Moors out of Spain."

"But you're not a Spaniard," his companion said.

"I've got it!" Hemingway said. "I was in Toulouse one Friday when a bishop came in. There were no fish or eggs in the restaurant and he finally said, 'Oh, all right, bring me some meat. You don't have to fast when you're traveling.' Get it? I'm traveling now."

And Hemingway returned to his steak.

Otherwise, Hemingway made it a practice never to travel on Fridays or work on Sundays, if he could help it. He also had a habit of knocking on wood and black cats upset him.

Whichever were Hemingway's superstitions and whichever were his beliefs, there were hints that it was Pauline's Catholicism which came between them. Some reports, more readily denied than confirmed, had it that Hemingway and his wife were on opposite sides during the Spanish Civil War. Friends, however, said the reasons they drifted apart were much more personal. Nevertheless, Hemingway's sons and his surviving wives agreed that his romance with Pauline was a happy one while it lasted.

She bore him two sons, Patrick and Gregory, both by Caesarean section, and was told by doctors that she should not give birth again, an admonition complicated by her devout Catholicism. At the time of Patrick's birth, in Kansas City in 1928, Hemingway was in the midst of finishing *A Farewell to Arms*, and he wrote the pain of his wife's delivery into the final chapters of the book. But Pauline also has been memorialized in other Hemingway works, including *The Snows of Kilimanjaro*, in which she seems to appear as the wife of Harry, the writer, and in *Green Hills of Africa*, in which she is POM, or Poor Old Mama.

As POM, Pauline is described by Hemingway with undiminished affection. As Harry's wife, however, she is etched in acid. *"She shot very well this good, this rich bitch, this kindly caretaker and destroyer of his talent,"* Hemingway wrote in *The Snows of Kilimanjaro*. *"The steps by which she had acquired him and the way in which she had finally fallen in love with him were all part of a regular progression in which she had built herself a new life and he had traded away what remained of his old life."*

". . . No one who had read that book, in which the second Mrs. Hemingway figures, could fail to suspect in Harry's wife a less flattering portrait of the same woman," wrote Philip Young. And yet John, Hemingway's first son, insisted it was not. "I can't imagine—I don't think that Pauline is the prototype of the wife of Harry, the writer," said John. "I think it was somebody else and I think I almost heard the name mentioned as 'that bitch.' Papa and Pauline were just fine then. I don't think she is the prototype of that."

There is, in fact, some belief, if not evidence, that Hemingway might have created the characterization of Harry's wife from that of F. Scott Fitzgerald's, Zelda. Hemingway and Zelda had been enemies from the first. "Of all people on earth," Hemingway wrote to Fitzgerald in 1934, "you need discipline in your work and instead you marry someone who is jealous of your work, wants to compete with you and ruins you. It's not as simple as that and I thought Zelda was crazy the first time I met her and you complicated it even more by being in love with her and, of course you're a rummy." Hemingway, in fact, used Fitzgerald's name in the original Esquire version of The Snows of Kilimanjaro. At one point, he had the hero, Harry, thinking, "He remembered poor old Scott Fitzgerald and his romantic awe of [the rich] and how he had started a story once that began, 'The very rich are different from you and me.' And how someone had said to Scott, Yes they have more money. But that was not humorous to Scott." Fitzgerald didn't find Hemingway's public reference to him humorous, either. He told Maxwell Perkins, for example, that he had written Hemingway about the story, "asking him in the most measured terms not to use my name in future pieces of fiction. He wrote me back a crazy letter, telling me about what a Great Writer he was and how much he loved his children, but yielding the point—'If I should outlive him—' which he doubted. To have answered it would have been like fooling with a lit firecracker. Somehow I love that man, no matter what he says or does, but just one more crack and I think I would have to throw my weight with the gang. . ." Hemingway told Fitzgerald that he used his name in the story because Fitzgerald was then writing the narrative of his own disintegration in the Crack-Up articles, which also were running in Esquire. "Since I had chosen to expose my private life so 'shamelessly' in Esquire, he felt that it was sort of an open season for me," Fitzgerald told Perkins. Hemingway, nevertheless, later substituted the name of Julian for Fitzgerald's in The Snows of Kilimanjaro.

Whether Hemingway, too, was shamelessly exposing his private life with the publication of The Snows of Kilimanjaro in Esquire, the facts of it were at least partially written in the divorce records. Filled with a remorse that he would display only in his writing, compelled by a comparison that had grown in him for fifteen years and still wanting a daughter, Hemingway left Pauline to cover the Spanish Civil War. By the time the war was over, so was their marriage.

IV

"Martha Gellhorn sailed in and out in beautiful Saks Fifth Avenue pants with a green chiffon scarf wound around her head," wrote Josephine Herbst in her reminiscences about the press corps covering the Spanish Civil War. It was the same Martha Gellhorn, also from St. Louis, also wealthy, and also a former writer in the Paris office of Vogue magazine, who once had met Hemingway while a reporter in Key West. By the time she saw him again in Madrid, she already had been married to a French count, had written a book or two, had gotten her name in the Social Register and had traveled around the world several times.

Whether she met Hemingway by design or accident remains one of the questions she won't answer about him. There is one story that she went to Key West in interview him in 1937. There is another that her trip to Key West was part of her job as a federal relief investigator. And still another is that she went there to gather material for her book, *The Trouble I've Seen,* and chanced to make his acquaintance at Key West's Sloppy Joe's Bar, a habitat for writers. Not long afterwards, she was writing friends: "I have met the great literate citizen of Key West."

When she met him again, he was unhappily trying to save his marriage to Pauline. On the other hand, the beautiful, blonde-haired Martha, according to one correspondent at Madrid's Hotel Florida, "was trying to act like the girl Hemingway had invented." Amid the high explosive shells, Hemingway fell like another hemlock tree. The romance was to endure at least long enough for Hemingway to dedicate *For Whom the Bell Tolls* to her. Critic Philip Young, in fact, thinks that Maria, the heroine, was created by Hemingway to resemble Martha. Certainly she is discernible in Dorothy Bridges, the heroine of *The Fifth Column.*

In any event, Hemingway was divorced by Pauline on November fourth, 1940. Seventeen days later, he married Martha and they settled down together in his newly acquired *Finca Vigia,* where they wrote in separate rooms, he with a pencil and she with a typewriter. Later, for their honeymoon, they left to cover the Sino-Japanese War together.

"A writer," said Hemingway, assigned to China as a correspondent for the now defunct New York newspaper *PM,* "has to see a lot, because in writing, if you omit something you don't know about, your story is hollow and the emptiness shows. But if you omit something you do know about, it's all right, it's as though it's in. A story is like an iceberg. Seven-eighth of it is under water. Only one-eighth shows . . . In writing I try to make a touchable place, to get the smells and the tastes and the talk. I suppose that is why I am going to China. To continue my education."

On their honeymoon there, Martha's luggage consisted of a typewriter and a traveling bag, which, in addition to tramping boots, field glasses, flannel trousers, a sheepskin coat, sweaters and a few tailored dresses, also included an evening gown. "I doubt," she said, "that there'll be many formal affairs to go to in Chungking."

They had other fun together. Once, for example, she thought he was losing the hair on his head because he had too much of it on the very same chest that had caused Max Eastman so much grief. By a ruse, she got him to a Fifth Avenue skin specialist named Gloria Bristol. There, while he bellowed and fought, Miss Bristol removed some of the offending density by a short-wave process. Finally, Hemingway got up and left. He signed the register: "Ernest Gellhorn Hemingway."

Eventually, they quarreled. There were several causes, none of them documented, but one is said to have been Hemingway's unhappiness at Martha's decision to cover the war in Finland and the Nazi annexation of Czechoslovakia, leaving Hemingway alone in Cuba. These and other of Martha's constant attempts at literary competition began to trouble him. Afterwards, he decided that if a woman was going to be his wife, she was not going to be a writer as well. The next Mrs. Hemingway, in fact, although a writer, too, was to give up her career when she married him.

But still another factor in the estrangement between Hemingway and his third wife apparently was his growing wish to have a daughter. The story is told of how once, for example, Martha even approached a close friend of Hemingway and pleaded, "Can't you get him off it? He's almost obsessed with it. I can't have any children."

Whatever reasons Martha Gellhorn had for taking Ernest Hemingway's name, if not his by-line, she didn't choose to talk about them. Afterwards the wife of T. S. Matthews, a former editor of *Time* magazine, she made her home in London as well as on the title page of Ernest Hemingway's favorite work of art. As for her story of how Hemingway came to write it, there is none.

"I have absolutely no comment to make a-tall," she told the *New York Post* in a new-found British accent shortly after Hemingway's death. "That's to nobody! I do not write or report on anything in which I am personally involved. I don't write about myself. I don't write about myself ever. I write about other things. I'm a reporter. We all have our skills and our limits."

V

"In Papa's language," said John Hemingway, "any pleasing female person is called 'Daughter,' regardless of age."

Such a pleasing female was Marlene Dietrich.

"It was many years ago on a trans-Atlantic crossing on the Ile de France," she once said. "I had come down to the dining salon to join a dinner party. As I approached the table the men rose and I was offered a chair, but as I started to sit down I notice that there were twelve people in the party.

" 'Oh,' I exclaimed, 'I'm the thirteenth. You will excuse me if I don't join you. I'm superstitious about thirteen at dinner. I'll join you later.'

"I turned to leave, but my path was blocked by a large, trim man, who said, 'Excuse me. I don't mean to intrude. But I'd be glad to be the fourteenth.'

"That was Ernest Hemingway, and that was how we met, but even if I had never met him I would probably think him the most interesting man of my lifetime.

"That was in 1934 and we have been good friends ever since. We do not see each other often, but we write, and his letters are funny and sad and compassionate and sometimes so overwhelming I could die. It is a great pity I must be selfish about them and cannot share them with the world, so wonderful are they. I keep them in a fireproof strongbox, for they are the only possessions that have real value for me. My other possessions I have never cared about. But the letters are different. Sometimes I re-read them and enjoy them the way you enjoy certain classics, no matter how many times you have read them. . .

171

"We once met, Ernest and I, during World War II in Hurtgen Forest, which was the scene of one of the bloodiest actions of the entire war. Ernest was attached to the Twenty-second Regiment of the Fourth Division as a war correspondent, and I was roaming around the front entertaining the troops. Our meeting was brief, but I'll never forget the way he fished an old piece of paper out of his pocket and said that he had just scrawled a poem on it and would I read it so he could hear it spoken as it should be.

"It was a poem about war, beautifully written, and at the same time so overpowering an indictment of war, that I had to stop several times to compose myself. When I finished, I broke down crying.

"Hemingway has told me that he has left me the original of this poem in his will, and it is promised treasure. . ."

The friendship between Hemingway and Miss Dietrich was one of many which Hemingway cemented in the saloon society of his later years. As much as he hated the movies, and especially the movies made from his stories, Hemingway seemed to like the actors. Besides Miss Dietrich one whom he liked particularly was Gary Cooper, who had played in the original film version of *A Farewell to Arms*, complete with its rewritten, happy ending, and whom Hemingway chose to play Robert Jordan even before he had finished writing *For Whom the Bell Tolls*. Another close friend, and also one whom he called daughter, was Ingrid Bergman, who played Maria in *For Whom the Bell Tolls* and for whom Hemingway reportedly once wanted to fight a duel.

Among the movie stars, however, Miss Dietrich was his *best* friend. "Daughter, you're hitting them with the bases loaded," he would tell her, and they had a lot of Hemingway's style of fun together. Hemingway, for example, is once remembered to have gone chasing Miss Dietrich down a corridor of the then recently liberated Ritz Hotel of World War II Paris along with Mary Welsh in hot pursuit. It was Miss Welsh, nevertheless, who won the race, and she eventually became the fourth Mrs. Hemingway and the first Miss Mary. She was just as fond of Miss Dietrich as her husband was. Here, for instance, is a glimpse from Lillian Ross' *New Yorker* profile of how Mr. and the fourth Mrs. Hemingway greeted Miss Dietrich on a 1950 arrival at their New York hotel:

There was a knock at the door, and Hemingway got up quickly and opened it. It was Miss Dietrich. Their reunion was a happy one. Mrs. Hemingway came out of the bedroom and greeted the guest enthusiastically. Miss Dietrich stood back from Hemingway and looked at him with approval. "Papa, you look wonderful," she said slowly.

"I sure missed you, daughter," said Hemingway. He raised his fist to his face, and his shoulders shook as he laughed silently. . . .

"The Kraut's the best that ever came into the ring," he said as he handed me my glass. Then he pulled a chair up beside Miss Dietrich's, and they compared notes on friends and on themselves. They talked about theatre and motion-picture people, one of whom, a man, Hemingway referred to as a "sea heel."

Miss Dietrich wanted to know what a "sea heel" was.

"The sea is bigger than the land," he told her. . . .

Hemingway asked her about some recordings she had made, during the war, of popular American songs with lyrics translated into German, and said he'd like to have them. "I'll give you manuscript of new book for recordings if you want to trade even, daughter," he told her.

"Papa, I don't trade with you. I love you," said Miss Dietrich.

"You're the best that came into the ring," Hemingway said.

In addition to calling Miss Dietrich "Daughter," Hemingway obviously also called her "The Kraut." "She can melt a man with a lifted eyebrow and destroy a competing woman with a look," Hemingway once told magazine writer Bill Davidson. "She sets her own rules in life, and they are not very orthodox by most people's standards, but she never deviates from her own standard of conduct and decency. She knows more about love than anyone—and she expresses it in many different ways. But on the other hand, she's a thoroughgoing *Kraut*."

Or, as Hemingway also told Lillian Ross: "I love the Kraut and I love Ingrid. If I weren't married to Miss Mary and didn't love Miss Mary, I would try to hook up with either of them. Each one has what the other hasn't. And what each has, I love very much."

Leslie A. Fiedler, the novelist and critic, has written that although Hemingway was much addicted to describing the sex act, there are no *women* in his books. "In his earlier fictions, Hemingway's descriptions of the sexual encounter are intentionally brutal, in his later ones unintentionally comic," Fiedler wrote in *Love and Death in the American Novel*, "for in no case, can he quite succeed in making his females human, and coitus performed with an animal, a thing or a wet dream is either horrible or ridiculous. If in *For Whom the Bell Tolls* Hemingway has written the most absurd love scene in the history of the American novel, this is not because he lost momentarily his skill and authority; it is a give-away—a moment which illuminates the whole erotic content of his fiction.

"Hemingway is only really comfortable in dealing with 'men without women.' The relations of father to son, of battle-companions, friends on a fishing trip . . . Yet he feels an obligation to introduce women into his more ambitious fictions, though he does not know what to do with them beyond taking them to bed. All his life, he has been haunted by a sense of how simple it all was once, when he could take his Indian girl into the clean-smelling woods, stretch out beside her on the pine-needles (her brother standing guard), and rise to no obligations at all. . .

"In Hemingway the rejection of the sentimental happy ending of marriage involves the acceptance of the sentimental happy beginning of innocent and inconsequential sex, camouflages the rejection of maturity and fatherhood itself. The only story in which he portrays a major protagonist as having a child is one in which he remembers with nostalgia his little Trudy of the 'well holding arms, quick searching tongue,' and looks forward to the time when his son will have a gun and they can pop off to the forest like two boys together. More typically he aspires to be not Father but 'Papa,' the Old Man of the girl-child with whom he is temporarily sleeping. . ."

In *Across the River and into the Trees*, the hero is Colonel Richard Cantwell, a man fifty years old, which is what Hemingway's age was at the time he wrote the novel. The heroine in the book is the countess Renata, nineteen. In the novel, Colonel Cantwell and the Countess Renata are lovers.

Like Hemingway might have done, the Colonel calls her, "Daughter."

VII

Hemingway's first wife, Hadley, recalled, with a note of wistfulness in her voice, that if he wanted a daughter, "he never told me about it . . . I don't remember ever hearing that." As long ago as 1934, however, in *Green Hills of Africa*, Hemingway, describing a conversation with the Austrian trader Kandisky, wrote:

"And your wife?" asked mine.

"She waits at my house, the house of the maanger, with my daughter."

"Does she love you very much?" my wife asked.

"She must, or she would be gone long ago."

"How old is the daughter?"

"She is thirteen now."

"It must be very nice to have a daughter."

"You cannot know how nice it is. It is like a second wife. . ."

Pauline Pfeiffer Hemingway died in Los Angeles during a visit to her sister, Jinny, in 1950. She had been divorced from Hemingway for ten years, and the bitterness over their estrangement had long past. Hemingway helped make the funeral arrangements. Their sons Patrick, or Mousie, and Gregory, or Gigi, also had gotten over the bitterness. They remained close to Hemingway and sympathetic toward him. They knew he wanted a sister for them, too.

"I don't know when all that started," said Hemingway's first son, John, "but as for wanting a daughter, I think Papa just *did*. You know, he'd had three sons and he would have liked to have a daughter. I think that it got to be a thing he talked about and as he talked about it, it became important. It became, I guess, an obsession."

Hemingway's hopes for a daughter died long before him. By 1949, in *Across the River and into the Trees*, he could write of the girl he once had wanted only with some regret and irony.

"Did you ever have a daughter?" the nineteen-year-old countess asks.

"No," answers Colonel Cantwell. *"I always wanted one."*

175

CHAPTER TEN

The Illiterate Captain

IN THE World War II August of 1944, Ernest Hemingway dressed in the uniform of a newspaper correspondent but equipped with something more than words, decided that the Fourth Infantry Division wasn't moving toward Paris fast enough. With his head still swathed in the bandages of a London blackout taxi accident, suffered twelve days before D-Day, and with his helmet riding on the bandages high above his head, Hemingway commandeered a jeep, loaded it with his private stock of liquor and turned his pirate-bearded face toward the enemy lines. By the time he had gotten sixty miles past them, he was the new commander of a highly invisible, but highly lethal, group of some two hundred French irregulars. They were convinced he was a general but he told them he was a captain.

"This is a very low rank to have at the age of forty-five years," Hemingway remembered later, "and so, in the presence of strangers, they would address me, usually, as a colonel. But they were a little upset and worried by my very low rank, and one of them, whose trade for the past year had been receiving mines and blowing up German ammunition trucks and staff cars, asked confidentially, 'My Captain, how is it that with your age and your undoubted long years of service and your obvious wounds, you are still a captain?' I told him, 'Young man, I have not been able to advance in rank due to the fact that I cannot read or write.' "

When World War II broke out, the illiterate. Captain

Hemingway was busy working on some new illiteracy at his *Finca Vigia* in Cuba, sharpening seven No. 2 pencils a day and charting the progress of his illiteracy on the side of a packing case set against the wall—*450, 575, 462, 1250*. Each successive figure represented the number of words he had written on each successive morning, and yet that story he would later tell his French *Maquis* subordinate was not so far from the truth as other gentle exaggerations with which he has amplified the sound and fury of his life. The fact is that in the storage trunks of Hemingway's estate today is still the *tenente's* cape of the Italian *Arditi* that he wore, or that he told his sons he wore, during the first Great War. As a Red Cross ambulance driver, he had been an honorary lieutenant. When, later, after his hospitalization, he had joined the *Arditi,* he was still an honorary lieutenant. The Italians had wanted to commission him, but he could neither read nor write Italian. He had not been able to pass the Italian Army's literacy examination.

But he could pass any test on war. He had studied three since his days with the Italian infantry and he had participated to some extent in at least one of them. His homework in the interim had been with guns, hunting animal quarry that were just as hard to shoot as men, even if the animals didn't shoot back. He also knew how to fish, and it was as a fisherman that he joined World War II. Soon after Pearl Harbor, Hemingway volunteered himself and his forty-foot cabin cruiser, the Pilar, which he persuaded Naval Intelligence to turn into a Q-boat. Hemingway's fondest hope was that a German submarine, thinking the Pilar the easy mark of a fishing vessel, might surface next to it for a little Hemingway fun.

"Under various disguises, it cruised from 1942 to 1944 off the north shore of Cuba," wrote Spruille Braden, then the U. S. Ambassador at Havana and the man who authorized Hemingway's adventure. "Aboard the *Pilar* was a crew of nine, plus radio equipment, machine gun, bazooka and high explosives. Hemingway's objective was to be hailed and ordered alongside by a Nazi submarine, whereupon he would put a plan into operation that was designed to destroy the U-boat. This was an extremely dangerous mission, as certainly a fishing boat under normal circumstances would be no match for a heavily armed submarine. However, Ernest had worked out the plan intelligently and, I believe, would

177

have won the battle had he been able to make the contact. In fact, he would have made the contact had not my naval attache called him into Havana one day when he was on a location he himself had picked and where a submarine did show up within 24 hours. Even so he obtained valuable information on the location of German subs on various occasions, and the *Pilar* was credited with having located several submarines which were later reported by the Navy as 'presumed sunk.' So worthwhile was Ernest's contribution that I strongly recommended him for a decoration."

When Hemingway began to get bored with his fisherman's luck, he decided to accept *Collier's* offer to work as a war correspondent, which seemed as good a subterfuge as any to get him to a place where he could exercise his rightful, if illiterate, rank. The reason that he chose *Collier's* over the offers of other periodicals was that his third wife, Martha, was already working for the magazine as a writer in the Mediterranean theater. He was supposed to join Martha in London, and it was the Royal Air Force who, in the spring of 1944, provided Hemingway with transportation there. On his arrival, however, Hemingway did little more than change planes. He began flying with the RAF on bombing missions over Germany, but that was only to pass the time away until D-Day.

It was on May twenty-fourth, 1944, that Hemingway suffered another of his many head injuries when the car in which he was a passenger struck a water tank in London's blackout. According to Leonard Lyons, when Hemingway recovered consciousness after the accident he was in a hospital with a deep gash in his head and a surgeon stitching it.

"What is your name and occupation?" the doctor asked him.

Unable to speak clearly because of his injury, Hemingway was afraid to answer. He thought that an unintelligible reply might cause the doctor to think he was delirious, resulting in weeks of hospitalization. Instead he remained silent for two days, or that's what he told Lyons. Then, after the second day, he finally managed to say, "Let me up. I've got to get out of here in a hurry!"

Actually, there are photographs of him sitting up in bed and smiling with his head swathed in bandages, although it's true that he did leave the hospital before his injury was completely healed. D-Day was on June sixth, and he had a date to participate. Whether he did or not is another matter lacking complete documentation. There is one report that he was with the third wave to land at Fox Green Beach. But Malcolm Cowley reported that Hemingway actually didn't get to France until July twentieth, more than a month after the Allied invasion.

Officially, Hemingway was assigned as a correspondent to General Patton's Third Army, but he liked neither General Patton nor the job of writing weekly dispatches that were expected to be the equivalent of a latter-day *War and Peace*. The fact is that he wrote only enough articles to keep from being sent home and he studiously avoided Patton. At first, according to Cowley, Hemingway attached himself to an American pursuit squadron in Normandy but then he found the Fourth Infantry Division of the First Army gave him much better companionship. He also found good, if hectic, companionship in *Life* photographer Robert Capa, an old journalistic associate from the Spanish Civil War.

In Normandy, for example, he was riding along with Capa in a jeep when a German fighter plane appeared and began strafing the roadway. While Hemingway accused them of cowardice, Capa and the jeep driver dove beneath the vehicle for cover. For his part, Hemingway remained erect in his seat in the jeep, ignoring the bullets and apparently assuming that they would ignore him. When the German plane finally left, Capa crawled enthusiastically from beneath the jeep, announced that he had been taking pictures from his vantage point and ordered the driver to head back to a command post so he could fly his film to London.

"*What?*" shouted Hemingway. "*Go back?* I'm not going to retreat because of *Henry Luce!*"

Another time Hemingway and Capa were speeding along a Normandy road on a motorcycle with a side-car when a German machinegun opened up on them from its position covering a highway junction. The two men leaped into a roadside ditch, where they were pinned down by the bullets. After several anguished moments, Hemingway, in front of Capa and unable to move, ordered Capa to crawl back for aid. Capa, however, refused.

"Get back, goddammit!" Hemingway growled.

Capa stayed where he was.

"Get back, goddammit, I said," Hemingway growled again. But still Capa stayed where he was.

"I heard it from both of them," said Hemingway's son John years afterwards, "so I got both sides of the story. There was a small bitterness there, although they always stayed good friends. Capa said that he finally did go back and the only reason he stayed at first was so he could help Papa. But Papa always swore that the reason Capa didn't go back was because he wanted to be there to get the story and pictures of Papa getting it from the machinegun."

It was after the breakthrough at St. Lô, when the Fourth Division was sweeping eastward from Normandy, that Hemingway appointed himself a captain, took the jeep, moved through the German lines and began recruiting his French *Maquis*. Hemingway, the United States Office of War Information later announced, had enlisted in the French Forces of the Interior. When the Americans reached St. Michel, they found a sign on the cathedral: "Property of Ernest Hemingway."

"Papa knew a spot in St. Michel," said Jack Downey, another photographer who was then a correspondent for the OWI. "The owners, Monsieur and Madame Pouriard, hugged him when he stomped in. Soon we were all around a table with the Pouriards, wolfing down a twenty-five-egg omelet. Pouriard brought out the fine wines he had hidden from the Nazis. Everybody got stiff as a board, except Papa. He downed a canteen of gin every morning as an eye-opener.

"I remember Papa sitting on the porch, his weather-beaten face wrinkled in a grin as he watched German tracer bullets kicking up dirt. I remember him teaching French kids how to handle a Schmeiser and a Thompson. The U. S. Army gave the French underground only captured German weapons. There was a requisition stating that the weapons must have been captured. Hemingway would walk in with his big thumb over the word 'captured' and walk out loaded down with latest U. S. arms for the FFE."

Word began to seep back of some of his exploits. In one dispatch, he was reported to have entered a French village where townspeople told them six German Panzer soldiers were hiding in a basement. Accompanied by his jeep driver, Hemingway began to toss hand grenades down into the Germans' hiding place. The Nazis quickly exited with their hands in the air.

Incidents such as that, however, were only a small part

of Hemingway's routine. His jeep kept appearing in other unexpected places.

"I always keep a pin in the map for old Ernie Hemingway," said Major General R. O. Barton, commander of the Fourth Division, as he was briefing the other correspondents. Several days afterwards, the division reached the Seine above Paris. The Germans were in front and on both flanks. That, approximately, appeared to be Hemingway's position as well. "Old Ernie Hemingway is out there sixty miles ahead of everything in the First Army," General Barton told his staff. "He's sending back information. But now what do you think he says? He says that if he's going to hold out where he is, he'll need tanks."

Hemingway at the time was holding out in Rambouillet, a town thirty miles southwest of Paris. Arriving at the town August nineteenth, he had captured it with a patrol of his guerillas.

"The first time we entered Rambouillet," Hemingway wrote, "all but two of the men were naked from the waist up, and the populace did not greet us with any degree of fervor. The second time I went in with them, everyone was uniformed and we were cheered considerably. The third time we went through the town the men were all helmeted and we were cheered wildly, kissed extensively and heavily champagned, and we made our headquarters in the Hotel du Grand Veneur, which had an excellent wine cellar."

Hemingway and his guerilla band stayed a week in and out of Rambouillet and the reason for the Rambolitains' unhappiness at his presence was the added presence of heavy German tanks in the neighborhood. The Rambolitains feared that if the Germans learned the guerillas were there, the whole town might be wiped out. Hemingway, nevertheless, was confident he could defend his position, and he said so to Colonel David Bruce of the Office of Strategic Services, who had picked Rambouillet as a likely spot for carrying on his advanced reconnaissance.

"Ernest's bedroom at the Hotel du Grand Veneur was the nerve center of all operations," wrote Colonel Bruce. "There, in his shirtsleeves, he gave audience to intelligence couriers, to refugees from Paris, to deserters from the German army, to local officials and all comers. He had the help and advice of a French secret agent famous under his pseudonym of Mr. Sheep—M. Mouton. After posting guards on all the roads,

Hemingway's chief concern was to locate the German defenses south of Paris. He sent out armed patrols to attract German fire and civilian volunteers on bicycles to penetrate the German lines; some of them pedaled all the way into Paris and came back to Hemingway with sketches, reports and hatfuls of fresh eggs. Soon General Leclerc arrived in Rambouillet with the French armored division that had been chosen to enter Paris. Leclerc did not like American correspondents or French irregulars, but his chief of staff had dinner with Hemingway and M. Mouton. What they gave him was a detailed summary, with sketches, of the German defenses on all the roads between Paris and Rambouillet. I believe that this information had a determining effect on the successful accomplishment of Leclerc's march to Paris."

On the early morning of August twenty-fifth, one of Leclerc's French armored columns started out toward Paris, with Hemingway and his irregulars right behind. "Hemingway's unit was equipped with every imaginable American and German weapon," reported Robert Caps. "They carried more munitions and alcohol than a division would normally control. However, they were a very scraggly-looking lot who steadily improved in appearance as the fortunes of war smiled upon them." In his last dash for Paris, Hemingway followed the French column as far as the village of Buc, near Versailles, where he knew that it would be delayed by German resistance. By this time, his force riding in jeeps, trucks and some armored vehicles, numbered more than two hundred men, and Hemingway decided to lead them into Paris by the back roads. On the way, he taught them the same song he once had made his tiny son John commit to memory, more than twenty years before, so that John could find his way home again. The refrain became his outfit's marching song:

> Dix bis Avenue des Gobelins,
> Dix BIS Avenue des GOBELINS,
> DIX BIS AVENUE DES GOBELINS,
> THAT'S WHERE MY BUMBY LIVES.

When he reached the city, one of his first stops was at the studio of his old friend, Pablo Picasso, to find out if the Germans had harmed him. Before he left, Hemingway gave

Picasso four hand grenades. For his next stop in the city, Hemingway visited another old friend.

"There was still a lot of shooting going on in the Rue de l'Odeon, and we were getting tired of it," wrote Sylvia Beach, "when one day a string of jeeps came up the street and stopped in front of my house. I heard a deep voice calling: 'Sylvia!' And everybody in the street took up the cry of 'Sylvia!'

"'It's Hemingway! It's Hemingway!' cried Adrienne [Monnier]. I flew downstairs; we met with a crash; he picked me up and swung me around and kissed me while people on the street and in the windows cheered.

"We went up to Adrienne's apartment and sat Hemingway down. He was in battle dress, grimy and bloody. A machine gun clanked on the floor. He asked Adrienne for a piece of soap, and she gave him her last cake.

"He wanted to know if there was anything he could do for us. We asked him if he could do something about the Nazi snipers on the roof tops in our street, particularly on Adrienne's roof top. He got his company out of the jeeps and took them up to the roof. We heard firing for the last time in the Rue de l'Odeon. Hemingway and his men came down again and rode off in their jeeps—'to liberate,' according to Hemingway, 'the cellar at the Ritz.'"

While General Leclerc's column still hadn't gotten further than the south bank of the Seine River, Hemingway and his troop were fighting a skirmish with Nazi stragglers at the Arc de Triomphe. Leclerc's forces occupied Paris later that night and Robert Capa, who had been separated for some time from Hemingway, arrived with them.

"As far as I am concerned," wrote Capa, "I credit Hemingway and his unit with exclusively liberating the Hotel Ritz in Paris, for when I arrived at the hotel, along with General Leclerc's liberating forces, there was Red Pelkey, Hemingway's driver, standing guard outside the door. Speaking in Hemingwayese, Pelkey told me, 'Papa took good hotel. Plenty good stuff in cellar. You go up quick!'"

While he was remembering his old, favorite haunts in Paris, Hemingway also tried to liberate the Guaranty Trust Company. "I tried to take that bank and got smacked back," he said later. "I thought it would be awfully nice if I could take my own bank."

Hemingway's activities did not go unnoticed. While fighting its total war, the Army also decided to fight Hemingway. A complaint was issued and the Inspector General of the Third Army began an investigation to determine whether Hemingway had violated the Geneva Convention governing the non-combatant limitations of war correspondents. The investigation began September second, 1944 and endured for eight weeks. In the meantime, Hemingway was assaulting the Siegfried Line.

"When I checked in at Army headquarters at the front," reported John Groth, the artist, telling of Hemingway's adventures at the time, "I was told to proceed to Hemingway's farmhouse which was designated on the headquarters map as *Task Force Hemingway*. The farmhouse, I discovered, was smack on the front lines, and the Germans frequently sent patrols into its yard. Two French kids had attached themselves to him. I called them the Hemingway Irregulars. The house we called the *Schloss* Hemingway, and over this road the breakthrough came. German patrols came within fifty yards of this house at night and we always expected attack. At night we locked the German owners of the house in the cellar. Papa was in charge of the house and its defense.

"The first night I was there, Hemingway stood guard all night, after having given elaborate orders for cross-fire defense against every conceivable attack. Hemingway gave me a ration of hand grenades just as I was getting into bed and wished me a good night's sleep. Needless to say, I had some trouble falling asleep. There was the Hemingway I had read so much about, downstairs on guard with a tommygun and with grenades hanging from his belt. All this was exciting and a little unbelievable.

"The following day, while I was at dinner with Hemingway and several officers at the Regimental Command Post, which was close to the Nazi lines, German eighty-eights suddenly began to break their way in. I heard one shell go krrrunk outside and a soldier was killed twenty yards away. To a man, everyone hit the floor in the accepted fashion and groped for their helmets and kept covered until the shelling ceased. That is, I *thought* everyone had, but when the candles were lit, I was stunned by what I saw. There was Hemingway still at the table, bareheaded, his back to the firing, still eating his dinner, all alone."

One night, according to Groth, Hemingway was out on a

motorcycle when shellfire caused him and several others to dive into some brush. When patrols couldn't find Hemingway, everyone thought he had been killed. Finally, Groth said, the patrols discovered his hiding place.

"He was spread out on his belly, with his shoulders full of leaves," Groth said. "He'd been lying there watching the machine-gunning. The bullets which passed only a few inches above his head cut off the leaves. The leaves dropped down on him.

"One day he went to interview a Kraut in town, in his capacity as correspondent. While he was interviewing the Kraut, the Hemingway Irregulars cleaned out the Kraut's cognac from his cellar very quietly. They came up to Hemingway and whispered, 'We got three cases, Papa.' Hemingway nodded very gravely to the Kraut and said, 'All right, that'll be all the questions.' That was the end of the interview."

At *Task Force Hemingway*, there was a stream of visitors. One was a psychiatrist with the rank of captain who greeted Hemingway with a long psychoanalysis of Hemingway's writings. At the end of his consultation, the psychiatrist accused Hemingway of endowing war with false glory. In his polyglot uniform and from his professorial, steel-rimmed, GI eyeglasses, Hemingway stared back. Those present thought that Hemingway would punch the psychiatrist. Instead he issued a denunciation as long as the psychiatrist's and much more literate, despite his liberal use of four-letter words. The psychiatrist tried to apologize, but Hemingway refused to accept the apology. He ordered the psychiatrist from the farmhouse and into the shell-lit night.

"Everybody knew Hemingway's jeep," said Robert Capa, later killed photographing the Indo-China War. "From a string of fox holes or from out of the woods, you could hear hundreds of GI's voices saying, one after another, 'Good morning Mr. Hemingway.' It was like a royal procession."

Meanwhile, not back at the farm but in Paris, the Inspector General's eight-week investigation was continuing, and in October Hemingway was called back from the Siegfried Line to be interrogated. It was a harrowing experience and it was only with the help of fellow correspondents, who, in Malcolm Cowley's phrase, "testified like gentlemen," that Hemingway pulled through it. The other correspondents told the Inspector General that they had never seen Hemingway carry weapons or other armament. Finally, the case was closed. The investigation, according to the Inspector General, "disclosed no violation by him of the existing regulations for war correspondents." Instead, Hemingway, much later, would get the Bronze Star.

"In the next war," Hemingway told his friend, Colonel C. T. "Buck" Lanham, "I'm going to have the Geneva Convention tattooed on my ass in reverse, so I can read it with a mirror."

While he was still in Paris, Hemingway was stricken with pneumonia. He also was stricken with the news that his son John, then a second lieutenant in the OSS, had been wounded and captured while guiding a German spy back through the enemy lines.

"I received a message at my office at *Stars and Stripes*," remembered Jimmy Cannon, one of Hemingway's close friends. "The scrawl on the note advised me to contact Hemingway at the Ritz. I called. 'Come alone,' Ernest said."

Cannon found Hemingway, still in his uniform, lying bulkily beneath the covers. His eyes were red, watery and tired. His head was wet with perspiration. Each breath was a rasp and an effort. His voice was a groan.

"Got goddamn F - - - ing cold," said Hemingway, talking in what Cannon described as Hemingway's spoken cabelese.

"You ought to be in the hospital," Cannon said.

"I'm all right," answered Hemingway, "but they took my kid. He was hit. They threw grenades. That's all I know."

Cannon sat with Hemingway through the night. On the floor was a carpet of newspapers. Hemingway seemed to be strangling on the congestion in his lungs, and he kept spitting on the newspapers. But it wasn't the pneumonia, Cannon said, which troubled Hemingway. Yet each time Cannon tried to console Hemingway about his son, Hemingway began speaking about something else. He also kept drinking from a bottle of cognac.

"I'm going to be killed," Hemingway said.

"You will if you don't go to the hospital," answered Cannon.

"In combat," Hemingway said. "I know it." Then, referring to the Inspector General's investigation which was still going on, Hemingway added: "They're trying to ruin me, but I want you to promise that you will tell how it was.

I want someone I trust to do it. I won't live to defend myself."

Then Hemingway fell asleep.

Hemingway's favorite outfit during the war was the Fourth Division's Twenty-second Regiment, commanded by Lanham, who later became a brigadier general and the prototype for Colonel Cantwell in *Across the River and into the Trees.* When Hemingway wasn't with his Irregulars, he was with Lanham's men and he even wore a Fourth Division patch on his field jacket. Hemingway was still in Paris when the Twenty-second entered the Hurtgen Forest, just across the German frontier, in November of 1945, beginning a battle that lasted eighteen days.

"It was the bloodiest battle of the war," Lanham later said. "The Fourth Division was one of those listed as destroyed. Of course it wasn't. Hemingway refused to believe it. He got a car and a driver and came racing up to the front while all the other traffic was going the other way. When he got in he had a raging temperature of one hundred and four degrees."

When his jeep pulled up before Lanham's Hurtgen Forest command post, Hemingway stepped out coughing and slapping both pockets of his field jacket. In each was a bottle of cognac.

"My doctors," he said, slapping the bottles again, "cured me."

The Battle of Hurtgen Forest continued to rage after Hemingway's arrival, and, out of a regiment of thirty-two hundred men, the Twenty-second suffered more than twenty-six hundred casualties. Four battalion commanders were lost within thirty-six hours but, as Malcolm Cowley wrote, "Hemingway stayed with the regiment until the end of the battle, sharing all its dangers and hardships except deprivation of alcohol. To prevent that final misfortune he carried two canteens on the *Gott-mit-Uns* belt he had taken from a dead German. One canteen was filled with gin, the other with dry vermouth, and he poured them together to make lukewarm but powerful Martinis."

For a good part of the invasion years, Hemingway's war correspondence was limited to writing letters home for his jeep driver, a farmer, who said he couldn't express in writing what he felt about the war. Instead, the driver would tell

187

Hemingway and Hemingway would express it. Otherwise, Hemingway's dispatches included description such as this:

The division had not advanced beyond its objective. It had reached its objective, the high ground we were now on, exactly when it should have. It had been doing this for day after day after day after week after month now. No one remembered separate days any more, and history, being made each day, was never noticed but only merged into a great blur of tiredness and dust, of the smell of dead cattle, the smell of earth new-broken by TNT, the grinding sound of tanks and bulldozers, the sound of automatic-rifle and machine-gun fire, the interceptive, dry tattle of German machine-pistol fire, dry as a rattler rattling; and the quick, spurting tap of the German light machine-guns —and always waiting for others to come up.

History now was old K-ration boxes, empty foxholes, the drying leaves on the branches that were cut for camouflage. It was burned German vehicles, burned Sherman tanks, many burned German Panthers and some burned Tigers, German dead along the roads, in the hedges and in the orchards, German equipment scattered everywhere, German horses roaming the fields, and our own wounded and our dead passing back strapped two abreast on top of the evacuation jeeps. But mostly history was getting where we were to get on time and waiting there for others to come up.

When he came back from World War II, Hemingway, the illiterate captain, did not look upon it as he had looked upon his youthful search for manliness on the Lower Piave.

"Most of this last war made sense," he said, "while the first one made little sense to me. Also I had such good companionship. I had never known such fine people and it was the first time I ever had a chance to fight in my own language."

CHAPTER ELEVEN

In Defense of the Title

I

EARLY IN 1950, Ernest Hemingway, accompanied by his wife Mary and hugging a leather briefcase that had been skinned many times over, left *Finca Vigia* for a New York that he never really liked. Boarding a plane in Havana, he found himself sitting next to a small, wiry man named Myers who was returning from a business trip in Cuba. Hemingway, at one point during the flight, reached into his briefcase, covered and recovered with travel stickers, and pulled out a manuscript. He handed it to Myers to read.

When Hemingway arrived at Idlewild Airport, he was greeted by Lillian Ross, who was then gathering the material for her now-famous *New Yorker* profile of Hemingway. As Miss Ross later reported the scene, Hemingway was waiting at the luggage gate for her with one arm hugging his briefcase and the other hugging Myers.

"He read book all way up on plane," said Hemingway. "He like book, I think," and Hemingway sort of tightened his hug.

"Whew!" said Myers.

"Book too much for him," Hemingway said. "Book start slow, then increase in pace till it becomes impossible to stand. I bring emotion up to where you can't stand it, then we level off, so we won't have to provide oxygen tents for the readers. Book is like engine. We have to slack her off gradually."

"Whew!" said Myers again.

"Not trying for no-hit game in book," Hemingway said, releasing Myers from his hug. "Going to win maybe twelve to nothing or maybe twelve to eleven . . . She's better book than 'Farewell.' I think this is best one, but you are always prejudiced, I guess. Especially if you want to be champion."

Hemingway shook Myers' hand.

"Much thanks for reading book," he said.

"Pleasure," said Myers, and he walked away.

The manuscript which Myers had read was of *Across the River and into the Trees*, the fruit of Hemingway's fiftieth year in life. It was during this visit to New York that Hemingway told Miss Ross:

"It is sort of fun to be fifty and feel you are going to defend the title again. I won it in the twenties and defended it in the thirties and forties, and I don't mind at all defending it in the fifties."

II

He was an expatriate again. With one eye on the fins of the Gulf Stream and with another, perhaps, on the federal government's non-resident income tax exemptions, he had moved to Cuba, becoming, eventually, that country's most prominent non-citizen. Cuba, of course, was then, as it remains, only ninety miles away from Key West and he had paid an abundant number of visits to Havana beginning with his deep water fishing days in the late 1920s. He had, in fact, written a good portion of *A Farewell to Arms* in Room 511 of Havana's Hotel Ambos Mundos, and by 1941 he still kept himself registered all year round in the room, both as a matter of sentiment and as a place to store old luggage. "The Ambos Mundos," as he later said, ". . . was a very good place to work in."

Hemingway already had rented *Finca Vigia* by the time Pauline divorced him in 1940, and he even had written a portion of *For Whom the Bell Tolls* there. As part of her divorce settlement, Pauline kept their Key West house, later opening a gift shop in the city, and anyway Hemingway had been troubled by the constant stream of visitors and other interruptions in Key West. After his marriage to Martha Gellhorn in Cheyenne, Wyoming, Hemingway decided, nevertheless, to return to the Gulf Stream. So, putting ninety miles of open sea between him and his second wife, he bought *Finca Vigía*. During his first years there, his prominence had a hard time catching up with him.

"Not long after his marriage to Marty, I went down to see him," reported Earl Wilson. "I got a taxi in Havana, rode the twelve miles to San Francisco de Paula and began inquiring for him at once. But to my astonishment, nobody knew him. Neither the police nor the merchants—no, and not even the old reliable bartenders—had ever heard of him. And he had merely written most of *The Bell* right in this town! Anyway, it was a lot of fun looking for him. My cab driver, a regular bloodhound, refused to give up. He went 'Hssst!' at some card players in an open-front coffee bar and waved tiredly to them to come out. That's the way you ask directions in Cuba, and perhaps the reason you don't get many. The card players stated positively that no Ernesto Hemingway lived there.

"'*Famoso, famoso!*' I protested, flaunting my high school Spanish daringly, but they only shrugged.

"So we whipped on to the next town, Cotorro. There we interviewed the Cuban Telephone Company—a nice, snapping-eyed girl operator sitting at one lonesome switchboard which must have been adequate to handle the traffic of the four or five phones in the village. We asked whether she had ever heard of Ernest Hemingway.

"She said no at first. Then her face lit up. She pointed back toward San Francisco de Paula. '*Sí,*' she said, '*Señora Marta!*' With Señora Marta to front for him, Hemingway had absolute privacy. Later I found that the natives knew him vaguely as '*el Americano.*' The little operator had only known the name Hemingway because of some telephone calls from the outside, or from him personally. His neighbors, however, were suspicious. They never saw him hitching up a team of Cuban mules. They had seen him fishing and hunting and training his fighting cocks for matches at Club Gallis Tica, the cockfighting society in Havana. And with their own eyes they had seen him playing tennis on his own tennis court, which was buried in tropical foliage. They thought he was a loafer.

"But that was just the way Hemingway wanted it. He moved to Cuba, he said, to get away from doting admirers, postmen and people accursed with telephonitis."

To discourage visitors such as Earl Wilson, Hemingway made use of his Room 511 at the Ambos Mundos and of his friendship with the hotel owner, Manuel Asper. Anyone approaching the hotel, which stood on Obispo Street, overlooking Morro Castle and the waterfront, would have found Asper denying that Hemingway even existed. Behind the room clerk's desk, however, and atop a small safe there could be found a cardboard with papers and letters clipped to it. On the clip someone had scratched, with a shaky hand, the words "Correspondencia de E. Hemingway." It was there that Hemingway received his mail, and every four or five days he would stride in to pick up the accumulation.

This facade, however, was only one of the inventions that Hemingway designed to keep himself at work. As Hemingway told Jimmy Cannon, "Here in Havana, I have my own stool against the wall in a corner of the bar where I can see who comes in or who gets out of a car in the mirror. Nobody treats me like a writer." Treating himself like a writer, Hemingway established ruses to discourage himself from spending too much time on that stool. Purposely, he berthed his cruiser, the *Pilar*, at the town of Cojimar, fifteen miles beyond San Francisco de Paula and twenty-seven miles from Havana. His plan was to make it adequately difficult for himself to escape for his usual afternoon of fishing and twice as difficult to get back to Havana for an evening at the saloons. Writers, he said, should write alone and see each other only after their work is done, and even then not too often. "Otherwise," he said, "they become like writers in New York. All angleworms in a bottle, trying to derive knowledge from their own contact and the bottle."

For a while, anyway, Hemingway was able to write without too frequent interruptions at *Finca Vigia*. Although a part of the village, the estate remained well hidden within it, despite its fifteen acres, and, behind a wall of foliage and the thatched roofs of his unlettered neighbors, he had comparative seclusion. He also had a pleasant view. At the entrance to *Finca Vigia* was an old gateway of blanched stone pillars framing a driveway that curved upward to the white, Spanish tower of a house that stood on the summit of a hill. At the base of the house were imported mango trees, thirty of them, with a terrace that was high but accessible to the doorway. Still another tree, a Ceiba, sacred in voodoo rites and with smooth bark the color of an elephant's hide, stood as part of the terrace, overlooking the green, mowed lawn that reached into the remainder of Hemingway's acreage.

On these grounds were the tennis courts and a swimming pool, to which he walked each afternoon with a knotted walking stick and in which he took a daily half-mile swim. The house itself had some fifteen rooms, each with floors of cool, yellow-tinged tile and some with balconies. From the balcony of Hemingway's workroom at the top of the fourth-story tower, reaching up from the house at its southwest corner, he could see, through a scape of royal palms, the capital dome of Havana, twelve miles away. In his initial vigor, Hemingway at first made good use of this high retreat, but as he grew older his legs grew weaker and the steps to the top of the house increased. Through the years, consequently, he preferred to do his writing in his ground-floor bedroom and, after a while, he came to ignore the tower except when the presence of visitors and "characters" drove him there.

Divided into two alcoves by a pair of chest-high bookcases that reached out into the room from its walls, the bedroom was filled with a big, low double bed and, on clear days, sunlight. It was this which occasioned Hemingway, with his thin lids and sensitive eyes, to work with a green-tinted shade tied around his forehead and sometimes to sleep with it.

"When I am working on a book or a story I write every morning as soon after first light as possible," he told George Plimpton of the *Paris Review* in an interview years later. "There is no one to disturb you and it is cool or cold and you come to your work and warm as you write. You read what you have written and, as you always stop when you know what is going to happen next, you go on from there. You write until you come to a place where you still have your juice and know what will happen next and you stop and try to live through until the next day when you hit it again. You have started at six in the morning, say, and may go on until noon or be through before that. When you stop you are as empty, and at the same time never empty but filling, as when you have made love to someone you love."

By 1958, when Hemingway told this to Plimpton, his habits already had become engraved on each day's agenda. His bedroom opened on the sixty-foot-long parlor, its walls lined with the stuffed trophies of Hemingway's African safaris, and the door between the two rooms was kept ajar by a thick volume called *The World's Aircraft Engines* which was lying on the floor. Hemingway's over-sized slippers were at the foot of the bed while at the head of it a pair of bedside tables were piled high with books. More books overflowed from the bookcases and from additional white-painted shelves that covered each wall. There also were newspapers and magazines, outdated and late, which arrived each day in increasing quantities and which Hemingway somehow never failed to read.

It was on one of the bookcases, filled with bullfight journals and stacks of letters clutched by rubber bands, that Hemingway had his work desk, a chest-high area one foot square which had been hewn clear, like a back yard in a forest, although here the forest was of books, papers, pamphlets, manuscripts and mementoes. The clearing left enough room for a typewriter, a wooden reading-board, five or six pencils, and a husky fragment of copper ore that he used as a paper-weight, and when he wrote he would stand at this clearing in his loose fitting loafers on a rug made from the skin of a Lesser Kudu. In his boyhood, he had learned to compose on a typewriter, a requirement of the newspapers of his apprentice years. By the time he reached Cuba, however, he had fallen into the practice of writing his first drafts with a pencil because, as he said, "my pencil is the difference between a hand-made product and a machine-made product." As for his habit of standing up at his work desk, it became, in his later years, a necessity, the result of a back injury suffered in one of his African plane crashes.

He wrote dialogue quickly, sometimes so quickly that he had to shift to the typewriter for speed. "I wake up in the morning and my mind starts making sentences, and I have to get rid of them fast—talk them or take them down," he told Lillian Ross. ". . . When the people are talking, I can hardly write it fast enough or keep up with it, but with an almost unbearable high manifold pleasure. I put more inches on than she will take, and then fly her as near as I know to how she should be flown, only flying as crazy as really good pilots fly crazy sometimes. Most of the time flying conservatively but with an awfully fast airplane that makes up for the conservatism. That way you live longer. I mean your writing lives longer," and then he added, characteristically for him, "How do you like it now, gentlemen?" It was Hemingway's manner of saying, "Now what do you think of that?"

On a chart made out of the side of a cardboard packing case and placed against the wall beneath the nose of a mounted gazelle head, he kept count of his daily word output. "So as not to kid myself," he said. The number varied, but on some days there would be four hundred and fifty words and on the other days there might be twelve hundred and fifty. When he wrote twice as much as usual, he might take the next day off to go fishing in the Gulf Stream.

"People ask you why you live in Cuba," he wrote in *Holiday* magazine in 1949, "and you say it is because you like it. It is too complicated to explain about the early morning in the hills above Havana where every morning is cool and fresh on the hottest day in summer. There is no need to tell them that one reason you live there is because you can raise your own fighting cocks, train them on the place and fight them anywhere that you can match them and that this is all legal.

"Maybe they do not like cockfighting anyway.

"You do not tell them about the strange and lovely birds that are on the farm the year around, nor about all the migratory birds that come through, nor that quail come in the early mornings to drink at the swimming pool, nor about the different types of lizards that live and hunt in the thatched arbor at the end of the pool, nor the eighteen different kinds of mangoes that grow on the long slope up to the house. You do not try to explain about our ball team —hard ball—where, if you are over forty, you can have a boy run for you and still stay in the game, nor which are the boys in our town that are really the fastest on the basepaths. . .

"You could tell them that you live in Cuba because you only have to put shoes on when you come into town, and that you can plug the bell in the telephone with paper so you won't have to answer, and that you work as well there in those cool early mornings as you have ever worked anywhere in the world. But those are professional secrets. . ."

It was at *Finca Vigia*, despite his wish to be alone, that Hemingway eventually surrounded himself with two house boys, three gardners, a Chinese cook, a chauffeur, his ship's engineer, named Gregorio Fuentes, twenty-five cats, including one that he said wanted to be human and so he fed it everything but his blood pressure capsules, an additional, uncounted array of dogs, a few cows, a constant stream of visiting friends, crackpots and idolatry, and, inevitably, a parish priest.

"That was Don Andres," said Hemingway's son John. "He was a Basque priest who's now passed on. He had been one of the minor priests in the cathedral at Bilbao and when the Spanish Civil War started he had gotten up in the pulpit and made a speech telling everybody to get out in the streets and start shooting and to hell with staying in Church. He'd been a machinegunner on the Republican side for a while and then, when it was over, he was booted out of Spain and went down to Cuba. And of course, the church was a little rough on him and he got the poorest parish in town. He used to go down and bet on the jai-alai to make a living. He was a very nice old guy and very tough. But he was not with Papa in the guise of a man of God but rather as a friend.

"And then there were those escapees from Devil's Island who used to drop in occasionally, or at least they were 'claimed' escapees. One came through one time and Papa put him up and then for years afterwards various other people who claimed they were escapees, too, used to stop at the *Finca* as the first safe spot you could drop into and get a drink and a change of clothes."

The parade to the *Finca*, in fact, became an enormous as well as endless one because Hemingway, by this time, had earned his rank as Papa. With his beard growing and with its color turning first to iron and then white, he was living on a patriarchal scale that included the world and not just his estate, with its cats and dogs. He had become, in his time, not only a legend to *Sports Illustrated* and the readers of Leonard Lyons and Earl Wilson, but a legend of American literature. It was not to learn how to go marlin fishing that George Plimpton journeyed to San Francisco de Paula for an interview or that book reviewer Bernard Kalb wrote him questions begging answers or that college professors, young writers, high school students, and unabashed readers knocked unheralded at his *Finca* door. He was Papa Hemingway and he knew all the answers to whatever questions they might ask. Wherever they wanted to go, he had been there. Whatever they wanted to see, he could describe. He was Papa Hemingway of Oak Park, Illinois, weighing two hundred and eight pounds, wearing the trunks and color of eternity and they were fully expecting him to defend and *keep* the title.

196

III

Unlike Hemingway's previous wives, Mary Welsh didn't come from St. Louis. But she had, he found, other qualities.

"Miss Mary is durable," Hemingway wrote in *Look* magazine. "She is also brave, charming, witty, exciting to look at, a pleasure to be with and a good wife. She is also an excellent fisherwoman, a fair wing shot, a strong swimmer, a really good cook, a good judge of wine, an excellent gardener, an amateur astronomer, a student of art, political economy, Swahili, French and Italian and can run a boat or household in Spanish. She can also sing well with an accurate and true voice, knows more generals, admirals, air marshals, politicians and important persons than I know dead company commanders, former battalion commanders, rummies, coyotes, prairie dogs, jack rabbits, leaders of cafe society, saloon keepers, airplane drivers, horse players, good and bad writers and goats.

"Miss Mary can also sing in Basque and is a brilliant and erratic rifle shot. She has been known to be irascible and can say in her own perfect Swahili, *'Tupa ile chupa tupu,'* which means take away that empty bottle.

"When she is away, the *Finca* is as empty as the emptiest bottle she ever ordered removed and I live in a vacuum that is as lonely as a radio tube when the batteries are dead and there is no current to plug into."

She was born in Bemidji, Minnesota, the daughter of a prosperous lumberman, and if she didn't come from St. Louis she was still as much of a Midwesterner as her three predecessors. She also was a writer, although by the time they were married Hemingway put a stop to that. She had gone to Northwestern University in 1931, had worked for the *Chicago Daily News* and then had switched to the *London Daily Express*. In London, she met Noel Monks, an Australian then working for the *London Daily Mail*, and there was, in the proper terms of journalese, a merger. The marriage, however, didn't endure and before long she was separated from both Monks and the *Daily Express*. In 1940 she joined *Time* magazine as one of its London correspondents and in 1944 she met Hemingway there. Soon after she became the second Allied woman war correspondent to arrive in liberated Paris and coincidentally she stayed at the Ritz hotel. There, of course, she renewed her acquaintance with the liberator of the Ritz wine cellar.

In December of 1945, Hemingway obtained a Havana divorce from Martha Gellhorn on the grounds that she had abandoned him in London. He married Mary in Havana the following March fourteenth. "Pauline likes Mary," Hemingway said later after introducing his new wife to one of his old ones. "Pauline said to me, 'You ugly old baboon, you, how did you get such a nice wife as Mary? She's the nicest wife you ever had.'"

IV

He was working on what he called "the big book." His references to it were often, but vague. When Maxwell Perkins or Carlos Baker or dozens of other literary associates asked him about it, he would tell them it was about "land, sea and air." With Hemingway it was a habit, if not a superstition, to avoid any discussion of what he happened to be doing at the time. "I do not like to talk about my work when I am writing it," he once wrote to Bernard Kalb. "Some people do. But, unfortunately, I don't."

In December of 1946, he announced that he had completed twelve hundred pages of the book. "It's a big book," he said. "I've broken the back of it now. I'd like to write a good novel and ten or fifteen more short stories and not go to any more wars. I'd like to raise my kids." There were rumors that Hollywood had bought the rights to the big book for two hundred and fifty thousand dollars, sight unseen.

By 1949, Malcolm Cowley was reporting in *Life* that Hemingway had more than one thousand pages written. Cowley said that Hemingway wouldn't even tell his publisher what the big book was about. It was, in fact, fast becoming a mystery. Soon it would become several mysteries.

In 1952, Hemingway wrote Bernard Kalb:

Question: How is the writing going?
Answer: About the same as always. Some days better than others. I've worked two and a half years steady now and could use a vacation.
Question: How is the big book?
Answer: Very long. I am in no hurry about it.
Question: When may be expect it?
Answer: As and when it seems best to publish it.

By January of 1954 Leonard Lyons declared that Hemingway's "long novel is finished and is in a safe-deposit box in a Havana bank." That same month, Earl Wilson explained that the book "—his mammoth masterpiece—will be in five parts..." Again, in July, 1955, Lyons said: "Ernest Hemingway is devoting all his time to finishing the Big Novel." By the following September, Hemingway himself, leaving for Europe, talked affectionately to ship reporters about his "major job." Three volumes had been completed, he said, and "I have those nine hundred finished pages tucked away in a bank vault and I expect to do a lot more during the trip."

In September of 1956, Hemingway wrote in *Look* magazine:

> So ... having interrupted a book that you loved and believed in on the eight hundred and fiftieth manuscript page, to work four months on the script and photography of a motion picture of another book that you believed in and loved, you know that now you will never again interrupt the work that you were born and trained to do until you die. Since in almost any week you can read the obituaries of good dead friends, this is not much of a promise. But it is one that you can keep ... This is a situation report of how things go until we go back to work tomorrow on the long book. Three other books are finished, and this piece can tell how things go now and, after slightly bad times, I hope it is a little cheerful ...

More than two years later, Wilson reported Hemingway had told him: "Finished page six-sixty-seven today. By February I may have her done and in the bank. I've got three unpublished ones in the bank. This'll be the fourth. I put 'em away and let 'em ripen." Lyons then reported that Hemingway "has three more chapters to write and then his big novel will be finished."

By July third, 1961, Scribner's was still awaiting the manuscript.

V

With *Finca Vigia* quickly becoming the capital of the world, or at least of Hemingway's world, he began to seek other capitals. Hemingway was born at home, but not to stay there. He was an inveterate traveler, moving restlessly all his life, and even in the whitening years of it he kept shifting his stance, like a boxer. He wanted company and he wanted to travel, but most of all he wanted to write. When the interruptions at *Finca Vigia* became too frequent, he would seek another writing desk.

"The company of jerks is neither stimulating nor rewarding," he explained in *Look* magazine in 1956, "so for a long time you have tried to avoid it. There are many ways to do this and you learn most of them. But the jerks and twerps, the creeps and the squares and the drips flourish and seem, with the new antibiotics, to have attained a sort of creeping immortality, while people that you care for die publicly or anonymously each month . . . So Mary and I live here and work until visitors interrupt work so much that we have to leave. It was a nice life here for a long time, and it still is a nice life when we are left alone and we will always come back here from wherever we go. This is our home. And you do not get run out of your home; you defend it. Spain and Africa are good places, but they are being overrun. They are not too badly overrun yet and there are places that have not been ruined. But you have to find them . . ."

It was on one of these journeys, in February, 1949, that Hemingway, while duck shooting near Venice, was struck in the eye by a tiny fragment of gunshot wadding. Troubled all his life by eye injuries, Hemingway didn't even notice this one and it wasn't until several days later that he discovered he had been struck by anything at all. By that time a form of blood poisoning had set in and Hemingway with the fragment still lodged in his eye, was hospitalized at Padua. Although Hemingway himself later described the illness as erysipelas, the infection spread so rapidly that doctors gave him only a short time to live. Confronted with death, Hemingway worked out, in his mind, the theme of *Across the River and into the Trees*, the story of a fifty-year-old colonel who had a bad heart, faced death at any moment, and fell in love with that nineteen-year-old countess in Venice. According to his friends, it took sixteen million units of penicillin to save Hemingway's life and, during his convalescence, instead of returning to work on his big book, he instead began to write *Across the River and into the Trees*. When it came out in 1950, it sold seventy-five thousand copies, but certainly not on the strength of its reviews. Of the panning his book received, Hemingway wrote Leonard Lyons:

"They write this nonsense about champions, saying you never won a round. They should have been around a little and know you have to knock a champion out to beat him; that is if he really is one. And that it is one thing to be on the ropes and another to be on the skids . . ."

Hemingway suffered still another imprint on his body in 1950, when, during heavy seas and on a wet deck, he fell from the flying bridge of the *Pilar*. "We were coming in to anchor," he wrote to Leonard Lyons, "and I was going up to relieve Gregorio at the wheel. He swung her broadside to go in through the entrance to the channel between the two reefs at Rincon, just as I had my good leg over the rail. My head hit one of the clamps we hold the hooks of the big gaffs in, although I braced with my shoulders and took most of it there. Also hung onto the rail. But got the real up-spout fireworks. It amounted to a five-inch cut that reached the skull and severed the artery and about a Force Five Beaufort concussion. A friend who was along, and Mary, got the hemorrhage contained OK and we got to a surgeon in about five hours I guess. Anyway we avoided it being Just Another Tragedy of N. Y. Society."

A short time afterwards Hemingway told his big, sportsman, polo-playing friend, Winston Guest: "Wolfie, all of a sudden I found I could write wonderful again, instead of just biting on the nail. I think it took a while for my head to get rebuilt inside. You should not, ideally, break a writer's head open or give him seven concussions in two years or break six ribs on him when he is forty-seven or push a rear-view-mirror support through the front of his skull opposite the pituitary gland or, really, shoot at him too much. On the other hand, Wolfie, leave the sons of bitches alone and they are liable to start crawling back into the womb or somewhere if you drop a porkpie hat." And he broke into laughter.

VI

In April of 1936, Hemingway wrote an essay for *Esquire* entitled *On the Blue Water (A Gulf Stream Letter)*. In it he described what was to him the beauty and the mystery of deep-sea fishing in the waters between Key West and Cuba and especially of the inner thrill that there was in the observance and capture of the marlin which swam there. As part of his essay, Hemingway told, in a paragraph, a story which he once had heard:

Another time an old man fishing alone in a skiff out of Cabanas hooked a great marlin that, on the heavy sash-cord handline, pulled the skiff far out to sea. Two days later the old man was picked up by fishermen sixty miles to the eastward, the head and forward part of the marlin lashed alongside. What was left of this fish, less than half, weighed eight hundred pounds. The old man had stayed with him a day, a night, a day and another night while the fish swam deep and pulled the boat. When he had come up the old man had pulled the boat up on him and harpooned him. Lashed alongside the sharks had hit him and the old han had fought them out alone in the Gulf Stream in a skiff, clubbing them, stabbing at them, lunging at them with an oar until he was exhausted and the sharks had eaten all that they could hold. He was crying in the boat when the fishermen picked him up, half crazy from his loss, and the sharks were still circling the boat.

In that paragraph, of course, was the nucleus and plot of Hemingway's *The Old Man and the Sea*. For fifteen years, the incident had remained in his head until he could somehow determine the greater mystery of it. There is evidence that not only did Hemingway find in the story the old man's place in nature but his own as well. The allegory in the story is inescapable, and yet Hemingway, all his life, believed in stories and not allegory. His place in nature, he would say, was that of "a writer of hard cover books for money." For *The Old Man and the Sea*, he received sixty-five thousand dollars on the magazine rights alone.

"He was broke when my wife and I visited him in Cuba," said producer Leland Hayward. "I asked him what he was writing and he said it was a big book with four parts and a coda. He had finished two of the parts, but he didn't like them and was doing them over again. He was satisfied with the coda, and said, 'You want read?' He watched my face throughout the time I was reading. When I finished the tears were streaming down my face. I told him it was the greatest thing he had written."

When he dried his tears, Hayward said: "Papa, you've got to publish this."

"No," Hemingway answered. "It is meant to be a coda, as part of a book."

"That's all right," Hayward said. "You can put it in the

book when it is all finished. No one will mind. You need the money."

Again Hemingway refused and then Hayward, silent for a moment, asked: "Suppose I could get it published in *Life* magazine—complete in one issue without ads to break it up?"

"That would be impossible," Hemingway replied. Hayward, however, pointed out that *The New Yorker* had printed John Hersey's *Hiroshima* in a single issue.

"That's true," said Hemingway, and he paused a moment. Finally he said it would be all right with him if Hayward could get *Life* to agree. *Life*, of course, did, paying the aforementioned sixty-five thousand dollars and printing *The Old Man and the Sea* in its entirety in September of 1952.

From the book's hard-cover and movie sales, Hemingway earned thousands of dollars more and yet *The Old Man and the Sea* created a sharp division of opinion among its readers, and especially among its more demanding readers. Literary critics were as often at one another's throat about the book as they were at Hemingway's and *avant-garde* literary elements, the new enemies of Hemingway, couldn't agree on the worth of *The Old Man and the Sea*, with some young writers lavish in their praise of its mysticism and others condemning it as more of Hemingway's code boorishness.

As for Hemingway's usual apologists, they were exultant. But even in their ranks there was the explicit opinion that *The Old Man and the Sea* represented a Hemingway "comeback," as if literature had suddenly written off the white-bearded man in Cuba or as if, through his own recent writing, he had written himself off.

On the flying bridge of the *Pilar*, with four baited lines trailing into the stern, Hemingway was not exactly impervious to the discussion of his latest title fight, just as he would remain aware of all the literary criticism of his work until his death. If Hemingway's old man had fathomed anything in the Gulf Stream besides a big fish, Hemingway could not give the depth of it.

"I tried to make a real old man, a real boy, a real sea and a real fish and real sharks," he later told a *Time* magazine reporter over a couple of bottles of beer. "But if I made them good and true enough they would mean many things. The hardest thing is to make something really true and sometimes truer than true." Concerning any symbolism, Hemingway said: "No good book has ever been written that has in it symbols arrived at beforehand and stuck in."

Whatever else it might mean, *The Old Man and the Sea* was the only published fragment of Hemingway's Big Book during his lifetime. It came, as he told Carlos Baker, from the maritime section of his overall topic of land, sea and air. In the early 1950s, Hemingway's working title for the maritime section was *The Sea in Being*. He had been wrestling with it much the same as Santiago wrestled with his marlin.

"Half fish," he said. "Fish that you were. I am sorry that I went too far out. I ruined us both. But we have killed many sharks, you and I, and ruined many others. How many did you ever kill, old fish? You do not have that spear on your head for nothing."

VII

Ernest Hemingway's 1953 Christmas present to his wife Mary was a pair of plane crashes. They came without wrappings, except, perhaps, for a few bandages. Obviously, they were his to give. The circumstances of them couldn't possibly have accrued to anyone else.

The Hemingways were, as usual, evading interruptions at *Finca Vigia* with a tour to their other parts of the world. The tour had begun that 1953 summer in Spain, where Hemingway was finally readmitted by a Franco government willing to forgive almost anyone bearing a tourist visa. At the border, Hemingway had been apprehensive when the Fascist guard, looking at his passport, had asked if he were Hemingway the writer.

"A sus ordenes," Hemingway had answered, stiffening.

"I have read all your books and admire them very much," the guard answered, holding out his hand and smiling. "Let me stamp these and see if I can help you at the customs."

In Spain he had met Antonio Ordoñez, the son of Cayetano. "I could tell he was great from the first slow pass he made with the cape," Hemingway would later write. He had introduced Mary to bullrings he hadn't seen in some seventeen years and had been introduced himself to Luis Miguel Dominguin, then the ranking matador in Spain and Ordoñez's brother-in-law-to-be. It had been the first of the dangerous summers that Hemingway would later write about. Then came his dangerous winter.

By December of 1953, Hemingway and his wife were in the Emali-Laitokitok area of Kenya, where Hemingway was acting as temporary game ranger in the absence of a friend, one Denis Zaphiro. Because of his duties he was unable to travel into Nairobi for a Christmas gift for Mary and when January arrived she picked one out for herself. She wanted, she announced, a plane ride to the Belgian Congo. Hemingway was in the midst of hunting a goat-hungry leopard when he had to leave to deliver the present.

With their pilot, Roy Marsh, they took off from Nairobi on January twenty-fourth in a light Cessna 180 and flew over various points of interest, including the location of a film which Hemingway referred to as *The Snows of Zanuck*. With Mary photographing the scenery along the way, the trio decided to make the four-hundred-foot Murchison Falls one of their sight-seeing stops, and it soon became an unscheduled one. As pilot Marsh descended over the falls, a flight of large ibis birds caused him to take a sharp dive into an abandoned telegraph line and the plane crash-landed on a hill of trees.

Mary suffered two broken ribs in the accident, but kept them and her pain to herself. Surrounded by an elephant herd, Hemingway, his wife and their pilot took refuge in an abandoned poacher's shack, where the elephants, never forgetting the departed poacher's activities, kept them at trunk's length. Finally Hemingway spotted a launch, the SS *Murchison Falls*, which happened to be making its once-a-month trip down the river to Lake Albert. He hailed it, and the trio were rescued. Or that's what they thought.

The SS *Murchison Falls* was the same ship which had been used in the filming of the Humphrey Bogart movie, *The African Queen*, and, in its ancient way, it took the three survivors to a place called Butiaba in Uganda. There, Hemingway met the pilot of one of the planes which had been searching for him and the pilot offered to fly the trio to the next large city.

On takeoff, however, the rescue plane crashed, starting a bush fire, although Hemingway, his wife and both pilots escaped safely. As the legend goes Hemingway eventually made his way to civilization with a bottle of gin in one hand and a bunch of bananas in the other, causing Ogden Nash to write:

I land in the jungle by the teeth of my skeen.
Big gorilla walk up to me and talk very mean.
He put up his mits and I sock him in the cheen.
Witha bunch of bananas and a bottle of jeen.

Actually, Hemingway left the gin aboard the burning plane and, to his regret, watched it explode with a sickening pop. He had to suffer without it, in fact, for the entire long drive through the jungle to Masindi, and it wasn't until he reached a doctor that he received any. The doctor poured it on his wounds. "Gin is good for you, both inside and out," the doctor said.

Although only slightly hurt in the first plane crash, Hemingway was seriously injured in the second. In addition to being painfully burned, he suffered a skull fracture, a ruptured kidney and one broken and two compressed vertebrae. When he read the newspapers, however, he found he was believed hurt much worse than that. Search planes, spotting the wreck of the Cessna 180, had radioed back word that there was no sign of life. Throughout the world, newspapers had printed Hemingway's obituary. In his sick bed, Hemingway had the pleasure of reading them.

"Most of the obituaries I could never have written nearly as well myself," he wrote later in *Look*. "There were certain inaccuracies and many good things were said which were in no way deserved. There were, however, some rather glaring inaccuracies in the account of my unfortunate death. One in the German press stated that I had attempted to land the aircraft myself on the summit of Mount Kilimanjaro, which we call 'Kibo.' It seems that I was landing this aircraft accompanied by Miss Mary in an effort to approach the carcass of a dead leopard about which I had written a story in 1934. This story was called *The Snows of Kilimanjaro* and was made into a motion picture which I unfortunately was not able to sit through so I cannot tell you how it came out . . . We love Italy very much and more than that we love many individual Italians. None of those we truly loved wrote obituaries. They were instead, I believe, at Mass and many old friends would not believe that we were dead unless they saw the bodies . . .

"In all the obituaries, or almost all, it was emphasized that I had sought death all my life. Can one imagine that if a man sought death all of his life he could not have found her before the age of fifty-four? It is one thing to be in the proximity of death, to know more or less what she is, and it is quite another thing to seek her. She is the most easy thing to find that I know of. You can find her through a minor carelessness on a road with heavy traffic, you could find her in any full bottle of Seconol, you could find her with any type of razor blade; you could find her in your own bathtub or you could find her by not being battle wise. There are so many ways of finding her that it is stupid to enumerate them."

Hemingway laughed, pasted some of the obituaries into two zebra skin bound scrapbooks, and returned to *Finca Vigia.*

VII

Once upon a time there was a battered old prizefighter in Key West who wanted to make a comeback. The prizefighter asked Hemingway to referee.

"It was a Negro section," Hemingway later recalled, "and they really introduced me in the ring: 'The referee for tonight's bouts, that world-famous millionaire sportsman and playboy, Mr. Ernest Hemingway!' Playboy was the greatest title they thought they could give a man. How can the Nobel Prize move a man who has heard plaudits like that?"

Ernest Hemingway almost won the Nobel Prize for Literature the year before he finally did. His name had been up for consideration in 1953 but the Swedish Academy had decided instead to award the prize to Winston Churchill, in view of the British statesman's advanced age. While Churchill lived blissfully on, however, Hemingway was almost killed twice. Finally, in 1954, the Academy decided to award the Nobel Prize to Hemingway. "He was due to receive the award eventually," an Academy official explained, "and we might as well give it to him now before he kills himself in some adventure."

The official news came over the Cuban radio at ten-thirty in the morning on October twenty-eighth, 1954, and Hemingway was immediately deluged by notes of congratulations and the press. "I am very pleased and very proud to receive the Nobel Prize for Literature," he said at *Finca Vigia.* The citation read: "Ernest Hemingway for his powerful mastery, which has created a new style in modern literature, as recently demonstrated again in *The Old Man and the Sea.*"

With his Nobel Prize, Hemingway received a gold medal,

an illuminated scroll and thirty-six thousand dollars in cash. He was pleased, he said, because at the time he was eight thousand dollars in debt.

"As a Nobel Prize winner," he said, "I cannot but regret that the award was never given to Mark Twain, nor to Henry James, speaking only of my own countrymen. Greater writers than these also did not receive the prize. I would have been happy—happier—today if the prize had gone to that beautiful writer Isak Dinesen, or to Bernard Berenson, who has devoted a lifetime to the most lucid and best writing on painting that has been produced, and I would have been most happy to know that the prize had been awarded to Carl Sandburg. Since I am not in a position to—no—since I respect and honor the decision of the Swedish Academy, I should not make any such observation. Anyone receiving an honor must receive it in humility."

Because of the injuries Hemingway had suffered in his dangerous winter, his doctor would not permit him to go to Stockholm to receive the award. Instead he sent a message:

"Having no facility for speechmaking and no command of oratory nor any domination of rhetoric, I wish to thank the administrators of the generosity of Alfred Nobel for this prize. No writer who knows the great writers who did not receive the prize can accept it other than with humility. . . . Organizations for writers palliate the writer's loneliness but I doubt if they improve his writing. . . .

"For a true writer each book should be a new beginning where he tries again for something that is beyond attainment. He should always try for something that has never been done or that others have tried and failed. Then sometimes, with great luck, he will succeed. How simple the writing of literature would be if it were only necessary to write in another way what has been well written. . . ."

Hemingway already had received the Pulitzer Prize for *The Old Man and the Sea* the year before. He had been aboard the *Pilar*, riding out a squall with his radio tuned in for the weather report, when he learned of the award. "The Cuban radio had it on the air every fifteen minutes," he said. "I was glad I was not at home so as not to say anything wrong on the telephone. Imagine if you had asked me what my reactions were and I had said a lot of people, including myself, would have been happier if Native Dancer had won the Derby. But I am going to watch my goddamn mouth now for a couple of years and see what happens. Maybe I will get respectable. Wouldn't that be wonderful."

At the same time, however, he sent his five hundred-dollar Pulitzer Prize check to his son John, then an Army captain at Fort Bragg, adding the note: "It is the same as five months' jump pay."

VIII

To Mary Welsh Hemingway, life at *Finca Vigia* was a "perpetual weekend . . . involving time, space, motion, noise, animals and personalities, always approaching but seldom actually attaining complete uproar."

In 1947 when the Dodgers were training in Cuba, Hemingway, in addition to accompanying them to the Havana barrooms for their boxing matches, often would invite team members to his parlor, where his liquor supply was a match for any man. On one visit to his home, Hemingway challenged pitcher Hugh Casey to the same kind of pitching duel Hemingway once had with Kirby Higbe in a tavern doorway, except that this time it was to be with boxing gloves. According to Dodger third baseman Billy Herman, who was one of those present, Hemingway quickly donned his gloves and threw the first punch. Casey, who was in the midst of putting his gloves on, fell to the floor beneath the surprise attack but quickly got to his feet and started swinging back. "He knocked Hemingway over the furniture twice," remembered Herman, "sending bottles and everything flying." The noise attracted Mary, who rushed in from the next room, screaming the fight to a halt.

"That's all right, honey," said Hemingway, rising to his feet. "We're just having a little fun."

As the Dodgers were leaving, however, Hemingway patted Casey on the shoulder and said: "Let them go. You sleep over. We were both drunk tonight when you licked me, but in the morning we'll both be sober, and then we can have a nice little duel—knives, pistols, anything you want."

"Casey wasn't that drunk," Herman said. "He left with the rest of us."

There were other challenges.

"I was talking to Mrs. Hemingway at a diplomatic cocktail party and she asked me if I had ever eaten lion steak, which she described as succulent and tender and worthy of a gourmet's approval," wrote Edward Scott, then a columnist for the *Havana Post*. "I said I wouldn't willingly eat the flesh of any carnivora because they live on other animals. 'I know,' she said, 'it is because you are stupid. You are stupid and prejudiced just like all the rest of the British colonials.'

"I said nothing then but later I wrote a column that was not exactly complimentary to Mrs. Hemingway. Mr. Hemingway telephoned me. I identified myself on the phone and Hemingway said, 'I want to know if you're going to apologize to my wife for the things you've been writing about her.' I replied that I did not intend to apologize in a situation in which I obviously was the offended party. Hemingway isn't as handy with a telephone as he is with a pen or a typewriter, but this day he was in good form. 'Well,' he said, 'you said in your column that if I had said to you what my wife said to you, you would do this and that and so to me.' Then Mr. Hemingway went down a long list of names, none of them honorable connotation, which he thought should be applied to me. At the conclusion he said that he was waiting for me out at his residence. That I should go out there alone and he would be alone, and we would settle our differences man to man. I told Mr. Hemingway that the meeting would have to take place in some neutral spot, certainly not at his house.

"I then wrote him a formal letter in which I told him that I considered myself grievously offended by his language and conduct, and that I now challenged him to meet me with forty-five caliber pistols, the other details to be arranged by the respective gentlemen serving as seconds. I stipulated that each pistol should have one cartridge in the chamber and a full clip. Each principal would have the right to discharge the entire magazine irrespective of whether or not hits had been scored.

"On the evening of August twenty-first, following his several telephone calls in the afternoon, Mr. Hemingway again telephoned me. I told him that if he were looking for trouble he could set his mind at ease because trouble he was about to have. I then assured him that he would be hearing from my seconds within twenty-four hours. 'Oh,' Hemingway said, 'You're challenging me to a phony duel.' I replied there was nothing phony about forty-five automatics and a full clip. Hemingway then said that he did not want to kill me. I replied that that was a task which lay ahead of him. When we talked in the evening, which was the last time I spoke to him, he suggested several times that my real intention was to make a front-page story about the difficulties existing between us. I then told him that I had no intention of riding to fame on his shirttails or his shroud. All I wanted was an apology, or for Mr. Hemingway to give me satisfaction at a shooting party. He could take his choice. The following day, my representative went out to San Francisco de Paula to see Mr. Hemingway at his house. He was received courteously and a lengthy conversation took place. The relevant part of it is summed up in my representative's letter to me in which he said that Hemingway manifested no intention whatsoever of apologizing to me. At the same time, according to the letter, Mr. Hemingway said he had no desire to fight a duel with me, and furthermore stated that he did not consider me to have the qualifications to fight a duel with him. I pressed the matter in a subsequent letter to my representative and insisted that he challenge Mr. Hemingway formally to meet me and give me satisfaction. To this challenge Mr. Hemingway replied by registered letter which read as follows: 'For good and sufficient reasons I do not choose to meet Mr. Edward Scott on the so-called field of honor nor anywhere else. I will answer no challenges from him and will send no friends of mine to meet with his friends. If any tribunal interprets this as being motivated by cowardice I believe they would be in error. I am not a publicity seeker and I will not be provoked into something which can only lead to the worst kind of publicity. Aside from other considerations, my obligation at this time is to continue my writing and resume my health. At the present time I am fighting no duels with anyone. If any friends of Mr. Scott's consider that to be an act of cowardice they are at liberty to think so, but it is a decision made by a man who has served in war with honor, and is fully conscious of his obligations. Since I have let you know my decision, reached after mature consideration, and after talking with you, there is little point in explaining further. Signed, Ernest Hemingway.'"

At a Hemingway party at the *Finca*, there was likely to be Winston Guest, Alfred Wynne Vanderbilt, the bartender from Manolo's, members of the fleet, Ava Gardner, or her boyfriend Dominguin. "With few exceptions," said Mary, "the only parties we attend are those we give ourselves for two, twenty or two hundred people, one reason being, as Ernest says, 'You can't control the food and drink at other people's parties.'" As in Norman Mailer's complaint, Hemingway, issuing communiques on the progress of his Big Book through the medium of Leonard Lyons and Earl Wilson, seemed to become less the literary giant than the big bad boy of cafe society. But this was an oversimplification of which Hemingway was aware. "I'm not a solemn man," he said in 1954, "but I'm serious when I work. I don't expect to live more than five years more and I have to hurry." Caught between the Rotarian in him and the artist, he grew more and more irascible.

He put signs up at the *Finca* barring visitors without appointments. When the Cuban Revolution broke out, he erected a fence. Once a woman approached him on the terrace at Cojimar and said, "Oh, Mr. Hemingway, I want to tell you how much I enjoyed your latest book, *By Love Possessed.*" He glowered at her. When the woman's husband ran up and shouted, "Keep away from my wife!" Hemingway swung and knocked him out. Another time, Hemingway was in his Buick station wagon coming back from Cojimar with Sam Boal when two Cuban policemen stopped him to report that a maid from the *Finca* had committed suicide. "She's got some nerve interfering in my life," Hemingway said.

In 1952, a young critic, Seymour Krim, denounced *The Old Man and the Sea* in *Commonweal,* writing that Hemingway was, "by our living needs and standards, a true, brilliant, but very limited artist, and I believe that we have gotten all we can from him now." About seven years later Krim happened to be in Havana and, on a lark, took a taxi to *Finca Vigia* and knocked on the door.

"At first Hemingway chased me away," Krim remembered. "But I persisted until he let me in and then I said, 'How about a drink?' I can't get over how he looked, this tremendously husky torso on legs that didn't seem as if they could carry the weight. But what really amazed me was that he recognized my name instantly. He had read my review in *Commonweal* and after all those years he still remembered my name. Right off the bat, he told me, 'You don't know anything about literature.' Then he started arguing with me. I couldn't help thinking to myself, 'Here's this giant and he feels he has to defend himself against a young punk like me. This guy must really be insecure.'"

IX

The legacy of Ernest Hemingway is words. They are there, thousands of them, in trunks, suitcases and vaults, In Havana, Paris, Ketchum and perhaps in all the other cities of the world that he liked to call his home towns. There are some who say skeptically that in the last years of his life he did more talking than writing. It's true that in his labored meticulousness he refused to publish what he did not think ready for the printer. Sometimes he even burned manuscripts unsatisfactory to him. In those bank vaults, nevertheless, may be gold, from the richest Hemingway vein.

Carlos Baker wrote shortly after Hemingway's death that he apparently had been working on three projects. One was *The Dangerous Summer*, the account of the *mano a mano* bullfights of Ordoñez and Dominguin during the 1959 season, excerpts of which were published in *Life* in 1960. A second project was a book of Paris reminiscences from the Lost Generation 1920s.

"I inadvertently was responsible for that book," said Leonard Lyons. "I was three days late for an appointment with him in Paris. And while he waited, at the Ritz, the manager asked about the trunk he'd left in the basement long before the war. He'd forgotten about it. The trunk was brought up. It contained his old notebooks, about incidents and people with whom he was involved. 'Those notebooks opened up memories long locked in my mind,' he told me. One night in Havana, three years later, he read me four of the chapters—about Gertrude Stein, Scott Fitzgerald, and Ford Madox Ford. The book will be published soon." Also in the trunk, reportedly, was a submachinegun.

Carlos Baker said that his final communication with Hemingway was a telegram in which Hemingway asked Baker to delete an anecdote about Ezra Pound and the Russian novelists from a book which Baker was writing. Hemingway explained that he wanted to use the anecdote himself.

"The few who have seen it," Baker said, "agree that these sketches are of a very high order—so high, indeed, that they are likely to overshadow the innumerable literary autobiographies which have already appeared, and in which Hemingway himself was not infrequently an important character." Hemingway's publisher, Charles Scribner's Sons, admit that they had already received the manuscript for this book, tentatively called *Paris Sketchbook*, but that six months before his death Hemingway asked for it back to make further revisions.

And then Hemingway's third project, of course, was the Big Book.

"Some degree of mystery continues to surround the third volume (or volumes) which Hemingway left behind him," Baker wrote. "Ten years ago this spring he told the present writer about a long novel whose triple subject was 'The Land, The Sea, and the Air.' He made at that time a half-humorous, half-rueful apology for his temerity in having undertaken so ambitious a project, and went on to say that he had been trying out sections of it on his wife Mary. If she responded to any given passage with gooseflesh, he knew that he had succeeded. Although he seems to have had an almost pathological love of secrecy, particularly about the stories on which he was currently engaged, he was careful to give the impression that the book had already reached at least a penultimate form, that the work of cutting and polishing was then mostly behind him, and that the typescript had been deposited for safekeeping in the vaults of the National Bank in Cuba."

It soon became obvious that Hemingway was working on a project that he had never attempted before—something that was almost on a Proustian scale. It would be at last, perhaps, his challenge to the man with whom he once said he would never step into the ring—Tolstoy.

"I am a strange old man," said Santiago, the fisherman in *The Old Man and the Sea.*

"But are you strong enough for a truly big fish?" the boy asked him.

"I think so. And there are many tricks."

Immediately after the Nobel Prize announcement, Hemingway told Herbert Matthews of *The New York Times*, a fellow correspondent during the Spanish Civil war, that he was working on still a fourth project—a book of short stories about Africa. "He added that he started two months ago what was meant to be another short story," Matthews reported, "only 'it is running into a novel.'"

Shortly after Hemingway's death, his lawyer, Albert Rice, confirmed that there were manuscripts lying in various parts of the world. "I'm going to have a hell of a time digging them out," he said. "They might be in Cuba, Florida, Paris, Spain, Africa—all the places he's been. Whether they will ever be published is another question. That's up to Mary, me and possibly Scribner's."

"Writing, at its best, is a lonely life," Hemingway said in his message accepting the Nobel Prize. ". . . He grows in public stature as he sheds his loneliness and often his work deteriorates. For he does his work alone and if he is a good enough writer he must face eternity, or the lack of it each day . . . It is because we have had such great writers in the past that a writer is driven far out past where he can go, out to where no one can help him."

"*His choice,*" *thought Santiago,* "*had been to stay in the deep dark water far out beyond all snares and traps and treacheries. My choice was to go there to find him beyond all people. Beyond all people in the world. Now we are joined together and have been since noon. And no one to help either one of us.*"

CHAPTER TWELVE

The Only Ending

I

AT NINE-THIRTY one morning in November of 1960, two professors from Montana State University drove up to the bi-level, wooden, hillside lodge that was Ernest Hemingway's home during the Sun Valley duck hunting seasons at Ketchum, Idaho. Inside the lodge, beneath the fierce, wall-hung trophies of his aim, Hemingway was expecting them. When they stepped up to greet him, however, they found they had been expecting someone else.

He was still the same tower of a man, but he seemed a vacant tower. In the white-maned oval of his face, his spectacles slipped down his nose. From his shoulders, his body dwindled in a taper. When he opened his mouth to say hello, his teeth were yellowish with gaps of age between them. He spoke slow and haltingly and almost not at all.

One of the professors, Leslie A. Fiedler, who had written several appraisals of Hemingway's work, reached out for a handshake, bracing himself for the bone-grip of Hemingway's past. When Hemingway's hand clasped his, however, Fiedler could hardly feel it. The other professor, Seymour Betsky, felt merely that he was shaking the hand of a frail, old man. It was his first meeting with Hemingway.

"I had a feeling," said Fiedler afterwards, "that this must be not Hemingway but Hemingway's father, the ghost of his father. His legs seemed scarcely able to hold him up. His

216

eyes were the eyes of a poet who dreams of hunters. They were brown, soft, scared."

Hemingway invited the two professors to sit down and then brought out a bottle of wine. "It's Tavel," Hemingway said, indicating that it always had been his favorite. "A fine, little wine from the Pyrenees." Then he began to pour, and, forgetting the wine-tasting ceremony, filled Fiedler's glass. An instant later, he caught himself, poured a few drops into his own glass, put it to his lips and then filled Betsky's.

The two professors had come to ask Hemingway if he would address a group of their students at Montana State University, but Hemingway shook his head. "It's too hard for me to write," he said, "let alone talk. I don't want to talk about literature or politics. I talked once about literature and I became sick." He spoke the words slowly, and even in his slowness he hesitated over several of the words as if he were uncertain he would be able to pronounce them. When he finished he sat quietly, like an unsure schoolboy, and it seemed as if Hemingway had been disciplined at last. Then the two professors asked about his own literature and Hemingway again hesitated. He evaded the questions and avoided the answers, but not, it seemed, so much out of his habit of secrecy as out of a sudden vulnerability to the last ten years of criticism which had been directed against him.

"He was," Betsky remembered, "like a young writer working and agonizing over his first novel. He was really quite unsure of himself and quite unsure he had written anything worth anything."

Fiedler mentioned other writers, but all Hemingway would do at the naming of them was to nod. As his comment on the older ones, Hemingway would say, "He was a great guy—you should have known him." Of the younger ones, Hemingway would mumble, "That boy has talent." And all the while, Hemingway kept watching Fiedler with weary, anxious eyes, as if waiting for Fiedler to talk about Hemingway.

"It seemed," Fiedler said, "as if he were waiting for me to tell him he made it, that he was a figure of consequence. He was like a beginner waiting for a review of his first book, and I was the reviewer. I thought to myself, 'Who in the United States would know that he made it if Hemingway didn't know it?'"

For the hour and a half that the professors remained there, Hemingway's speech seemed to lose more and more coherence. "He had an almost desperate inarticulateness," Betsky said. "He couldn't seem to put a sentence together. We started to talk subjects in an effort to make conversation with him, but he didn't seem to be able to follow things. He looked so frail it seemed you could almost break him."

To Fiedler, Hemingway looked like a boy who, suddenly and overnight, had become an old man, a fragile, too-often repaired old man. And yet, just as Hemingway seemed to be waiting for some sort of word from the professors, they kept waiting for a word, just one old-fashioned word of his masculinity, from Hemingway. The word never came.

The two professors readied to leave. "Tell Norman Mailer," Hemingway said suddenly, "I never got the book. The mails in Cuba are terrible." They walked out to their car. Behind them, Hemingway started off absentmindedly. His wife, Mary, called to him:

"Don't forget your vitamin tablets, Daddy."

II

Several days later, on November thirtieth, 1960, a man who gave his name as George Saviers registered at Saint Mary's Hospital of the Mayo Clinic in Rochester, Minnesota. Soon afterwards, or as soon as he was placed in his hospital bed, a staff of physicians paid a visit to his room and examined him. The man, of course, was Hemingway. The name of Saviers was taken from his doctor, an old, elderly friend in Ketchum, who had discovered that Hemingway was suffering from a worsening case of hypertension, and who had sent him to the Mayo Clinic for treatment. The treatment lasted fifty-three days.

In addition to hypertension, there was a suspected case of incipient diabetes, the same disease which had afflicted his father years before. There were the effects of a 1959 case of hepatitis, which had kept him sick and bedridden for many weeks in Cuba. And finally, there were the accumulations of years and years of wounds, injuries, illnesses, drinking and brawling, an erosion of his body that only Hemingway's body had been able to survive. By early 1961, his body was wearing out.

When he came home from that winter's stay at the Mayo Clinic, his weight, which he marked daily on a chart along with his word-count, was down to one hundred and seventy-four pounds, and dropping. His diet, once as omniverous as any beast whose head hung in his trophy rooms, was restricted, along with his alcohol. He was unsteady with a gun and instead of hunting he went on long walks in the hills near his home.

He was living the year-round in Ketchum then. Although he had sympathized with Fidel Castro's Twenty-Sixth of July Movement during the Fulgencio Batista tyranny, he had maintained a strict neutrality in his *Finca Vigia* in Cuba. When Castro took power, he and Hemingway were several times in each other's friendly company. But then relations between the Castro government and the United States began to worsen. Silently, Hemingway moved to his lodge in Ketchum. On the pro-Castro side and among the forces against him, there was a clamor for Hemingway's support. But Hemingway remained silent at Ketchum. The only sound was from the trap-shooting in the back yard.

III

He was working, when he could, on the *Paris Sketchbook*. On Saturday nights, he watched the fights. "It's terrible what they make those boys do," he said. One night, on television, he was looking at the Academy Award presentations and, along with the rest of the nation, he got his first hint that Gary Cooper was dying. James Stewart, accepting a special Oscar for the absent Cooper, broke into tears. Cooper had been Hemingway's hunting companion in Sun Valley. His own illness had caused him to break a date several months before. Immediately, Hemingway went to the telephone and called Cooper in Beverly Hills.

"I'm sick, too," Hemingway said.

"I bet I'll beat you to the barn," Cooper replied.

IV

When, in 1960, he had been traveling the bullring circuit with his young friend, Antonio Ordoñez, who was then twenty-seven, Hemingway had been the victim of still another exaggerated report of his death.

"A Swedish radio station announced that Papa Ernesto had died in Spain," remembered Ordoñez. "He said, 'How silly, Spain is a country to live in, not die,' and then we went off to have some glasses of wine together to celebrate that he was still alive."

Hemingway had made reservations to attend the *Feria* of

San Fermín at Pamplona in July of 1961 as well. He had, in fact, begun to resent the presence of any American at the Pamplona bull-fights who hadn't been invited by him. But by April twenty-third, Hemingway was back in Rochester at St. Mary's Hospital, where he checked in this time under his own name. By June twenty-ninth, he had to cancel his Pamplona reservations.

His hypertension, among his other ills, had not been responding to treatment and Dr. Saviers feared he might suffer a heart attack. Hemingway also was depressed, and he was given shock treatments. His second visit to the clinic lasted until June twenty-fourth and then, accompanied by Mary and George Brown, his old friend and sparring partner, Hemingway drove in a leisurely trip back to Ketchum.

He arrived there July first. In his lodge, things were much as he left them, with zebra skins as carpets, hunting scenes on the wall, an autographed photo of light heavyweight champion Archie Moore. That afternoon, he spoke to his neighbor, Chuck Atkinson. That night, he joined Mary and George Brown in a drive into Sun Valley, where they dined at their favorite restaurant. Later, when they returned to the lodge, Hemingway was brushing his teeth in his room when Mary walked across the hall to join him.

"I have a present for you," she said.

The present was an Italian folk song, *Tutti Mi Chiamano Bionda,* which she hadn't thought of for many years. She began to sing it and when Hemingway finished brushing his teeth, he joined her in the last lines.

V

"All stories, if continued far enough, end in death," Hemingway once wrote, *"and he is no true story-teller who would keep that from you."*

At about seven-thirty in the morning of July second, 1961, Mary Hemingway was awakened in her upstairs bedroom by what sounded like a shot. She hurried downstairs. On the floor of the foyer in front of the gun rack her husband lay almost decapitated. Lying across his legs was his favorite twelve-gauge shotgun, one that was inlaid with silver and made especially for him. Both barrels had been fired. Of Hemingway's face, only his mouth, his chin and part of his cheeks remained.

At once, Mary telephoned her neighbor, Chuck Atkinson.

Then she called Leonard Lyons in Beverly Hills and asked him to notify the press. Afterwards, she issued a hasty announcement that read: "Mr. Hemingway accidentally killed himself while cleaning a gun yesterday morning at seven-thirty a.m. No time has been set for the funeral services, which will be private." The coroner, Ray McGoldrick, said the wounds were "self-inflicted" but that there would be no inquest. Hemingway had left no notes. There also were no gun cleaning implements near the body.

"Mary made a mistake in saying that he was cleaning a shotgun," said Hemingway's son John afterwards. "I mean, somebody said, 'What was he doing?,' and she said, 'Cleaning a shotgun.' There also was a big point made that the hunting season was over. But, hell, they used to shoot clay birds outside in the back all the time. Not only that, but if you have guns or anything else you like very much, you pick them up. You should be careful with them, but Papa was in *very* bad shape. So, there *is* a question of doubt, no matter what anybody may feel. There *is* doubt."

Still later, Mary granted an interview to four reporters in her living room. She announced that Hemingway had left behind at least two unpublished novels and had planned to work on one of them, kept in an Idaho bank vault, only that week. "He left a great many unpublished works—undone and unfinished," she said. "We don't even know where some of it is at the moment. He was never eager to publish. Why should you make your income tax go from seventy-five to ninety-five per cent. In a sense, it was his bank account."

She said that she wanted to set the record straight on a number of other things. She said the story that Hemingway once played a twenty-five-thousand-dollar bluff in a poker game with a pair of queens was untrue. She said that he had not stalked out of a theater in the middle of *The Killers*. And she said he had not emerged from the jungles after his African plane crashes with a bottle of gin in one arm and her on the other, saying, "I feel wonderful."

"The gun," she said, "was one of the favorite things he owned. He wasn't cleaning it, but he was certainly looking at it. I sometimes take out my camera and look at it although I don't plan to take a picture. . . . I feel certain that this, in some incredible way, was an accident."

Before her press conference was over, she broke down and hurried to another room.

221

VI

Ernest Hemingway was buried July sixth, 1961, beneath the awesome scape of the Sawtooth Mountains. In the small Ketchum cemetery near a federal highway, about fifty persons, mostly Idaho neighbors, gathered about the rose-covered coffin.

For the services, Mary and Hemingway's three sons had asked the priest, the Reverend Robert L. Waldmann of Our Lady of the Snows Church in Sun Valley, to read Hemingway's favorite passage from *Ecclesiastes*. The priest, however, did not understand the meaning of the request, and he read only the first line, quoting it in its different wording from the Roman Catholic Douay version.

"We were awfully disappointed," John said later. "But the priest just plain didn't realize. We were pretty upset."

"Oh, Lord," Father Waldmann prayed, "grant to thy servant Ernest the remission of his sins. Eternal rest grant unto him, O Lord."

Then he read the single line from *Ecclesiastes: "One generation passeth away, and another generation cometh, but the earth standeth forever."*

And the sun, of course, also rises.

NEW! From LANCER

ERNEST HEMINGWAY: *The Life and Death of a Man*   50¢
The first new biography published since the death of the giant
of American Letters. *By Alfred G. Aronowitz and Peter Hamill*

THE PIT AND THE PENDULUM   35¢
Taken from the big motion picture version of Edgar Allan
Poe's supreme work of terror, this book is filled with thrills,
suspense and horror.

A PECULIAR TREASURE by Edna Ferber   60¢
The greatest and most dramatic story by the world-famous
author of such beloved best-sellers as SHOWBOAT, CIMAR-
RON and GIANT.

MASTER OF SPACE by Arthur C. Clarke   50¢
This sensational space-flight classic by today's foremost author-
scientist has been called "One of the best space flight novels
yet written," by the New York *Times*. A remarkable book.

THE LUST OF PRIVATE COOPER by James Gordon   35¢
The harshly realistic novel about soldiers and their women that
has been compared in power and style to GOD'S LITTLE
ACRE.